THE ROLE OF SCRIPT SUPERVISION
IN FILM AND TELEVISION

A Career Guide

THE ROLE OF SCRIPT SUPERVISION IN FILM AND TELEVISION

A CAREER GUIDE

by

Shirley Ulmer and C. R. Sevilla

Illustrations by C. R. Sevilla and Robert Zentis

COMMUNICATION ARTS BOOKS

HASTINGS HOUSE, PUBLISHERS

Library of Congress Cataloging in Publication Data
Ulmer, Shirley.
    The role of script supervision in film and television.
    Includes index.
    1. Moving-pictures—Production   and   direction—Vocational   guidance.
2. Television—Production and direction. I. Sevilla, C.R. (Carol R.) II.
Title.   III. Title: Script supervision in film and television: a career guide.
PN1995.9.P7U45   1986   791.43′023′02373   82-21344
ISBN 0-8038-6366-7

Printed in the United States of America

To my knowledge, this is the first professional, thorough, legitimate book on the subject. It is indispensable!
In fact—after fifty years of writing and directing, I learned quite a few tricks I was not aware of.

Billy Wilder

Contents

     Multiple Camera Film
     Commercials
     Specialized Notation

     INTERVIEWS
     Morris Abrams, production manager 19
     Richard Hashimoto, production manager 64
     Peter Bogdanovich, director 80
     Leslie Martinson, director 138
     Ralph Schoenfeld, editor 159
     Thelma Preece, script supervisor representative .. 220

     CONCLUSION 267

     GLOSSARY 269

     INDEX 287

To director, Edgar George Ulmer, whose
tombstone bears only his favorite two words—
"TALENT OBLIGES"

Acknowledgements

INDIVIDUAL CONTRIBUTIONS FROM:

Morris Abrams, production manager
Johnny Alonzo, cinematographer
Dorothy Aldworth, script supervisor on *Happy Days*
Peter Bogdanovich, director
May Wale Brown, script supervisor
Ron Capell, IATSE local 871 representative
David Cipes, Vidtronics
Linda Day, director of *WKRP in Cincinnati*
Rudi Fehr, editor
Verna Fields, editor
Thomas Hailey, writer
Richard Hashimoto, production manager
John Hazard, commercial producer
Leslie Martinson, director
Allen Persselin, editor
Kit Parker, Kit Parker Films
Ilse Lahn, Paul Kohner Agency
Myron Meisel, lawyer
Thelma Preece, script supervisor representative
Leonard Regan, Enterprise Stationers
Rita Riggs, costume designer
Joan Rivers, director
Rita Riggs, costume designer
Marshall Schlom, script supervisor
Ralph Schoenfeld, editor
Stanley Sevilla, lawyer
Ray Stark, producer
Billy Wilder, director

PERMISSION TO REPRINT COPYRIGHTED MATERIAL FROM:

Comeback episode, "Herve Villechaize" © 1978 American International Television. Filmways Productions.

The Competition, screenplay written and directed by Joel Oliansky. Story by Joel Oliansky and William Sackheim. *The Competition* © 1979 Columbia Picture/Rastar Productions. Reprinted by permission.

"Prospecting . . . You're in business for Yourself" segment of the Ford Marketing Institute training tape produced by Interact Learning Systems and written by Allen Alch.

Recipe Dog Food Commercial Permission to use Lassie by Lassie Television, Incorporated, a subsidiary of Wrather Corporation. Recipe Dog Food courtesy of Campbell Soup Company.

Return to Macon County © 1974 American International Pictures. Written and directed by Richard Compton.

Roar by Noel Marshall and Ted Cassidy. Roar © 1981 Noel Marshall Productions.

S.W.A.T. from the "Courthouse" episode of the "S.W.A.T." television series—reprinted with permission from Spelling-Goldburg Productions. All rights reserved.

"The Hot Rod" episode of *The Waltons* television series, written by Scott Hamner. The Waltons © 1981 Lorimar Productions. Reprinted by permission.

"The Patter of Little Feet" episode of *WKRP in Cincinnati* television series, written by Blake Hunter. *WKRP in Cincinnati* © 1979 Mary Tylor Moore Productions. Reprinted by permission.

ASSISTANCE AND PERMISSION TO USE PHOTOGRAPHS FROM:

Collective Films
Warner Brothers
United Artists
National Telefilm Associates Inc. Distributors of *Detour* and *Ruthless*
Universal
Eagle Lion
PRC
Video Cinema Films

ALL PRODUCTION STILLS ARE FROM PICTURES DIRECTED BY
EDGAR GEORGE ULMER.

Preface

Nearly everyone just starting out on a career in motion picture/television production one way or another has heard the same advice. They have been warned countless times to try and gain as much experience as possible, to learn all they can about every aspect of production, and most of all, to remember always that the creative process of making films is a collaborative effort. Although the best way to heed this advice is to work directly on a film set, there are many other avenues as well. These alternatives, while clearly not as valuable as first-hand experience, are often more accessible.

Practical experience can be gained by taking on related jobs. A novice can learn about film crafts by cranking discarded film even if he or she is really interested in sound editing. Learning about making budgets is possible by typing them. Even a knowledge of the problems that are likely to arise in production can be gained by running errands.

At the same time, nearly all the additional information anyone could want about production is available on a piece of paper somewhere. Numerous specialized books are written about the various aspects of production, and there are detailed technical manuals for nearly all the film crafts as well as hundreds of published interviews with experts in their respective fields. If access can be arranged, a wealth of information can be found in business files, staff contracts, production reports (and even lawsuits!).

The one aspect that cannot be fully understood without extensive experience is what is meant by "collaboration." Making a film is a business of details. How the various craftspeople and artists working on a single television show or film attend to these details can make the difference between a well-made or a sloppy program. The foundation of the script supervisor's job lies in the complexities of this collaborative process.

Collaboration appears to be a simple enough concept. In producing a film, each of the various parts is created separately and then brought together to compose a single product—the tape or film. What could be easier? Every product-oriented business operates in a similar manner. Why then, do you constantly hear stories of crew-members who think they can do everything themselves and end up not being able to do anything? What explains the articles that appear almost daily in the trade journals announcing that projects are abandoned due to "irreconcilable differences" or "artistic disagreements" or "inadequate finances"? How do mistakes cause projects to go millions of dollars over budget? And why are production problems common occurrences rather than exceptions to the rule?

The list of questions goes on and on, but the answers are more difficult to pinpoint. The one thing all the questions have in common is that their answer rests in understanding the structure of the working relationships and how interaction can cause a gamut of unpredictable variables on the set.

Since script supervisors must address themselves to the continual influx of variables, the very nature of the job is problematic. As a result, to state that the script supervisor is merely in charge of continuity is misleading. There are any number of people on the set also responsible for what could be termed "continuity." The list includes the director, cinematographer, make-up artist, costumers, prop master, editors, hairstylists, sound recordist and actors, just to mention a few. Except for the director and cinematographer, each of these craftspeople is responsible for one very specific area of continuity. Because of this, the distinction between where the various craftspeople's jurisdiction ends and the script supervisor's begins becomes of primary importance in performing the latter's duties.

A competent script supervisor understands his or her place in the structure of the film crew. It's not enough simply to memorize the defined responsibilities on the set and the technicalities involved directly in handling those duties. To perform the job efficiently, a script supervisor must also understand the scope of the interaction with the various persons that she or he will come in contact with on the set and off.

In a typical production company, the producer is the owner of the ship, the director is the captain, and the craftspeople are the various members of the crew. In some cases, the producer may be called an associate producer, the line producer, an executive producer or even the network. If a star owns ten percent of the gross profits, the star as well as owns a good part of the ship, not to mention who is the real owner in the case of an auteur writer-director-producer. Regardless of title, the working relationships remain constant for the most part. Some individual or individuals take on the role of producing, others the directorial duties and the rest divide up the crew chores.

Bearing this in mind, the script supervisor as a member of the crew is directly responsible to the director, assuming responsibility for whatever is necessary to aid in a smooth link between the directorial workmanship (or what is shot), and the cutting room. Further definition of a script supervisor's function on a film depends on what everyone else is doing. If the cinematographer is concerned with preserving continuous directional patterns, or the costume designer watches that the actors are all wearing the correct costumes for the Tuesday classroom scene, then the script supervisor's responsibility doesn't go beyond confirming. If, on the other hand, the cinematographer is more concerned with achieving a particular look in a shot or the costumer is too busy setting up the next scene's costumes to worry about the "students," the script supervisor's jurisdiction is expanded. In other words, the definition of a script supervisor's function often depends on what everyone else is doing. The job becomes even more complicated in that what everyone else is doing varies from film to film.

The key word is *flexibility*. A good script supervisor has to be healthy, dedicated, a bit of a psychologist and impervious to criticism, deserved or not. He or she is the liaison between camera, sound, editor, the Girl or Boy Friday to the director, the friend and coordinator for the rest of the crew. A script supervisor must adapt to a new director, actor and set of circumstances on every shoot—often many times in one day.

Usually, film artists are a sensitive group. Many directors like to hug their set up close to their bosoms and are very secretive about what's next. This is very hard on a script supervisor. Many a cinematographer, due to a language barrier, has been unable to communicate verbally. A German old-timer was known for calling out to his operator, "Raise the camera lower, please." Perhaps the most sensitive area is dealing with the actors. Some will like going over their lines with the script supervisor while others may not. Some mingle with the crew. Others work better staying aloof. The really talented artists are usually well-balanced professionals and friendly; yet others are childishly difficult. It is the script supervisor's job to feel them out and adjust attitudes accordingly.

The question naturally arises of what possible use is a manual on script supervision. How can any book prepare a novice for all situations that may come up? Doesn't the unpredictable nature of the job defy the very purposes of a "how-to" book? If even the most experienced script supervisors have difficulty handicapping the odds of when or what will happen next, how is any novice going to be able to do so by reading this book?

The intention of this book is not to anticipate all the possible requirements of a motion picture/television production, but merely to offer the basic tools necessary to perform the job. With these tools, beginning script supervisors can start to develop their own working styles with whatever methods work best for them. The only thing that distinguishes a good method from a bad method is that a good method *works*. The concepts discussed in the following chapters are compiled from our personal experiences in the film business together with tips from our colleagues designed to present several time-proven methods. Interviews and quotes from highly successful filmmakers corroborate the theories in the five chapters from divergent perspectives.

Parts of this book may seem overly simplistic. Many of the principles are so obvious that it may even appear questionable to mention them. Other concepts may seem more appropriate to cinematographers, directors and screenwriters than to script supervisors. Still other sections may appear to pose questions but not supply the answers. In a visual art such as filmmaking the underlying concepts *are* for the most part simplistic, and some of the most important principles *are* obvious. The problem is rarely that the questions have no answers, but that they have many answers. A basic understanding of these underlying concepts provides a sound orientation to thinking in visual terms. By reading the following chapters about the theories of continuity and how to implement them, a common visual sense can be developed that will furnish the answer to the majority of problems a script supervisor may encounter.

THE ROLE OF SCRIPT SUPERVISION
IN FILM AND TELEVISION

Chapter One

The Theory of Continuity

On a picture called *Captain John Smith and the Slave Girl,* a scene takes place where the villain tries to trap the hero by planting an explosive in a cave. Instead, the cave explodes with the villain inside. The villain finally stumbles out much the worse for wear, only the entire crew didn't know how much worse until considerably later. For some practical reason, the exterior of the cave was shot prior to filming the explosion inside. The villain's coat was torn and dirt was thrown over his clothes and hair so that he would look the part as he emerged from the cave. When the crew eventually filmed the interior, the unexpected happened. As the villain appeared at the mouth of the cave, he was covered from head to foot with a thick layer of white dust. He looked like a snowman! How were they able to cut from the "snowman" to the slightly disheveled villain? Easy. A cut was added in which the villain's sidekick runs in and brushes him off. So much for continuity. Unfortunately, a crew can't always count on the availability of easy solutions. One crew member—the script supervisor—must be assigned to take charge of observing the film's continuity. In order to assume responsibility for such a comprehensive area, the script supervisor needs to be well-acquainted with all the various theories and techniques of filmmaking.

Screen continuity is based on the premise that during the filming of a motion picture, the screen story evolves independently of the world around it. If a superhero jumps off a wall, but through the lens it looks as if he scales an impenetrable fortress in a single bound, then he is scaling a fortress because the camera's point of view prevails. Similarly, when shooting a documentary dramatizing the plight of the hungry, the camera captures the images of starving Biafrans even if they are actually well-fed actors. What happens in reality has no importance.

1

A film narrative is compiled of continuous visual images. The story is made up of a series of shots which, when put together, comprise a sequence. A series of sequences forms the complete story. The over-all action will flow smoothly from shot to shot only when the individual components meld so that together they depict the picture in a coherent manner.

Unexplainable changes from one shot to the next are disruptive to the reality created by the film. If the viewer has to stop to decipher why, in one shot, the house is green and in the next blue, then the illusion will be destroyed. Mismatched use of costumes, set dressing and props is often jarring. Inconsistencies in dialogue or facial expressions tend to add to the confusion. With enough discrepancies, the cumulative effect prevents the viewer from remaining involved in the story.

It is the script supervisor's job to address his- or herself to the care and attention of maintaining continuity. Although the director or the cinematographer often will play a substantial role in protecting against continuity errors, the ultimate responsibility lies with the script supervisor. A committed script supervisor will develop a thorough knowledge of the basic theories of continuity—*continuity of motion, continuity of space,* and *continuity of time.*

CONTINUITY OF MOTION

The importance of maintaining proper screen motion cannot be overestimated. How an actor travels across the frame, where a policeman looks at fleeing robbers, and in which direction an airplane flies when it's heading west are just three examples of what to look for. Special precautions must be taken to ensure continuity in these cases and countless other examples of moving subjects.

Continuity of Moving Subjects

There are three basic types of screen direction for moving subjects. Keeping in mind that it is only how the action appears through the camera that matters, all three directions are defined in terms of where in the camera frame they occur. From the camera's point of view, subjects move from *camera left to camera right,* from *camera right to camera left* or in *neutral* directions.

How a subject moves from camera left to camera right varies. It can enter the frame from camera left and head in the direction of camera right. It can start center frame and move towards the right or even exit the frame right. A subject can move diagonally from the top left side, across the frame, and exit the lower right corner. It can enter the middle of camera left and exit the top right corner. All these plus any of the other possible combinations constitute a camera left to camera right direction.

Subjects can move camera right to camera left in the corresponding combinations of directions. The following diagram presents several of these possibilities:

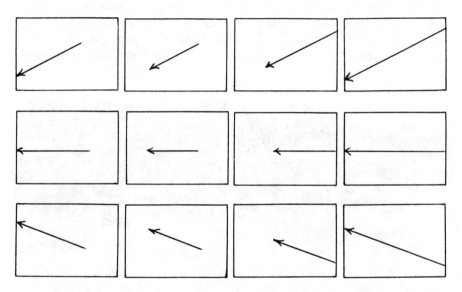

A neutral direction is neither to the right nor to the left. The most common examples are when the subject moves toward the top of the frame and toward the bottom of the frame. Again, there are several combinations of which all are considered neutral directions. The next diagram shows a number of these:

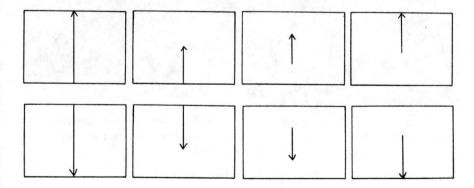

Other typical examples are *tail-away* and *head-on* shots. These terms refer to subjects heading directly toward the camera or directly away without moving up or down the frame. Generally speaking, once established, a directional should be maintained until there is a reason for altering it.

Choosing a Directional Pattern

Directional patterns are chosen for numerous reasons. Some companies work from detailed shooting scripts where all directional patterns are carefully mapped out well in advance of principal photography. Others plan how to photograph each sequence just prior to filming

CL to CR Travel Pattern of Hannibal's army crossing the Alps in Warner Brothers' *Hannibal,* starring Victor Mature.

CR to CL Travel Pattern with Rosie, the head elephant, in *Hannibal.*

Tail Away view of Hannibal's army lining up for battle.

Head-on shot of the elephant as Hannibal and his men are ready to attack.

Hannibal © Warner Bros. Inc. 1959

it. Although there are no absolutes that dictate why a subject should move in one direction over another, several principles are traditionally accepted. Ignoring these common patterns will often result in what would appear as continuity errors.

Moving vehicles illustrate one example of a traditionally accepted principle. If a vehicle travels from camera left to camera right in one shot, then the left to right pattern must be continued in all subsequent shots. For example, a sequence is established by a long shot of a car zooming down a deserted road from camera left to camera right. The next shot is an interior view focusing on the driver inside the car. The driver should either be facing camera right or in a neutral direction, because facing camera left would be confusing. While continuing down the road, the driver glances out the window. The view outside the car is a panorama of the nearby foothills moving in a direction consistent with the driver's point of view.

A second example involving the same principle is more flexible. This time an *enclosed vehicle,* a dilapidated panel truck, heads north toward New Mexico camera right. Inside the back of the truck, half a dozen illegal aliens hide out, chatting noisily among themselves. In the first interior shot, the directional pattern should remain consistent with the initial camera left to camera right. As the scene progresses, the camera angles vary because it is no longer necessary to limit the shots for directional continuity. The illusion of traveling in one direction will be preserved. On the other hand, when the camera cuts back to the truck's passenger compartment, the camera right pattern resumes. If suddenly the direction switched to the opposite direction, right to left, then the audience might think that somehow the aliens were being taken back to Mexico. Whether cars, trucks, planes, boats, trains, stagecoaches or spaceships; the outside, inside, and view out the window of moving vehicles should be directionally consistent.

A similar principle of directional continuity applies to *chases.* In a full shot, a macho cowboy rides camera right to camera left, chasing a yet-to-be-seen subject. The camera pulls in close to capture the look of determination on his rugged face. The next shot tracks with the cowboy as he masterfully increases his speed to catch up to his challenger. Finally, we're shown the object of the chase, a steer running frantically to escape the cowboy. Imagine the effect if the camera cuts to a shot of the steer running in the wrong direction. The mismatch would result in one stupid-looking cowboy.

The opposite principle occurs when two subjects confront each other. In a chase, one subject follows after the other while in a *confrontation,* both subjects approach each other. Directional continuity is preserved individually for each. The only difference is that one travels in one direction while the other moves in the opposite direction. In this way they will appear to be nearing each other. When a large, commercial airplane flying camera right to camera left is intercut with a small private plane flying camera left to right, the possibility of a crash is implied.

A second example of a confrontational pattern is less clear-cut than the possible airplane crash. A film's demolition derby sequence consists of a mish-mash of head-on collisions between masochistic maniacs. The sequence expresses the futility of senseless risk. Amidst shots of crashing metal and flying car parts, it's sometimes difficult to distinguish the winner from the loser. By establishing Maniac A in one direction and Maniac B in the opposite, the confusion will be significantly reduced.

Destinations occasionally define a directional pattern. Audiences tend to have preconceived notions about how geographical locations are laid out. Young men who go west generally are expected to travel camera right to camera left. Flying back east means camera left to camera right. Of course, these theories are for the most part ignored nowadays, but in a case where there is constant traveling back and forth, it might be easier to keep track of the story if directional patterns are maintained.

There are just as many preconceived notions about *comings and goings* as there are for geographical locations. When the tenor enters the concert hall, he is expected to exit the same door but this time going in the opposite direction (unless he has been forced to slip out the backdoor). The same line of reasoning dictates that when Sally leaves town to seek her fame and fortune, she will come back from the opposite direction when she returns home to visit. If *coming* is one direction, then *going* is the other.

Whether it is a moving vehicle, a chase, a confrontation or comings and goings to specific destinations, proper directional continuity should be observed. Although the types of shots and camera angles vary, a basic directional pattern should be established. When followed consistently, the pattern will ensure directional continuity until a reason arises to alter the pattern.

Changing Directions

There are as many reasons to change directional patterns as there are to create them. All directors and cinematographers have their own definite ideas about why a pattern should be broken. It is not the script supervisor's job to insist that a pattern should be altered or preserved. Most often, the director or the cinematographer will suggest the change; however, a script supervisor who is on top of things should recognize when an alteration might be needed.

The most common reasons to alter directional patterns are *thematic*. A pattern is frequently shifted when the storyline calls for a change.

Some directors prefer to start each new sequence with a fresh directional pattern. This method imposes a visual device to differentiate between the individual events of the plot. Changes are not limited to appearing only between sequences. If a driver pulls up to a gas station, he has reached his first destination. When he steers off into a new direction, the continuity is not broken because he now heads toward a new destination. During a Keystone Cops chase, the robbers' car spins 180° and zooms off in the opposite direction in an attempt to lose the cops. The town drunk meanders in no particular direction as he walks aimlessly in circles. Directional changes dictated by the plot rarely pose continuity difficulties.

Production problems sometimes make it necessary to switch a directional pattern. Often there is only one possible direction to set-up the scene due to the physical layout of the location. For example, it is dusk on the last shooting day at a particular location. The main character has been traveling camera right to camera left in the previous scenes. A crucial scene to the sequence has yet to be shot, but the sunset poses a problem on the camera lens. The location cannot be switched because it must match the rest of the sequence. In this case, altering the directional pattern is unavoidable. The physical layout has made it impossible to do anything else.

The unpredictable nature of filming on location inevitably affects screen continuity. The physical layout nearly always determines an array of filming requirements from directional patterns to available camera angles and even to scheduling. One of today's finest script supervisors, Marshall Schlom, illustrates how from his past experience:

> When Michael Ritchie, the director of *The Island*, held his pre-production meeting, he told the key production personnel that because of foreseeable weather and logistical problems, shooting on the small Caribbean island of Antigua, no sequence would ever be considered finished until the wrap day of shooting. The first day of filming, it rained so hard that water inundated our principal set and destroyed it, forcing us to change our schedule while it took five weeks to rebuild. We discovered after the next few days that the sun would be out in the morning, the clouds would come in after lunch, and it would remain overcast until sunset. Since Michael wanted the whole look of the film to be dull and gloomy, we would have to switch our shooting daily, and sometimes hourly, filming interiors or controlable exteriors for a few hours, then move to something else when we had poor light which necessitated changing locations and moving the company all over the island. This resulted in my having to confer constantly with Michael and coordinate with the assistant director, Michael Cheyko, how he would plan our shooting each hour of the day. It became a huge puzzle, with my being responsible for making sure we had all the pieces by the end of the picture.

In a third example, the physical layout of the location determined scheduling, directional patterns, and available angles. A commercial was filmed featuring a car racing along various baracaded city streets on a simulated race course. The features of the car's interior was the subject of one shot. The camera had to be mounted on the passenger side of the car angling toward the driver who comments on the car's features. This was the only logical angle to cover both the car interior and capture the driver, which limited the directional pattern to left to right. In another shot, a helicopter-mounted camera tracks with the car as it speeds up a bridge and around a turn. Because of nearby trees and street lights lining the bridge, for safety reasons the local police department only permitted the helicopter to fly on one side of the bridge, resulting in a right to left pattern. In addition, weather conditions dictated when the helicopter could fly while traffic conditions prevented many of the other shots from being filmed at peak traffic hours. Similarly, certain angles such as severe head-on shots were limited because there weren't enough police on hand to block off additional streets in the background. The car's travel path, available camera positions and scheduling were all at the mercy of the location. The director was faced with no economical or practical choice but to settle for directional inconsistencies by making the most of a montage effect.

A great many changes are due to *stylistic reasons*. The most common of these is providing *visual variety*. A picture shot all in one directional pattern would bore its audience. Even if the entire picture deals with the journey from Virginia to the Golden West, who would want to watch two hours of camera right to camera left?

Another typical stylistic reason is establishing a *time-passage* quality. During a series of short running visuals, a fugitive travels in all directions. Although the fugitive is actually going in only one direction—away from the law—the combinations give the sequence the feeling of transcending time.

Creating a visual design is a reason less frequently cited. In a 60-second commercial set to bicycling, the design concept requires the bikes to wheel in all directions from shot to shot. The resulting effect creates a starburst formation.

Creating a design effect, enhancing visual variety and expressing the passage of time are only three of the many types of stylistic reasons to vary a previously established pattern. Whatever the reason, whether stylistic, thematic or due to production problems the director may opt to alter a directional pattern. The script supervisor should watch for how the alteration is carried out. A well-implemented change of direction will not break the continuity of the sequence.

Methods for Changing Directional Patterns

Most successful methods for changing directional patterns recognize the disruptive consequence of presenting an inconsistent travel pattern. They try to provide the viewer with a visual explanation for an alteration. If the device is effective, any audience confusion will be warded off before it has a chance to form.

Perhaps the most obvious solution is *changing directions on camera.* By presenting a clear motivation, a subject can switch directions in a single shot. An Indian, for example, walks into a courtyard. Across the wide expanse of lawn, he sees a cowboy approaching him. Panicked, he spins around and darts off away from the courtyard. In this case, no one wonders why the Indian is now heading in a different direction because they already have seen why.

Sometimes nothing specific in the story causes a change in direction. Presenting a motivation offers an inappropriate solution. This change of direction can be explained in a single shot. *Turning a corner* or *following a curved path,* for example, are two possibilities.

The following example illustrates how corners and curves switch directional patterns:

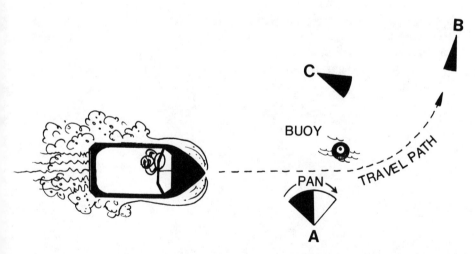

The first diagram is a top view of a speed boat turning a corner. Each letter represents a camera position and the arc indicates in which direction the camera is angled. Camera angle A pans with a boat as it travels toward a buoy camera left to camera right. After reaching the buoy, the boat turns and heads away from the camera. Angle B picks up the boat heading straight at the camera. Angle C follows the boat as it continues camera right to left.

The front views of camera angles A, B, and C look like this:

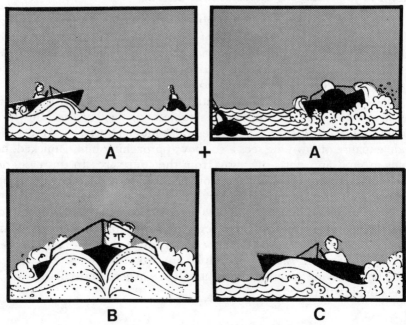

Camera angle A changes the pattern from a clear left to right direction to a neutral. Camera angle B sustains the neutral direction so that camera angle C will be accepted as a continuous right to left pattern.

The second diagram accomplishes a similar change of direction.

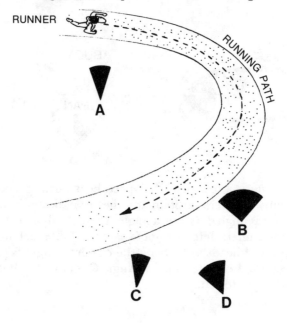

In angle A, a long distance runner sprints camera left to camera right. The curved running path causes the runner to exit the frame of angle B on the left side of the camera. Angle C shows the runner heading camera right to camera left and slightly towards the bottom of the frame. Angle D includes the opposite direction from A. The front views illustrate the change in direction:

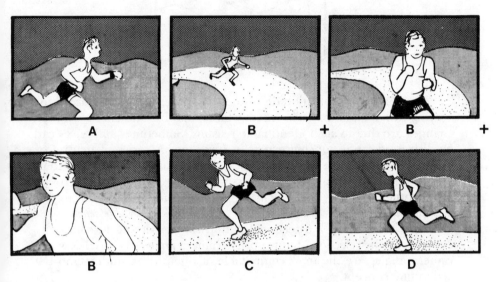

The last diagram portrays a curved, mountain path. It shows how within a single shot, the subject can change directions as many times as desirable. The only directions that matter are how the subject enters the frame, and how the subject finally exits the frame.

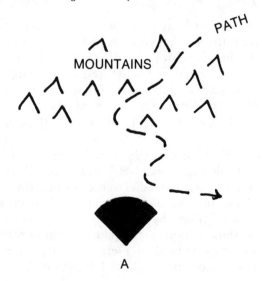

The aerial view from the front shows how the pattern is altered despite the many switchbacks in between.

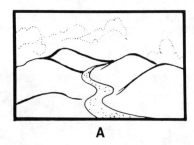

A

The changes of direction discussed so far present visual reasons for varying directional patterns readily accepted by audiences. Not all changes are due to such identifiable reasons. Sometimes audiences can be distracted from noticing errors in direction. A series of neutral or unrelated shots hides inconsistencies. Directional patterns are commonly shifted when a character passes through a doorway or crosses into another room. *By removing as far psychologically or sequentially as possible one direction from another, the effect of the inconsistency is lessened.*

Whether altering a directional pattern or preserving it, continuity depends on the selection of appropriate camera angles. To predict which camera angles are the most compatable, it's helpful to understand the action line concept.

The Action Line

The *action line,* an imaginary line drawn across the playing area, provides a strict division between acceptable and nonacceptable angles. As long as the line is drawn parallel to the subject's travel path, the camera can be positioned at any desired angle along one side of the line. Moving the camera to the opposite side of the line results in inconsistent directional continuity. "Crossing the line," "going over the action axis," and "breaking the T" all refer to these improper uses of camera angles.

A simple example of drawing an action line appears on the opposite page. In this picture, a man walks in a straight line. The action line is placed alongside a fence parallel to the path in which he walks. Cameras A and B capture the man traveling away from and toward the camera respectively. Since they are neutral angles, they are compatible for both left to right or right to left patterns. On the other hand, angles C, D and E can only be used in a left to right pattern while angles F, G and H are only good for a right to left pattern.

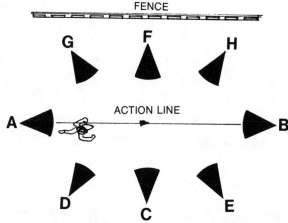

Transferring the example from a top view to frontal views would look like this:

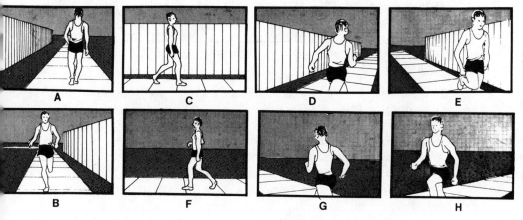

All camera angles on one side of the line, in this case angles A, B, C, D and E remain directionally consistent to each other. The angles on the other side, A, B, F, G and H, are consistent to each other as well, but not to the first group.

Inserting a shot from the wrong side of the line into an otherwise consistent series causes continuity problems. Notice that in the following front views, angle F has a jarring effect and seems to stop the action.

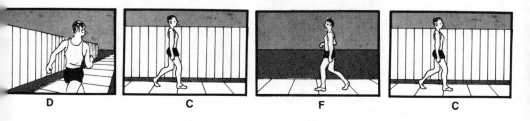

Although all angles from one side of the line are directionally consistent, not all flow together. When side by side, camera angles D and E would look odd.

D   E   D   E

Camera angles A and B might appear equally ridiculous.

A   B   A

Under the wrong conditions, the fence seems to leap back and forth to the opposite side of the frame.

The actual order of the shots isn't determined until after assembling the footage. The script supervisor's only concern in these cases is providing compatible footage. The editor must have adequate coverage in order to cut the shots into a continuous sequence.

Re-ordering the shots presents a better coverage of the action.

  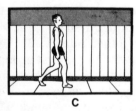

A   D   C

E   B

Here, camera angles A and B are far enough apart to avoid clashing. D and E become much more fluid when they are separated by C. The sequence works better because it is a good combination of directionally continuous shots taken from one side of the action line.

So far, assuring directional continuity seems easy, but circumstances aren't always as controllable as in the clear-cut examples outlined in the preceding pages. Other examples are more difficult to predict.

Problematic Examples of Directional Patterns

Crowds, changing backgrounds, and *moving two-shots* require special care in choosing camera angles. Each of these cases poses problems unique to its own particularities. Previous techniques of observing directional patterns by using an action line does not always provide the best way to ensure continuity.

When dealing with crowds, often it's easier to think of the directional patterns as left to right, right to left or neutral rather than trying to pinpoint an action line. If a crowd breaks up and disperses, why bother with an action line when the scene is obviously neutral? If a mob splits up just before the camera so that half of the mob exits the frame camera right and the other half exits left, then the pattern is neutral. Plotting the action line for these examples would be a waste of time.

Subjects exit the frame left when they pass the camera.

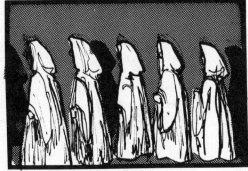

Subjects head camera left en masse

Camera tracks with the mob
resulting in a neutral shot.

A crowd splits up resulting in a
neutral directional pattern.

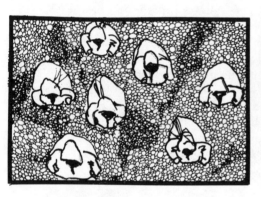

High angle creates a neutral
pattern.

Crowd disperses in all directions and hence, no direction or
neutral.

A series of traveling shots set against changing backgrounds is particularly tricky to film. Without adequate coverage, the sequence is impossible to edit. If in each new shot the subject remains center frame,
there is no illusion of the progression from one location to the next;
the subject appears to hop around to unrelated locations. Instead, the
subject should travel out of the frame in one location and enter the
frame in the other if the illusion of progression is to be preserved.
Progression is as much a part of motion continuity as directional patterns. There can be no progression if the necessary footage was never
shot.

Moving two-shots require similar attention. The filmed subjects must
be watched for their position in the frame and the order in which they

enter. When two doctors approach the main entrance to the hospital, one enters the doorway first. Weeks later, the interior hospital scenes are filmed. The same doctor had better enter the lobby first if the shots are going to flow together.

A moving two-shot's action line is expanded into a T formation. Neutral shots are still on either end of the travel path, but acceptable camera angles are determined by a second axis. The top of the T or second axis is formed by drawing a line through the moving subjects. Any angles on one side of the second axis are compatible.

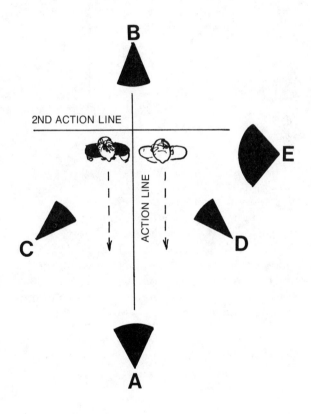

Even though the subjects will be traveling in opposite screen directions, the audience will not be confused if the scene is first established by a shot showing that the two men are walking side by side.

E   A   C

D   B

Before returning to the next step of the travel sequence, the camera angle which depicts the previously established direction should be used to provide a smoother transition.

Crowds, changing backgrounds and moving two-shots are just some of the problems involved in motion continuity. The major part of a motion picture can be considered stationary. From a literal point of view, a talking head moves, but for our purposes, a distinction will be made between a moving subject or *one which travels,* and a basically stationary subject or *one that doesn't travel.* From this premise, it's easier to identify stationary subjects as those which comprise *film space.*

MORRIS ABRAMS INTERVIEW

Morris Abrams started in the entertainment industry during the late silent film days as a script supervisor. After scripting many films including *Billy the Kid, The Big House* and *Tarzan of the Apes,* he moved into other areas of production. For the last twelve years, Morris Abrams has worked as a first assistant director. His credits include a number of features and television programs. Among the television credits are *Kojak, The Brady Bunch* and *Love American Style.* His production managing credits include the *Trapper John* pilot, *Rivals, Slaughter's Big Rip Off* and *J.D.'s Revenge.* More recently he has worked as a financial production representative and as an executive in charge of production. His thorough knowledge of production requirements along with his early experience as a script supervisor makes him a perfect person to ask about the importance of a script supervisor on the set.

ABRAMS: This is a hell of a day. It's too beautiful to be inside. My wife said don't talk too long and the first thing I did was rip my pants coming out. With that opening, I should be in a fairly rotten mood, but I'm not. I'm really flattered that I get to tie up your time by talking to you.

To give you a little background, I guess I'm one of the few people in the industry today who kept script on silent films. It happened because I was trying to get a little bit of high school in before eleven o'clock a.m. daily. When I wasn't going to school, I worked as an office boy in the M.G.M. production office. I got in one day and the management said, "That darn Charlie is falling asleep on the job again. Go down there and keep script." That was my entire training period.

The producer-director was a wonderful, marvelous man by the name of Lucien Hubbard. When matching and slating began to fall apart all because of my ignorance, he said, "All right, Morrie, when we finish this picture you're going in the cutting room. You'll sit in a corner and help us find the right takes, and show us how to match the shots."

Instead of firing me which would have been the natural thing, they educated me. I saw where they cut to the close-ups. I saw how they worked reverse shots. I learned about progression and directions while they tried to figure out how to take care of the mistakes I'd made.

19

STUDENT: When did you start to feel at ease with the job of script supervisor? Surely, not everyone was as patient as they were on the first film.

ABRAMS: Of course they weren't patient. They hazed the hell out of me. But it was a young industry. There was room for error, and the cutters were magicians at editing out mistakes. It took almost a year of on-the-job training to really master the mechanics of the job. I guess what I'm trying to tell you is that after you've mastered the fundamentals, your mind and your creativity are two of the most important things you can give. For instance, I'm going to tell you a story about Harry Beaumont that happened just after a new thing called "sound" came into the industry. I was still pretty excited about the whole business of being on a set. Harry was a pretty hard-bitten guy. He would direct a scene, and I'd see something, or I'd think of some piece of business, and I couldn't contain myself. I would say, "Mr. Beaumont, what if you did so and so with this? Would it be better?" And he'd just look at me out of the corner of his eye and say, "You trying to direct this picture?" Afterwards he'd deliberately walk over to the actors and say, "Look, if you do this, it'll be better." Then he would look back in my direction as if daring me to open my mouth. What he was really doing was very smart. He was making me think and analyze before I would offer a suggestion. Of course, being young, I couldn't contain myself. I'd come up with another suggestion, and he'd say, "Huh, trying to direct the picture again." And he'd go back among the actors. So I was helping make the picture. It was a long time afterwards that I learned that, after every picture, Harry would go into the production office and say, "I want that boy on my next picture." But he wouldn't tell me. So, if you can get on a relationship with the people around you, starting with the director—as long as you're careful only to speak when you've really got something to say or you don't cornball it up with top-of-the-head suggestions—when you see something that can really help, you can become very valuable.

STUDENT: Things must be a lot different now from the time you started as a script supervisor?

ABRAMS: When I started work as a script girl, script bitch, script clerk, "Hey Script," or whatever they called me, I did essentially everything a script supervisor does today except I didn't have to worry about dialogue. There wasn't any. When sound came in it was very tough to watch action, hear words and memorize dialogue well enough to catch where they might blow a line or mumble. It may interest you to know that there was no such thing as a second assistant director at M.G.M. then. The script clerk had to make the call sheets, help herd the extras, make production reports, and sometimes on night calls, pay the extras in cash. I'll never forget working on the first Viva Villa in 1933 down in Mexico. Our accountant got drunk, and who do you think ended up handling the money as well as keeping script? Morrie. Since then, I've seen an evolution where jobs have become more specialized; and new departments with additional jobs have developed as the industry became more complex. But basically, if there's anything I would want to stress, it's that whatever job you're in, soak up anything that isn't nailed down. I don't care if it's another guy's jurisdiction. Learn his job and how it relates to the rest of the package, and then build good relationships.

STUDENT: I would think that the other crew members would get angry if the script supervisor was constantly stepping on their toes.

ABRAMS: Ultimately, there's really no such thing as other people's toes. We have to work together in varying circumstances with varying skills and varying personalities. If a line is blown, it's the script supervisor's problem. If an actor comes in with the wrong shirt, somebody's likely to say, "It's wardrobe's jurisdiction—not my fault." That isn't the point. Basically, the script supervisor is the back-up. The script supervisor must be observant enough to catch the mistake and prevent it from causing trouble. And this is the kind of training that has slipped away in the industry with everybody trying to grab more authority and exclusive control in order to become more important and get more money. But in the end, cooperation, collaboration, contribution—and understanding the other guy's job and his problems—will be your key to advancement because this isn't the last job you're going to hold.

STUDENT: What other recommendations would you make for script supervisors just starting out in the business?

ABRAMS: Some things come to mind. I got tired of having applicants come into a studio and say, "I'm a great assistant," or "I'm a great script clerk," or whatever it took to get the job. After they landed the job, they'd come in and say, "What's your paper work like? Where are the departments? Where's the ladies' room?"—all the damn things that a professional checks out before ever getting onto a show. If you're going to apply for a job, tell whoever is hiring you that you want to put in a couple of days on your own time. Get a map of the lot, find out what their paperwork is, how they handle it, how the set operation works and their other needs—at your own expense. And tell your employer that the reason for this is because when you first walk in, you want to be able to go to work immediately and not lose time at his expense. I suggest this to you as a way of selling yourself. Everyone of you is in competition with every other one. The only thing I say about competition is keep it clean; don't wear spikes when you run over each other. Play it fair. I'm sick and tired of paying out money for "hardly-ables" who come in and say, "Take me by the hand and lead me around." To get top money and deliver top results, you make your own investment. I still do. I come in a day ahead or two days ahead. I still read the script on *my own time. I still study out what I think the problems are so that I can negotiate intelligently for myself; but also so that I'm all ready to function the minute I drive in that gate. I recommend that philosophy to you.*

STUDENT: *How far would you extend this philosophy to the creative side? I guess what I'm trying to get at is if you think that a script supervisor has to be responsive to a director's vision?*

ABRAMS: *Your usefulness to yourself, and your usefulness as filmmakers will depend on developing a sense of dramatic values. Many filmmakers don't consider the technicians and the support people in the industry important enough to involve them in the creative process. As a support person, I find that, whether you agree with the creative people or not, if you understand their concepts, you will help the picture. Even the indirect benefit of anticipating and meeting creative people's needs will make a difference. And the script supervisor can play a part in this.*

The more in tune you are with the effort of the creative people—the director, the actors, the producer, the editors—the more you can anticipate, have things ready, and above all, help to make a better film. I don't know whether most of you recognize this: 85 percent of the time is used up by the support troops. The remaining 15 percent of the time is rehearsal and takes. I'm not arguing as an efficiency man. I'm arguing from the standpoint of making a better film. Filmmaking is a business and an art of details. It is a synthesis of many efforts and impressions, many of them subliminal. That is what makes it possible to say that a script supervisor who feels a responsibility to know everything possible about every aspect of production can help make a better film. If the little things are handled so that you can work smoothly and have a little sense of momentum on the set, then you get a better film. If you get a better film, you get better sales. If you get better sales, you get a crack at better money. It's as simple as that.

CONTINUITY OF SPACE

The concept of space continuity overlaps many of the other topics outlined in this book. The elements of continuity are so interrelated that it is difficult to discuss one aspect without going into others. Both continuity of time (with which we will deal later), and continuity of direction play major roles in continuity of space.

In the same way as for moving subjects, directional continuity must be observed when the subject being filmed is stationary. The direction in which the subject looks should be protected against inconsistencies. If during an exam, a student sneaks a peak at Suzy's test on the right, then the student should continue to look toward the right each time he cheats. Every portion of the action must match throughout the sequence if the spatial relationship between the student and Suzy is to remain consistent.

Once acceptable camera angles are selected, they will again fall into neutral, left to right or right to left patterns Left to right and right to left patterns operate in much the same way as for moving subjects.

CL to CR FACIAL DIRECTION of Isadore Cashier in *Green Fields,* a Collective Film Production.

CR to CL FACIAL DIRECTION of Max Vodnoy in *Green Fields.*

A neutral direction occurs when a subject looks above, below or straight into the camera lens. Neutral looks are not as universally used for stationary subjects as for moving subjects because most audiences find it disturbing to have an actor gaze at the lens.

NEUTRAL FACIAL DIRECTION of Isadore Cashier in *Green Fields*.

NEUTRAL FACIAL DIRECTION from *Green Fields*. Notice that this woman's gaze directly into the lens tends to be far more puzzling to the audience than the slightly camera right look of Isadore Cashier.

Whether left to right, right to left or neutral, the principles of continuity that apply to moving subjects also apply to stationary subjects. Changes in direction made accountable by on-camera explanations pose no problems in directional continuity. Neither do inconsistencies that are obscured by cutaways or neutral shots. Ensuring directional continuity can be accomplished in the same manner as for moving subjects by drawing an action line.

The difference between a stationary action line compared to a moving one is that the stationary line doesn't follow a travel path. Instead, the line is set by the physical relationship of the subjects in the center of attention. By using the action line device, the direction a subject faces or looks will automatically be consistent. *Matching the look* is the primary concern of directional continuity for stationary subjects.

Matching the Look for One or Two Subjects

An action line for two subjects is chosen the same way as for one subject. For two subjects, drawing a straight line through the subjects forms the division between acceptable and non-acceptable camera angles. For one subject, the line is drawn through the object towards which the subject is looking. Both create a boundary where camera angles are consistent within 180°.

The first diagram shows a man and a woman sitting alone at a table in a crowded restaurant. Although the camera focuses on these two, other diners sit at nearby tables scattered in the background. A top view appears on the top of page 25.

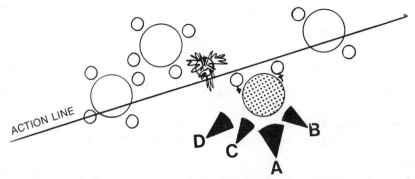

Angle A captures both main actors sitting together. This angle establishes a relationship between the two. Angle B focuses on the man as he faces toward the woman. Angle C is the reverse angle focusing on the woman. Angle D includes both, but favors the woman.

Crossing over the line results in a mis-matched relationship between the two actors. Remember that the woman should appear on the

right side of the man. Placing the camera on the wrong side of the action line makes her appear as if she were talking to the man at the next table.

The next diagram shows a detective peeking through a window at an off-camera clue. In this example, there is only one subject, the detective. Still, the spatial relationship between the detective and the clue must be preserved in order for the direction in which the detective faces to remain consistent.

A top view of the line would look like this:

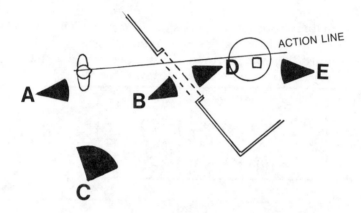

Whether the camera is positioned outside of the house as in angles A, B and C or inside as in angles D and E, complementary views must be shot from only one side of the line. Notice that in the front views the detective consistently appears on the camera left side of the clue.

The spatial relationship between two stationary subjects or a stationary subject and an object of interest can easily be observed by drawing an action line. This action line shifts as the subjects move around the set into new physical relationships, but for each segment of the scene, the line provides a boundary. This device will ensure consistent camera angles throughout the scene or until a new character enters.

Matching the Look for Three Subjects

An action line for three subjects poses different requirements than for one or two subjects because the line is not always drawn straight. Most often, the subjects form a triangular pattern. Each side of the triangle is treated the same as any two-shot.

In the following example, Alice speaks to Tweedledee and Tweedledum:

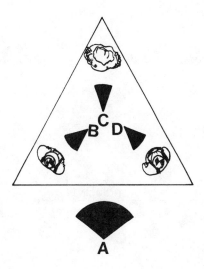

Camera angle A includes Tweedledee, Tweedledum and Alice in a full shot. Camera angle B shows Tweedledee facing toward the right as he relates to Alice. Angle C is the corresponding shot of Alice relating back toward Tweedledee camera left and then turning to Tweedledum camera right. Angle D presents Tweedledum looking toward Alice in the opposite direction. By using these angles, all three characters share the weight of the scene with Alice taking slightly more focus than the twins.

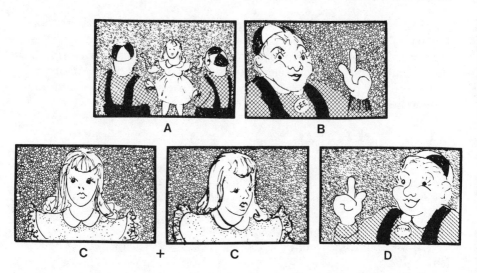

If the same scene were structured differently so that Alice ad-
dresses Tweedledee and Tweedledum as a pair, then only one line is
needed.

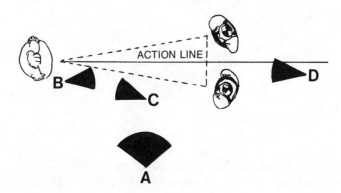

In the above diagram, all fat boys look alike to Alice so together they
become a unit. The line is drawn between this "unit" and Alice. The
front views resemble the spatial relationships of a two-shot.

Whether one subject dominates the action or all three equally share the scene, the same principles for directional continuity apply. The spatial relationship between one subject and the next must be preserved whether the other subjects are on screen or off. When more subjects are added to the group, these principles are put to further use.

·*Matching the Look for a Group of Subjects*

When filming a group of subjects, special attention must be devoted to preserving the direction that each person faces. Particularly complex scenes require considerable advance planning of camera angles from the director. When Joan Rivers, the comedienne, decided that she wanted to direct her comedy script, *Rabbit Test*, she addressed herself to the problem of matching looks by first hiring a production illustrator early in pre-production. The illustrator made sketches of every scene. Joan also hired May Wale Brown as her script supervisor several weeks before shooting was to commence. The three of them carefully went through the script scene by scene planning camera angles and important visual approaches.

Rabbit Test is the story of a young man who becomes pregnant which makes him the laughing stock of the world. When the world suddenly recognized the "miracle" of his pregnancy, he is showered with honors, and he becomes the ambassador of the world.

In one scene, Lionel, a young man played by Billy Crystal, finds out that he is pregnant. Segoynia, a gypsy girl, invites Lionel to tea in order to meet her gypsy family, consisting of her mother, Imogene Coca, her grandmother played by Roddy McDowell, her father, and two zany brothers. As they sit around the table, the grandmother tells Lionel's fortune by reading tea leaves.

Group scenes around a table are usually complicated because the angle of the master decides which side of the camera each individual must look toward the others during closeups. Sometimes a second master is necessary to ensure that they continue to look toward each other in a natural manner instead of forcing their looks too far camera right or camera left.

Joan Rivers came to the set well-prepared for this complicated scene due to her pre-production efforts. She told her script supervisor, "May, you and I are attached at the hip. Don't ever leave my side." She carefully arranged the main characters around the table for group shots, two shots and closeups. The other characters could be covered with quick reaction shots. Since, of the gypsies, only the mother and daughter speak English, they had to find a nasty-sounding word that Grandmother could spit at Lionel to tell him he is pregnant. Lionel only spoke English. The word they came up with was *curva*, the Hungarian word for *whore*.

Roddy McDowell was so funny when he shot Billy Crystal a piercing look and snarled "curva," and Imogene Coca's reaction of outrage was so hilarious that the two of them broke up laughing during each attempt at the master. It got so bad that as soon as Roddy looked toward Billy everybody around the table cracked up. Finally, Joan Rivers and the crew couldn't stop laughing either.

Eventually, all the carefully laid plans of how to shoot this scene easily and economically had to be abandoned. They had to start with Roddy's closeup, keeping Imogene completely out of his sight. The master angle became the last shot of the sequence when everyone finally could control their laughter.

The filming of a group scene is comparable to filming three subjects. The members of the group either share or dominate the focus. The following diagram, for example, represents a teacher lecturing to a classroom of students. If the teacher leads the scene as the students merely react en masse, then one action line suffices. The line is drawn from the lecturer through the center of the students.

Angle A masters the scene with the lecturer on the left of the frame and the students on the right. Angle B captures the teacher looking toward camera right where we've just established the students. The final angle, C, catches the students facing the lecturer.

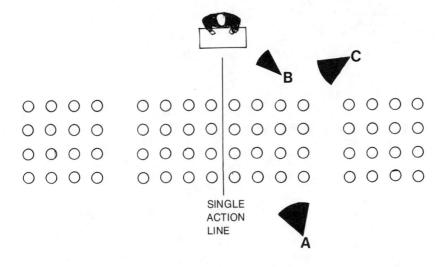

The frontal views are directionally consistent.

If, on the other hand, the students' individual reactions were important to the scene, a new line should be drawn for each two-shot.

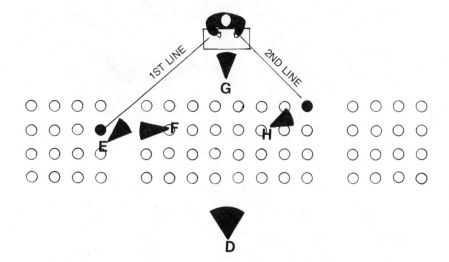

Angle E, F, and G presents a consistent physical relationship between the students and the lecturer but only if the lecturer faces the marked student on the first action line. Switching to the second line requires a shot to explain why the lecturer's direction is altered. A fluid sequence from the first line to the second might appear like this:

In this arrangement, the lecturer turns his head in camera angle D when the second student raises his hand. The new direction is established automatically.

When selecting camera angles, it is important to remember that the action line is only a means to an end. Many directors disregard rules of directional continuity altogether and observe their own theories. A director might claim that the eye has a natural tendency to follow motion which compensates for inconsistencies in direction. Another might consider a large object in the frame enough for physical orientation regardless of which direction a subject faces. Another may jump the line frequently with the intention of cutting out the problematic inconsistencies such as crosses or entrances in the final assembly. Sometimes it is perfectly acceptable to cross the line while shooting singles as long as the actor cheats his look to the proper side of the lens when relating to his offscreen companion. Still, most directors feel very strongly that observing these basic rules of directional continuity avoid needless disruptions in a film's illusion. Choosing directional patterns is only part of the requirements for space continuity. *Continuity of time* also plays a major role.

CONTINUITY OF TIME

Unlike space and motion, continuity of time is hard to define. The abstract concept of time can only be defined through tangible means. Time continuity must be observed through those physical clues which tend to express the passage of time.

There are several different types of time. Time can be *actual* where actions filmed take as long as in reality, or *accelerated* where only the highlights of the action are filmed. A sequence can occur during the *past*, the *present* or the *future*. Each of these can be further broken down into days or partial days. A picture such as *Petulia*, for example, may take place in the present interspersed with flashbacks in the past. Another such as *Klute* may start with a scene in the future, followed by a series of events occurring on consecutive days in the present. As the days in the present progress, they catch up to the future. Unless the physical indications of time are consistent in both examples, it is difficult for the average audience to follow the storyline.

The most common way to express time is through costumes, makeup, set dressing and lighting. *Lighting continuity* is perhaps the easiest to keep track of. If a sequence occurs during the day, the light is relatively bright compared to a sequence that occurs at night. If a second shot happens shortly after a first, then its light should more or less match the first. It's that simple.

Academy award-winning cinematographer, John Alonzo, expresses his opinion about how script supervisors help him trace nuances in lighting continuity in the following quote:

> I take advantages of the script supervisor beyond their innumerable duties. They are seldom given credit for actually collaborating with their director of photography, not only tracing time progression and movement, but also in their grasp of the mood of a scene. Because a good script supervisor reads the script so many times, between setups I use them as a good source to bounce ideas off. While lighting, a script supervisor's short descriptions such as "late afternoon going into night" help me determine the nuances of lighting. I rely on a script supervisor just as much for out-of-continuity matching, keeping track of lens information, and helping my assistant keep up on numbering and print instructions. To sum up, a good script supervisor has always been the unsung hero or heroine for me and I would be greatly handicapped without one.

Continuity of make-up is also simple. A character shaves off his beard in one scene, so in every following scene the beard is absent. A black eye becomes progressively healed as time passes.

Set dressing continuity involves more details. A lamp that appears on one side of a desk should remain on the same side throughout the office interiors unless we see it moved. If an apartment is dressed with a carefully-laid-out array of junk when the occupant leaves in the morning, the array should remain intact when the character returns that evening. The next day, the junk may be rearranged, indicating that time has passed. A candle that burns throughout a conversation becomes progressively shorter as the time elapses.

Costume continuity poses the same problems as set dressing, if not more. A character who leaves in the morning returns in the same clothes. When a coat is taken off, it should remain off until the end of the sequence, or until it is put back on or lost or any number of other explanations. Details further complicate the picture. How many buttons are done? What jewelry is she wearing and where? Which side of his shirt is stained with blood? Is the boa over her right shoulder or the left? How does the train of the evening gown drape as the queen sits? All these factors and many more are evidence of the passage of time.

Rita Riggs, who has spent the last 20 years designing costumes from feature films to a decade of Norman Lear television comedies, tells an interesting story about how continuity affects the costume designer's job.

> Between setups during the filming of *Psycho* and *The Birds,* Alfred Hitchcock often launched into impromptu dialogues on "movie-making." How lucky was I, a costume apprentice under Edith Head, to be

included in these sessions involving editing and continuity disciplines. Aspiring designers quickly develop a respect for continuity responsibilities on the set. After three months of matching a floating chiffon scarf in high wind, a fledgling costumer may never again establish costumes so mobile that they waste time and takes, and craze both the script supervisor and the performers. A twenty-odd-year career later, I once more found myself daily begging forgiveness from one of the best and busiest continuity professionals on a picture called *Yes, Georgio* for using scarves again. A team of artists combined effects to create the larger-than-life grandeur of the tenor of the decade, Luciano Pavarotti. The script supervisor nicknamed this wonderful genius, "The wind—my throat!" Throughout the film as we traveled across America from Boston to San Francisco, from L.A. to New York, scarves were yanked out of my trunks and wrapped protectively around Pavarotti's sensitive throat. Everytime that silk fluttered in the breeze, I genuflected three times toward the script chair and received a pained blessing in return. Coming from his operatic background, Mr. Pavarotti was unaccustomed to shooting out of sequence. "Matching" became a new game of challenge to him. He quickly became the first to catch us up on continuity details in dress. And Luciano's final comment after seeing the first rough cut and looping was, "Now I know how a movie is made. First you loop, then you make the movie."

Watching to see that these costume, lighting, set dressing and make-up details remain consistent from shot to shot may sound too obvious to merit discussion, but don't be fooled. Remember that a film is rarely shot in sequence. Some scenes may be shot weeks or months apart even though they take place within seconds in the script. The company may shoot a traveller entering a train station's exterior in August, and not shoot the corresponding interior until December. This tends to make time continuity far less obvious during the process of shooting.

Continuity of time, space and motion are interrelated. The elements of one overlap to the others, and they all share the same goal. The main objective is to present the most coherent and dramatic presentation of the story as possible.

Audiences have strong expectations of what is required to achieve a logical flow from shot to shot. Only unaccountable changes cause continuity problems. Inconsistencies, mismatches, unexplained alterations in established patterns all interrupt the flow of a picture by breaking the illusion of the film's reality. Putting these principles of continuity to use as a script supervisor will be outlined in the following chapters.

Chapter Two

The Preparation Period

With a better idea of what is meant by continuity, we are now ready to tackle the job of script supervision. Starting at the beginning, a script supervisor's job commences upon receipt of a script. Before actual filming begins, a number of days are required to prepare.

The duration of the script supervisor's preparation period varies depending on the length, quality and budget of the script. A feature-length assignment may include a two-week preparation period while an hour television drama may only have two and a half days. Commercials usually don't have more perparation time other than a short period before the first camera set-up. The quality of a screenplay determines how much time is allotted because certain treatments of a subject naturally require more than others. A gory thriller about the Manson murders with 500 action-packed scenes invariably takes longer to prepare than an intimate story with few locations and characters. Since the time factor will determine how much can be accomplished, for the purposes of this book, we'll consider the preparation period to be at least one week.

A preparation week put to good use proves invaluable not only in making the shoot easier for the script supervisor, but for every member of the crew. A major part of mastering the job of script supervision is learning how to use the preparation week to the fullest. The importance of studying and memorizing every possible detail of the script cannot be stressed strongly enough. A thorough knowledge will be acquired naturally as the script supervisor goes through the process of *gathering and organizing the equipment, preparing the working script* and *taking advantage of pre-production.*

GATHERING AND ORGANIZING THE EQUIPMENT

The success or failure of a script supervisor partially depends on having adequate equipment. Some of the script supervisor's equipment is standard while others depend on individual tastes. The following list is designed to offer guidelines for selecting necessary and time-saving scripting equipment. Since the magic word when it comes to organizing the equipment is *time,* perhaps the best place to start is with an ordinary *wristwatch.*

Wristwatch

The need for a wristwatch shouldn't be ignored just because it's so fundamental. Filming is highly schedule-oriented and knowing the exact time is important for every member of the crew. The script supervisor, in particular, requires a dependable watch in order to fill out forms among other continuity duties. Constantly hounding co-workers asking for the hour is annoying. The only mandatory feature is that the watch keep accurate time. Some script supervisors find it helpful to have the date on their watch. Others like to have a second hand, in case their stopwatch breaks.

Stopwatch

Unlike a wristwatch, a *stopwatch* requires more specific features. Nearly every experienced script supervisor will recommend investing in a quality instrument. Three main characteristics to look for are *convenience, silence* and *accuracy.*

For convenience, a stopwatch should be sturdy enough to bang around and easy to read. Some face styles are easier to read than others. Whether a digital, a 30-second, or a 60-second face, certain disadvantages should be avoided. Stopwatch dials that measure time in units of film footage rather than in seconds aren't necessary; script supervisors mostly deal in time. Any such "extra" gadgets tend to clutter up the watch face, and they slow down the process of recording time. A script supervisor has to be able to read the time by quickly glancing at the watch.

Another feature that simplifies reading a stopwatch is a minute gauge. Many cheaper watches only have a second hand and no device to measure minutes. These watches won't do. A busy script supervisor can't possibly keep track of how many times the second hand has passed "60."

The stopwatch should also be convenient to operate. A watch with an automatic return to zero seconds, for instance, is simpler to use.

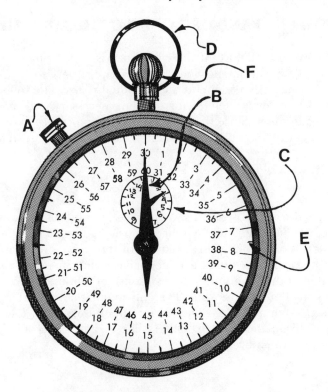

A. AUTOMATIC RETURN TO ZERO
B. SECOND HAND
C. MINUTE GAUGE
D. HANGING RING, (FOR CHAIN OR CORD)
E. HALF-SECOND MARKS
F. STOP AND START BUTTON

Often, there won't be enough time between takes for the script supervisor to run the second hand back to the zero mark before the watch can be used again.

A final convenience is accessibility. A script supervisor can't afford to waste time searching for the watch. One technique widely used by experienced script supervisors is wearing the stopwatch on a chain or a cord around the neck. This also helps avoiding the problem of juggling the watch with an armload of other equipment.

Wearing the watch as a necklace also reduces possible unwanted noise during filming. A stopwatch can't be accidentally dropped when it's securely hanging on a neckchain. A noisy stopwatch may ruin a take if the microphone picks up the ticking noises. Sometimes, it's difficult to avoid ticking during a particularly intimate scene. To solve this problem, the stopwatch's chain should be long enough for the script supervisor to shield the watch under an arm.

In addition to silence and convenience, a stopwatch should be checked for accuracy. Periodic *vibograph inspections* from a watch specialist can ensure that the stopwatch keeps an even beat. A vibograph readout indicates to the split-second if the stopwatch is running properly in various positions. Watches sometimes run fast or slow when the stem is up, for instance, but not when the stem is down. Sideways, it may run at a completely different rate. A well-tuned watch runs accurately regardless of the position.

While currently the majority of script supervisors use mechanical stopwatches, digital stopwatches work just as well. Digital watches should include the same features. They should be sturdy enough to knock around, convenient to operate with one hand, easy to read at a glance, accurate and silent. Digital watches operate on batteries which emit a faint electrical hum, rather than a ticking noise. Unlike ticking, the electrical hum rarely interferes with a film's sound. On the other hand, similar to a calculator number display, most digital time displays can only be seen from straight on; the display seems to disappear when viewed from even a slight angle. This is especially true in a glare. Even worse, the display may be misread when viewed from an angle. A three, for instance, may appear as an eight. Some script supervisors still prefer having a digital display rather than reading a second hand. Nearly all expensive and inexpensive digital watches record time to the 1/100th of a second which makes digital watches ideal for commercials. Choosing a digital stopwatch over a mechanical stopwatch or visa versa is a matter of personal preference.

A *split feature* which is available on both digital and mechanical stopwatches often comes in handy for the script supervisor. Say, for example, the script supervisor wants to time two overlapping actions. The first action runs fairly smoothly, but the actor begins to stumble during the second half of the scene. At this point, the script supervisor doesn't know whether the first part of the scene should be timed or the complete scene. A split feature permits both timings simultaneously. On the digital watch, the script supervisor punches a split/reset button at the end of the first action. The time display freezes at the moment after depressing the button, but the timing continues. When the stop button is pressed, the display switches to the timing for the entire action. On the mechanical stopwatch, an extra hand marks the place where the split button was depressed. By having both timings available, the script supervisor can ask the director which part of the scene is useful and record the proper timing.

Having an accurate, silent and convenient stopwatch is imperative. Certain minimum features are required if the script supervisor hopes to perform his or her duties effectively. While the stopwatch requirements rarely deviate from job to job, a script supervisor's other equipment is less defined.

Instant Camera

Sometimes an *instant camera,* such as a Polaroid, proves invaluable in matching set, make-up, hair and costume details [see union still photographer pg 74]. The cliché, "a picture is worth a thousand words," really holds true. A script supervisor could write a detailed description in the continuity notes and still fail to record as much information as a single instant photograph. As a result, instant photographs are commonly used as matching guides. The effectiveness of the photographs depends on how well they are organized into a convenient system.

By punching holes in the photographs, they can be hung on a large ring and worn on a belt loop. Three-by-five file cards separate the photographs into locations or sequences. Any notes regarding changes made after a photograph has been taken can be written on the back. Scene numbers should also be noted.

While a limited number of conveniences is helpful, an excess has the opposite effect. Some script supervisors even try to lug around a chair. A script supervisor who carries too much will become overburdened. Instead, he or she should be selective when choosing which supplies are the most necessary.

Miscellaneous Supplies

All other supplies that are not immediately needed on the set can be kept in a briefcase or satchel out of the way. Stationery supplies commonly included are paper clips, tape, hole reinforcers, dividers, a stapler, envelopes, carbon paper, manilla envelopes for turning in forms, and paper. Extra film and spare forms should be kept on hand. A cliplight or flashlight makes night shooting easier, while a clear plastic bag helps in the rain. Extra clothes, a wallet, timecards and personal belongings also can be set aside during most of the shooting day.

Miscellaneous supplies, an instant camera system, a stopwatch, and a wristwatch are pretty straight-forward items. The next items on the equipment list are more subjective. Organizing the following equipment depends on developing a working notation system.

Fully Equipped Notebook and Clipboard

A script supervisor's notation system is built around a *fully equipped notebook*. Generally speaking, the notebook should be a *three-ring binder* which allows script pages and forms to be subtracted and added easily. This flexibility will come in handy as scenes are rewritten, and as daily continuity notes are recorded into a workable order. Additional stationery supplies such as pens, pencils, erasers and liquid correction fluid can be kept in a pocket of the notebook. Some script supervisors prefer to wear these supplies in a pouch fastened to their belts. Dividers help organize the script. A ruler that is tied to the notebook by a short cord won't make noise hitting the ground if it falls. Effectively arranged supplies won't be left behind accidently when moving from location to location.

A *clipboard* is commonly used in addition to the script supervisor's notebook and accessories. Flipping between notebook pages is too time-consuming and noisy, yet a script supervisor often has to note records in two places at the same time. Using a clipboard beside the notebook pages alleviates this problem. Running lists such as editorial notes and daily production records can be kept conveniently on the clipboard.

Both a script supervisor's clipboard and notebook are instrumental to successfully performing continuity duties. The specifics of equipping this notebook can only be pinpointed as the script supervisor establishes a working routine. The best method for tailoring equipment to individual scripting systems will become clearer as the script supervisor prepares the working script.

PREPARING THE WORKING SCRIPT

Selecting the most effective system for the working script depends on the type of script used. There are various types of shooting scripts. The most common are *split-page, storyboard* and *full-page* formats.

Split-Page Format

Split-page scripts make a distinction between audio and visuals by dividing the page in half vertically. On the left side, only the visuals are described. The right side includes the dialogue and the narration. This audio-visual distinction is ideal for video projects or heavily voice-tracked films and for commercials. An example of the split-page format appears on the opposite page.

This script was used by American International Television on their series, *Comeback,* whose episodes dramatize the stories of famous people who have had the courage to make comebacks in their careers. Each episode is comprised of stock footage, film or tape excerpts, and original footage. On-camera interviews and narration tie together the miscellaneous pieces. The split-page format lends itself perfectly to this type of story. It provides an at-a-glance reference to what will be shot.

<u>TEASER</u>

1. EXT. RODEO DRIVE, CROWDED WITH PEOPLE. | WHITMORE (VO): This is the way the
   WE'RE TRACKING FORWARD, AND THE CAMERA | world looks when you're 3 feet 11
   IS PRECISELY 3 FEET 11 INCHES OFF THE | inches tall.
   GROUND AS WE <u>MOVE</u> THROUGH THE CROWDS.

2. INT. THE PRODUCTION CENTER. WE'RE | This is the way the world looks
   STILL <u>TRACKING FORWARD</u>, AND WE'RE | when you're 3 feet 11 inches tall,
   STILL 3 FEET 11 INCHES HIGH, ONLY NOW | and you're an actor...
   WE'RE MOVING PAST OFFICE DOORS READ- |
   ING "CASTING" AND "AGENTS". | and you want to work.

   AND NOW THE CAMERA <u>COMES UP</u> TO ONE
   PARTICULAR DOOR MARKED "CASTING"
   AND THE DOOR IS OPEN. AND THEN THE
   DOOR SLAMS RIGHT IN OUR FACE.

3. EXT. THE BURBANK STUDIOS, AND WE'RE | And this is the way the world looks
   REVERSE TRACKING ON HERVE VILLECHAIZE | when you're Herve Villechaize, and
   WALKING BETWEEN THE SOUNDSTAGES, AND | you've finally overcome people's
   HE'S WEARING HIS <u>BIONIC MIDGET</u> T- | prejudices about being different.
   SHIRT.

   AND NOW HERVE SPEAKS O.C. | HERVE: Finally, I'm being taken
   | seriously as an actor. They don't
   | consider me a freak anymore.

   FREEZE FRAME.

   OPENING CREDITS, BILLBOARD AND
   COMMERCIAL #1.

<u>ACT ONE</u>

4. INT. STUDIO. WHITMORE WALKS PAST | WHITMORE: I'm James Whitmore, and
   BLOWUPS OF OTHER SUBJECTS AND WE | this is <u>Comeback</u>, true stories of
   <u>TRACK</u> WITH HIM AS HE COMES UP TO | people who've been hit by adversity
   LORETTA AYEROFF'S STUDY OF HERVE | just when things were going great,
   LEANING AGAINST A POLE, A KERCHIEF | and then had the courage and determin-
   AT HIS NECK, AN INSOUCIANT EXPRES- | ation to fight their way back. This
   SION ON HIS FACE. WHITMORE STOPS | time, we're going to learn about a man
   BY THE BLOWUP. | who's fought to be accepted on his own
   | terms, and who refused to be limited
   | by people's vision of him: Herve
   | Villechaize.

Storyboard Format

A storyboard format also differentiates between the audio and the visual.

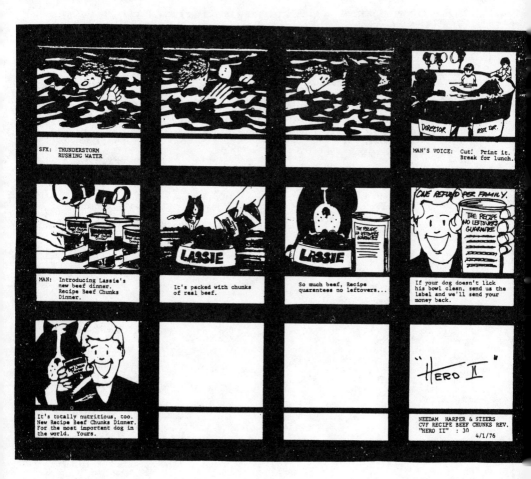

Instead of offering a description of the visual on one side of the page, the storyboard presents the visual in picture form with the dialogue and sound effects written below each corresponding picture. This layout stresses the visuals and is used primarily for commercials.

Full-Page Format

The type of script used most often for features and filmed television productions is the full-page script.

```
                    RETURN TO MACON COUNTY

        FADE IN:

   1    EXT. ACCESS ROAD - CLOSE UP - A COW - DAY              1

        looking directly into CAMERA.  OFF CAMERA we HEAR the
        SOUND of an ENGINE REVVING.  CAMERA PANS OFF the cow
        ONTO a car parked nearby on the access road.

        The car is a yellow 1956 customized Chevy.  The rear
        end is jacked up high, riding on over-sized tires.

   2    CLOSE-UP - ENGINE COMPARTMENT OF THE CAR               2

        We are LOOKING at a solid chrome, full-race power-
        house, which has been tilted to one side to make
        room for a blower which feeds this engine a lethal
        mixture of high-octane gasoline and ether.  The en-
        gine revs...

        ...VARROOM!

        A hand comes INTO the FRAME with a screwdriver, makes
        a slight adjustment on the injection system.  CAMERA
        WIDENS to INCLUDE...

        ...HARLEY McKAY.  Harley is twenty-one years old,
        wears blue jeans rolled at the bottom and carries
        a pack of Camel cigarettes in the sleeve of his T-
        shirt.  Harley cocks his head, listens for a beat,
        then smiles.

   3    INT. YELLOW CHEVY                                      3

        Sitting behind the wheel we SEE BO HOLLINGER, twenty-
        two years old, tall and ruggedly handsome.  He wears
        a red windbreaker and fashions his hair in the style
        of the late James Dean.

                          BO
                    (looking out the
                     window, shouting)
              Oh, Mother!  Is that sweet music.

   4    BO'S POV                                               4

                        HARLEY
              You called it, Dad.  The injector
              is tuned like a fine watch.
```

This style integrates audio and visuals together, making distinctions only through the use of differing type styles. The dialogue is set apart from the rest, indented in the middle of the page. Camera moves, music and shot descriptions are upper cased.

For simplification, we'll deal with full-page feature scripts in this chapter and other styles in Chapter Four. The process of setting up the working script is similar for all three formats when a problem-solving approach is used. By first identifying a problem and finding a solution, the techniques of a full-page format can easily be transferred to the others.

Problem One:

DEVISE AN EFFECTIVE WAY TO NOTE ANY NECESSARY INFORMATION QUICKLY DURING THE SHOOT

During the filming of a feature a multitude of continuity notes are recorded. These notations nearly always are taken in a time-pressured situation. Script supervisors can save themselves considerable grief by preparing their scripts for swift notation before filming starts.

One system of fast notation for people who write sloppily is to add a sheet of transparent, onion-skin paper between each page.

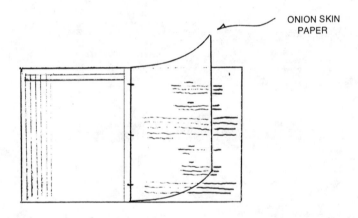

ONION SKIN
PAPER

Some of the continuity notes recorded aren't required by the editors such as the majority of hair, costume, make-up and set dressing notes. These, along with sloppy or obsolete notations, can be left on the onion skin paper. Essential notes should be transferred neatly when the final continuity script is needed by the editor and turned. While the onionskin is discarded.

Inserting a duplicate page between the original pages of the script provides the same type of solution as the onion skin paper. This duplicate page should be folded in half so that it lines up with the original page.

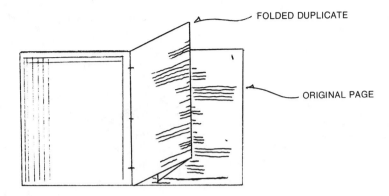

FOLDED DUPLICATE

ORIGINAL PAGE

Temporary and sloppy notes can be jotted on the folded pages while the original page is reserved for crucial editorial notes. Again, at the end of the shoot, the duplicate pages are discarded.

When adding extra pages is too bulky, a photocopy filtering system offers a better solution. Many photocopy machines won't copy a light blue color called "photoblue" or light pencil. All the sloppy notes can be written in a blue pencil so they won't copy. Whenever there is a free moment between set-ups, the important markings can be rewritten in black ink. The advantage to this method is that a script supervisor never loses any of the original markings. At the end, the pencil can be erased, leaving a clean-looking script.

There are many more methods for providing an effective notation system. If all else fails, a script supervisor can always rewrite the notes nightly in a fresh script. After spending a 12 hour day on the set, very few script supervisors opt for this method. Perhaps one of the most convenient solutions is to write all extraneous notes on the opposite side of the script page. The availability of this method depends on how our next problem is solved.

Problem Two:
MAINTAINING EDITORIAL NOTES
SEPARATELY FROM OTHER CONTINUITY NOTES

A system should be set up to accommodate editorial notes both in the script and on daily editorial reports. Most of these systems vary only slightly from one script supervisor to the next. This is because the information recorded must make sense to the editor. Unless the format adopted is similar to standard, accepted methods, the editor may have difficulty deciphering the script supervisor's notes. During the preparation week, script supervisors need only concern themselves with setting up forms. The form can be used for both the script and daily editorial reports.

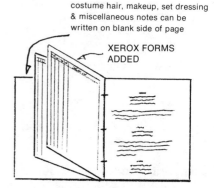

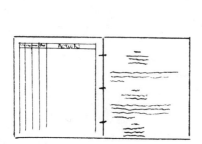

A number of commercial forms are available. Sometimes a company will insist on using one of its own forms, or an editor might have a preference. Otherwise, a script supervisor can use whichever form is most familiar.

There are several ways to prepare the working script for editorial forms. In one common method, the script supervisor copies the form on the backside of the opposite page. In another method, a Xerox copy of a form such as one of the two following examples is inserted between the script pages.

SCRIPT PAGE _____						
SLATE #	TAKE #	TIME	COMMENTS	CAM ROLL	SND ROLL	ACTION

```
                        SCRIPT  NOTE  FORM
                        ─────────────────

 JOB ·· _____ TITLE _____ DIRECTOR_____

 CAMERA_____ A. D _____ SCRIPT_____

 DATE_____ SET _____
```

SCENE	TAKE	SND	PRINT	TIME	LENS	ACTION

By using the latter method, a second form can be added if there is more than one page of editorial notes. Also, the blank side of the previous script page is available for continuity notes. On the other hand, adding extra pages may end up being too bulky on a lengthy script.

Some script supervisors prefer to use blank pages rather than a columned form.

```
 date   SL #                    SC #--Int. Kitchen -- Day
        1-:06 inc NGA           description written out in a
        2-:08 inc NGS (good up  paragraph with details applicable
              to line 26)       to all of the takes including
        3-:00 inc false start   lens, focal length, and camera
        4-:35 cmpl sloppy dial. roll information
        (5):31 cmpl print
```

The date of the shot, the slate number and the individual take results are listed on one side. The other side includes a description of the shot. Since this method requires no advance preparation, it is very popular.

In the next chapter, learning how to fill out the forms will be covered. In the meantime, we'll continue preparing the working script.

Problem Three:
PROVIDE AN EASY REFERENCE TO SEQUENCING

Since time sequencing plays such an important role in preserving a film's continuity, a script supervisor should identify how each scene falls into the total picture. It would be impractical, if not impossible, to memorize all of the various times and locations of each scene. A script supervisor should use other means to accomplish the same goal. Writing simple notations on the script pages helps keep track of which actions occur when and where.

There are several methods for recording *sequencing notations*. All the methods should identify *when* in the picture's fictional time span each scene occurs. Because many shots may take place in a single location, interior and exterior location notes also help to clarify sequencing.

For a simple script, it may only be necessary to write sequencing notations on the top right hand corner of the script pages. Any further notations would be superfluous. A good example of this type of script is the following page from Spelling/Goldberg Productions' television series, *S.W.A.T.* The episode is titled "Courthouse."

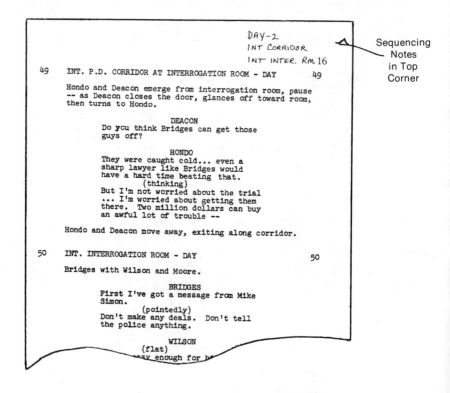

In this example, scenes 49 and 50 occur during day two. Scene 49 takes place in the interior hallway outside the interrogation room while scene 50 takes place inside the interrogation room. The corridor and interrogation room sets may have no physical relationship at all; one could be in a studio and the other could be some place across the city. Although both scenes occur during fictional day two, one could be shot on shooting day one and the other on shooting day seven. Having these sequencing notations on the top of the page will serve as a handy at-a-glance reminder.

For a more complicated sequence, further notation may be necessary. A different page of the same *S.W.A.T.* script illustrates how much more information helps keep track of fictional time. Here, night one switches to day two.

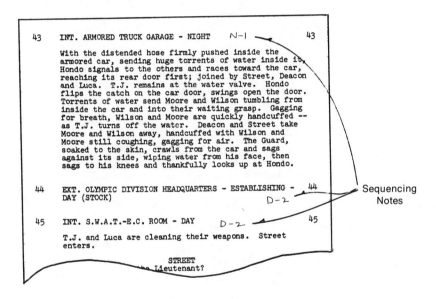

Although this *S.W.A.T.* page presents a fairly simple change of fictional days, other examples are not so straight-forward. Imagine, for instance, a scene between a psychiatrist and a patient. Every time the patient begins to describe an event in the patient's past, the event is dramatized in a flashback. The story keeps skipping back and forth from a day in the present to flashback day one, two, three, four, five, six and so on. Unless the time at each scene is identified, confusion will result.

A third *S.W.A.T.* page presents a complicated switch in locations. Several scenes within an action sequence alternate from the interior garage to the adjacent exterior compound. The specific locations are not immediately clear whenever the camera positions change. If each scene were shot with the exact angles described in the script, there would be no problem because the camera would simply be re-angled toward the described subject. However, since filming rarely follows the shoot-

---

9.

27   STREET'S POV - ARMORED CAR   ExT compound N-1   27

        parked, partially sideways about a hundred feet away
        in the garage; GUNFIRE issuing from the gunports in
        its side.

28   ANGLE - T.J.   InT garage N-1   28

        BULLETS spatter perilously close as he rolls to cover
        beside Street. The gunfire stops.

29   EXT. ARMORED TRUCK CO. COMPOUND - NIGHT·   -1   29

        Hondo, with Deacon and Luca poised near entry to
        garage, reacting to the abrupt stop of gunfire from
        within garage. He glances to Deacon and Luca, hesi-
        tates, then nods pointedly. Deacon poises, darts at
        crouch out into garage -- followed by Luca -- and then
        Hondo.

30   INT. ARMORED TRUCK CO. GARAGE - NIGHT   -1   30

        The scene. As Deacon, then Luca, then Hondo dart in
        from outside, at crouch and find cover -- GUNFIRE seeks
        them from the armored car. The bullets miss.

31   ANGLE - STREET, T.J. AND HONDO   InT garage N-1   31

        as he darts in, takes cover beside them.

                              STREET
                         (grim; to Hondo)
                 It's gonna take a king-size can
                 opener, Lieutenant.

        Hondo grimly studies the setup, then sees something
        and concentrates on it thoughtfully.

32   WHAT HONDO SEES - FIRE HOSE   InT garage N-1   32

        affixed to water line, rolled and hanging against a
        wall about twenty feet from the armored car.

33   BACK TO HONDO   InT garage N-1   33

        eyes fixed on the o.s. fire hose.

                              HONDO
                 Maybe we can cool 'em down, Deacon.
                         (MORE)

                                               (CONTINUED)

ing plan verbatim, a script supervisor must know precisely where each portion of the action happens. Notice how adding simple notes such as those on the previous example page can help clarify where the actions occur. This is typical of an action sequence.

In addition to making notations on the script pages, *one-liners* provide an easy reference to sequencing. One-liners are short, concise de-

S.W.A.T. ONE LINERS

SC #	LOCATION	DESCRIPTION	CAST	TIME
41.	Int Garage	TJ turns on water	TJ	N-1
42.	Int Armored Car	Water gushes in	Wilson, Moore	N-1
43.	Int Garage	SWAT team catches Moore and Wilson	Wilson, Moore, TJ, Deacon, Luca, Hondo, Street	N-1
44.	Ext Headquarters	to establish--stock	stock	D-2
45.	Int E.C. Room	TJ and Luca tell Street about the $2,000,000	TJ, Luca, Street	D-2
46.	Ext House	to establish	--	D-2
47.	Int House	Simon and Peterson talk about Wilson and Moore	Simon, Peterson	D-2
48.	Int Interrogation Room	Interrogation until attorney enters	Hondo, Wilson, Moore, Deacon, Bridges	D-2
49.	Int Corridor P.D.	Deacon & Hondo speculate about Bridges	Hondo, Deacon	D-2
50.	Int Interrogation Room	Lawyer plots strategy with clients	Bridges, Wilson, Moore	D-2
		END OF ACT ONE		
51.	Ext Courthouse	Street meets Diane	Street, Diane	N-3
52.	Int Restaurant	Diane tells Street about marriage doubts, Hondo joins	Street, Diane, Hondo	N-3
53.	Int House	Bridges and Simon discuss Wilson and Moore	Bridges, Simon, Peterson, Peggy	N-3
54.	Ext Headquarters	to establish--stock	stock	D-4
55.	Int E.C. Room	team suspects possible breakout	Hondo, Street, TJ Deacon, Luca	D-4
56.	Int House	Peggy and Simon talk about going away, Winters is briefed	2 heavies, Simon, Peggy, Winters, Bridges, Peterson	D-4
57.	Ext Courthouse	SWAT team prepares	Hondo, TJ, Deacon Luca (Street=off)	D-4
58.	Ext Courthouse	to establish	--	N-4

scriptions of every scene in consecutive order, prepared by the script supervisor. The scene number, location, action, list of cast members, costume numbers and relative time are all included in the one-line breakdown. The list will provide a sequencing reference for the entire picture as opposed to just page by page.

Using the one-liner reference, a script supervisor can quickly check on a number of continuity matters. A typical example is the director who, out of the blue, asks his script supervisor if a particular shot occurs before or after the star shaves his beard. The one-liners can be used to determine in what scene the beard was shaved. Flipping through the script pages obviously takes too much time. This is a single example of the many advantages of using one-liners. Other examples will become apparent as the next two problems are identified.

Problem Four:
DESIGN A METHOD FOR KEEPING TRACK OF COSTUME REQUIREMENTS

Only an over-zealous script supervisor bothers drawing complicated charts or lists of costume requirements. This is the job of the wardrobe people. The sheer number of characters in an average feature film makes the chore of recording every character's costumes an enormous undertaking. Each costume has countless details. In addition, costumes typically change up to the very moment they are filmed. A wise script supervisor will obtain most of the pertinent costume information on the set; however, there are certain basic costume requirements with which the script supervisor must be familiar. These fall into two basic categories—*sequencing requirements* and *story requirements*.

We have discussed how, when breaking down the continuity script, the script supervisor divides script events into ficticious days and nights. These same divisions are used as the basis for costuming. Many of the divisions are set arbitrarily. The script supervisor must be sure that the director sets all arbitrary or ambiguous time sequences and that the information is distributed to the various crew members such as the wardrobe people who rely on the information.

Often the story calls for costume changes in addition to those required by the time passage. A character may change clothes from pajamas to a business suit before going to work. Someone could fall into a mud puddle and wear muddy clothes for the rest of the day. Once all the time and story requirements are identified, reference numbers are assigned to each costume.

In the "Courthouse" episode of *S.W.A.T.*, Street wears his S.W.A.T. uniform when he first appears night one. The costume is assigned the number 1. Later that night, combat accessories are added to his basic uniform and the costume is numbered 1A. Day two, he wears his basic uniform 1 again. His street clothes are numbered 2 for night three. Street returns to costume 1 for day and night four. Day five and night six, he wears street clothes numbered 3 and 4 respectively. Diane doesn't appear until day two when she wears her first costume in court, labeled 1. Her next two appearances are on separate days again in court, so she wears costumes 2 and 3. The final costume is a street dress for night six, identified as number 4. The remaining characters' costumes are labeled in the same manner. These identification numbers are the basis for observing costume continuity.

After these identifying numbers are set by the costume department, most script supervisors enter them into their continuity script.

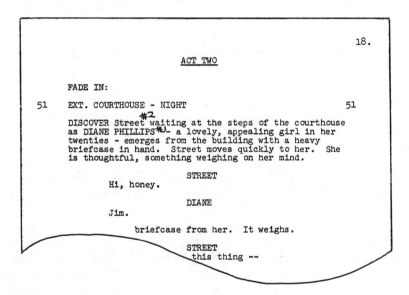

Other script supervisors transfer the costume identifying numbers to the one-liners.

Both systems provide a quick reference to the detailed costume descriptions that the script supervisor will be recording later during the shoot (see pages 96–98 & 148).

S.W.A.T. ONE LINERS

SC #	LOCATION	DESCRIPTION	CAST	TIME
41.	Int Garage	TJ turns on water	TJ #1B	N-1
42.	Int Armored Car	Water gushes in	Wilson, Moore #1A-B	N-1
43.	Int Garage	SWAT team catches Moore and Wilson	Wilson, Moore, TJ, Deacon, Luca, Hondo, Street #1B-C	N-1
44.	Ext Headquarters	to establish--stock	stock #1A #1A #1A	D-2
45.	Int E.C. Room	TJ and Luca tell Street about the $2,000,000	TJ, Luca, Street	D-2
46.	Ext House	to establish	-- #2 #2	D-2
47.	Int House	Simon and Peterson talk about Wilson and Moore	Simon, Peterson #1A #1C	D-2
48.	Int Interrogation Room	Interrogation until attorney enters #C	Hondo, Wilson, Moore, Deacon, #1A Bridges #1	D-2
49.	Int Corridor P.D.	Deacon & Hondo specu- late about Bridges	Hondo, Deacon #1A #1A	D-2
50.	Int Interrogation Room	Lawyer plots strategy with clients	Bridges, Wilson, #1C Moore #1C #1	D-2

Whichever system is adopted, a similar system can be used for the fifth problem.

Problem Five:
ADOPT A SYSTEM FOR KEEPING TRACK OF PROPS AND SET DRESSING REQUIREMENTS

Unless the script supervisor has an excess of free time, it's just as excessive to draw complicated prop and set dressing charts as costume charts. Continuity is a tough enough job without duplicating all other crew members' paperwork. Ensuring the availability of all physical requirements on the set is the job of the assistant director. A script supervisor offers reminders on the set when necessary. Unfortunately, in order to be effective when reminding other crew members about prop needs, the script supervisor requires a sound familiarity with the props involved throughout the script. There are many shortcuts available. Some script supervisors put key props on the one-liners. Others famil- iarize themselves with the scheduled scenes just prior to shooting them. Many cheat a bit by referring to an assistant director's breakdown on the call sheet.

```
O'HARA PRODUCTIONS                              PER SCRIPT REVISION
                                                DATED APRIL 23, 1981

                        "O'HARA'S WIFE"

                        SHOOTING SCHEDULE

Executive Producer:  Michael T. Murphy          Start Date:
Producers:           Peter Davis -
                     Bill Panzer                May 13, 1981
Director:            Bill Bartman
Production Manager:  Frank Beetson              Est. Finish:
Assistant Director:  Richard Rothschild         June 24, 1981
```

DATE	SET/SCENES		CAST	LOCATION
1ST DAY WEDNESDAY 5/13/81 & 2ND DAY THURSDAY 5/14/81	INT. BEDROOM Scs. 20, 20A Night - 7 5/8 Pgs. Discuss vacations, meaning of life, etc. Call from Gloria; Harry collapses.	#1 #2	BOB HARRY	McKINNEY RESIDENCE 515 S. NORTON L.A. (HANCOCK PARK) PROPS Dom Perignon Glasses Airline Tickets Rucksack St. Christopher's Medal, Chain & Card Phone Travel Posters (5 Duplicates Each) Nightstand & Lamp WARDROBE Sherlock Holmes Coat Gloves Corduroy Pants Crewneck Sweater White Cloth Shoes CAMERA Blurr POV
	INT. O'HARA BEDROOM Scs. 94A, 94Bpt, 94C, 94E Night - 1 3/8 Pgs. Call Bob, Jr.; ask him to visit.	#1 #2	BOB HARRY	SAME AS ABOVE PROPS Phone

```
        END OF 1ST & 2ND DAYS - TOTAL PAGES:  9
```

The real focus of the script supervisor's attention to props doesn't come into effect until the shoot, where a complex system of observation, notation and instant photographs are put to use (see pages 96–102 & 135). For now, we'll continue with the next problem.

Problem Six:
PLAN A WAY TO PROJECT WHETHER A FILM
IS RUNNING LONG OR SHORT

One of the important duties of a script supervisor is to estimate whether a film is running over the desired running length. The length of a television program is regulated exactly by station requirements. The majority of feature exhibitors also prefer specified lengths, usually no longer than 110 minutes.

Obviously, script supervisors don't have control over the running length. They don't choose the desired running time, nor can they control the outcome of the filming. The final length is ultimately determined by editing. Still, as in laying bricks, if each step is a little off, by the end of the project, a massive problem could result that few editors could overcome. It is the script supervisor's job to keep from running significantly over or under the desired running length.

Most script supervisors time their script before shooting starts. Sometimes this timing period is considered separately from the preparation week and sometimes not. IATSE, the union representing script supervisors, negotiates pre-timing of scripts independently from all other script supervisor duties. Either way, the script supervisor should time each scene individually, guessing at what pace the scene will eventually be performed.

Once the script is timed, the timings serve as a guideline during the filming. As the filming progresses, scenes are usually added that weren't included in the original script while others are omitted or condensed. With estimated timings, the script supervisor can determine if the cumulative time of the scenes shot exceeds the time of the script scenes covered.

Another system used to estimate a film's progress is counting pages. To maximize accuracy, each page is divided into eighths. When only 5/8ths of a page are printed, it constitutes 5/8ths rather than a full page. Next, all the eighths throughout the entire script are added to equal a total script page count. Many script supervisors mark total page count beside each scene during the preparation week. If scene 28 has 3/8ths of a page and 4/8ths of a page on scene 21, then 7/8ths is marked in the margin at the beginning of scene 28. These markings come in handy when the script supervisor adds up page credits daily during the shoot (see page 153 "The Shoot"). For now, the script supervisor need only be concerned with taking as accurate time and page counts as possible before continuing with the other preparation.

Problem Seven:
CREATE A QUICK REFERENCE TO DIALOGUE

While recording continuity notes, the script supervisor often will have to match action to dialogue. Which line an actor last spoke before the director called "cut," what phrase was fumbled and on what word did the star pick up the gun are three examples. Most script supervisors make references to lines by choosing key words. Others, in order to save time, assign reference numbers to the dialogue during the preparation week.

```
                                                          32.

65   CONTINUED:                                           65

     They start to burn -- as Peggy enters, clad in a very
     revealing bikini, grinning delightedly, posing.

                    PEGGY -5
          Hey, honey -- you think those
          Frenchmen will like this?

                    SIMON-6
               (grins)
          What do you want to do -- start a
          riot?

     She giggles delightedly.


66   EXT. BUILDING MAINTENANCE YARD - DAY                 66

     Several closed vans (with "Building Maintenance" I.D.
     painted on their sides) are parked.  We DISCOVER
     Winters as he emerges from a nearby building -- makes
     his way to a van.  CLOSE to him as he gets into the
     van at the wheel, slots the key into the ignition --
     then freezes abruptly as the muzzle of a revolver is
     pressed against the nape of his neck.  ADJUST to
     include Peterson behind him in the van -- with the
     two Heavies.  Peterson has his gun at Winters' nape.

                    WINTERS-1
               (terrified)
          What do you want?

                    PETERSON-2
          Drive.  I'll tell you where.

                    WINTERS-3
               (quailing;
                protesting)
          I already did what he told me.

                    PETERSON-4
          Now you do what I tell you -- and
          if you're lucky, you might even
          ___ alive.
```

In the preceding sample from *S.W.A.T.*, every line is given a number in consecutive order. When the scene switches to a new location, the numbers start over with 1.

Numbering the dialogue, timing the script, breaking down the costumes, props, and set dressing requirements, writing one-liners, making sequencing notations, setting up editorial forms and preparing the script for rapid notes are all common scripting techniques that can be implemented before filming commences. The script supervisor should select the best combination of systems to suit the requirements of the script. After choosing complementary methods, the script supervisor can attend to the final problem.

Problem Eight:
ENGINEER A METHOD TO FIND EVERYTHING FAST

All the continuity records in the world won't do any good unless a script supervisor knows how to use them. A script supervisor with unorganized notes might just as well have no notes at all. Unless a needed piece of information can be found quickly, the entire company suffers.

Say, for instance, that a picture is running way over budget. The director and camera crew are in a hurry to complete the last part of a highly emotional scene before losing the light. If they don't finish the shot immediately, the entire scene may have to be reshot because the actress can't duplicate the emotional level of her performance. The producer anxiously paces and worries that an extra day's shooting will run the budget up another X amount of dollars. With only seconds to squeeze in the shot, a question arises as to whether or not the actress is wearing the proper costume. The wardrobe person is not on the set. Everyone turns to the script supervisor. Fifty impatient eyes glare in disbelief as the nervous script supervisor flips through page after page trying to figure out what the actress is supposed to be wearing.

All script supervisors organize their working scripts into a system that works best for them. Most divide sections of the script by *tab dividers*. Suggested divisions include: a section for editorial reports, daily production reports, prop and set dressing plots, one liners, costume charts, and running lists of needed retakes, wild tracking and projections. Production information such as shooting schedules and contact sheets should also be tabbed as well as extra forms and blank paper. But the main divisions, of course, should be for the script.

Tabbing the script is a matter of personal preference. Many script supervisors tab every new location throughout the script. Others find all these extra tabs unnecessary—they make the other divisions stand out less. Whichever method is adopted, the script supervisor must be able to find information as quickly as possible.

What all these methods for setting up the working script have in common is that they attempt to provide practical solutions to problems that typically arise during filming. The more a script supervisor prepares for potential problems, the easier the job will be during filming. Setting up the working script and organizing the equipment are only two ways to prepare. Additional preparations can be accomplished before the filming starts.

PRE-PRODUCTION MEETINGS

Although the jobs performed by the various crew members on a film are similar from project to project, everyone has a different way of working. During pre-production, the script supervisor should try to gain insight into co-workers' working preferences. By talking to fellow crew members and asking questions, a script supervisor can avoid many needless confrontations.

In addition to honoring co-workers' preferences, the script supervisor should also observe currently accepted protocol. In the old days, for instance, a script supervisor treated the director with tremendous respect. By "old days," we mean back in 1948 when Shirley was involved in shooting the film *Carnegie Hall* on location in New York City. Shirley's husband, Edgar G. Ulmer, was directing the film, and she was holding script. Although they had been married for more than ten years, Shirley still addressed Edgar on the set as "Mr. Ulmer." Many people were not even aware of their personal relationship, which soon caused some consternation. As filming progressed, a wild rumor began to spread that the director was too close to the script supervisor. They had been seen together in the same room night after night! This illustrates how very formal things were on the set only about 35 years ago.

Even in the casual setting of today's features, certain courtesies should be observed. On Carol's last feature, the cameraman, a fine cinematographer from an acclaimed motion picture family, was stumped. Rarely a year passed that his father's name didn't appear on the Academy Awards list for "Best Cinematography." Following in his father's footsteps, he also collected decades worth of impressive feature credits and Academy Awards Nominations. Coming from this highly professional background, he couldn't understand why any experienced crew member would wear a white shirt on the set, light colors tend to cause reflection problems for the camera lens. Still, on a particularly bright and sunny day of filming, the crew showed up in their summery white clothes including two members who work closest to the camera—the first assistant cameraman and the guilty script supervisor.

Following protocol extends to varied areas of production. When scouting locations, the average crew member should not sit in the front of the bus. There is an unspoken rule that the first three seats are for the director, first assistant director and the cinematographer. No crew member should ever block the view of the cinematographer during rehearsals. This is not as easy as it sounds when a cinematographer dashes around the set searching for the best angle. The poor script supervisor has to watch the blocking, throw lines to the actors and dodge the cinematographer all at the same time. It's just as inexcusable to blurt out uncalled for comments which make *any* crew member feel insecure about his or her work.

Rudi Fehr, who has edited such prestigious pictures as *Dial M for Murder, Key Largo, Humoresque,* and *One From the Heart,* tells of an interesting mishap.

> I had one very nasty experience with a script supervisor who shall remain nameless. When I had just finished editing a feature, she begged to see the first cut. Naturally, nobody was supposed to see it until the director had his chance, but after literally pleading, I gave in. I was very surprised when I learned that she had sent a note to the director, who happened to be Alfred Hitchcock. In this note, she expressed her reaction to what she had seen, which was not favorable. After Hitchcock saw the first cut, he told me about the note and said, "I don't know what this girl's talking about. There is nothing wrong with your cut." The script supervisor still made me feel uneasy because I didn't see where my editing had gone wrong. That was just an isolated incident and a very unfortunate experience. On the whole, I am very fond of script supervisors. The only way I can perform my job as an editor is with the help of a good one. I was very fortunate to have been associated with many excellent script supervisors. I have learned to appreciate them. There is a close affiliation between continuity and editing. There has to be. We work together and we're lost without each other.

An accomplished editor who has worked with skilled directors from Hitchcock to Hawks to Coppola should not have to worry about the unsolicited opinion of a script supervisor.

Extending professional courtesy is as important for the star as well as the cinematographer. Shirley once incurred Hedy Lamar's enmity by correcting her publicly for a line misread. The next day, Hedy had her revenge. An important prop in the film, *Loves of Three Women,* was a large ring worn on her third left finger. Shirley let her walk through a difficult master-take without noticing the ring on her right hand, a real boo-boo. As the director called, "Cut and print," Miss Lamar laconically announced, "The script supervisor was certainly in another world. Now we have to do the whole thing over again." There are so many beautiful memories of helpful stars that it seems foolish to mention this petty behavior which, in actuality, was brought on by Shirley for publicly scolding a leading lady for a bad reading.

The reason idiosyncracies should be learned during pre-production meetings, (rather than relying on good judgment), is because a script supervisor should *never assume anything*. When it comes to working preferences, there is no such thing as good judgment. Remarks considered common courtesy to one actor, for example, are annoying to another.

Some actors like to be left alone and some like to be nursed through every step. When Shirley had the experience of working with George Sanders, she learned just how much attention some actors demand. As many shooting days as there were, that's how many spare scripts were required. The company continually had to supply extras. Mr. Sanders would lose his script every night like clockwork. Still, for the sake of harmony on the set, his script was replaced daily, (even though he never considered looking at it in any case). After the hundredth take of a scene with George Sanders, any script supervisor must realize how much cannot be assumed about working methods.

The most important working preferences to be learned as soon as possible are those of the crew members with whom the script supervisor will be in closest contact. These include the director, camera and sound operators, editors and assistant director. Since the director is the captain of the ship, it is most important to have a good rapport with the director.

When meeting the director for the first time, several topics should be discussed. The experienced script supervisor lets the director know that he or she will always be available to provide whatever technical assistance may be needed. In other words, the director should be assured that the script supervisor is enthusiastic and ready to help.

The next subject to be broached is getting the director's reaction to the takes. Sometimes directors are so involved in their creative process they don't even take time to tell their script supervisor whether a take is no good or a print. The script supervisor is either forced to disrupt filming or leave holes in the editorial notes. By pointing out at the first meeting the importance of knowing what method the director wishes to use, accurate and complete editorial notes are possible. In any case, the script supervisor must stress that he or she will try and accommodate the director's method to achieve the best result.

RICHARD HASHIMOTO INTERVIEW

Richard Hashimoto started in the business initially as an assistant cameraman. He soon moved into assistant directing. Most of his early credits were television pilots for Universal. Later feature credits as an assistant director include *Rooster Cogburn, Airport '75, Big Wednesday* and *Gauntlet.* During the last five years, he has moved into production managing strictly for independent feature productions. *Nine to Five, Hardcore, Carney, Heartbeat, On Golden Pond, White Dog* and *War Games* are among his most recent films. Through a very short period of time, Richard Hashimoto has gained the reputation as being one of the finest in his field. His interview will provide a clue why.

HASHIMOTO: I guess the best way of describing a script supervisor's importance from a production standpoint is by saying that really good ones are worth their weight in gold. When we hire a script supervisor, usually it's the director's choice. Established directors often have two or three people that they always work with. Whoever is free at the time is the person who comes on to the show if an acceptable arrangement can be reached. In the past, I have probably hired more script supervisors than normal, only because the directors didn't have regular people that they worked with. It was left for me to bring the script supervisors in for interviews with the director.

My experiences often have been with first-time directors. As a result, the kind of production companies that were calling me had projects with first-time directors. The telelphone calls were always prefaced with, "We've got a first-time guy and we've really got to get good people with him to make sure he doesn't get in trouble." That's how studios protect themselves from giving an inexperienced director a six to ten million dollar movie. They spend top dollar to get a production manager, cameraman, editor, assistant director, script supervisor, you name it; and surround the director with so much expertise that he can't do anything wrong.

Although I have a few favorite script supervisors that I push on most shows, a lot of times the script supervisors' and the directors' personalities have to be meshed together. Sometimes, you'll get a script supervisor who is too strong and a director who is intimidated. Pretty soon, after working long hours in tight situations, they become very antagonistic, and the director begins to feel that the script supervisor is directing his movie. The balance of personalities of any crew members who work closely with the director is so critical that considerable time has to be spent with the director to determine who will be his script supervisor.

STUDENT: *When you're making the script supervisor selection, why would you opt for one of your favorite script supervisors who charges a top-of-the-line salary rather than a qualified script supervisor who gets scale?*

HASHIMOTO: *To sum it up, it's experience. I believe you are referring to one particular script supervisor whom I hired on the last few shows, and in many respects, is known as the dean of script supervisors. His name is Marshall Schlom. Marshall is often faced with the same problem as all of us in the sense that he ends up working with many relatively new and inexperienced people. Marshall's importance to the smooth operation of a film is that he is attentive to filmmaking rather than just concerned with his own particular job. If you're going to make a mark in this business, then that's what you've got to do. The typical response that will automatically make me not hire somebody again is to hear the excuse that "It's not my job." If it's not your job, that's why you get paid scale. Over scale is paid to people so that they are conscious of everybody's job. For me, it's very important that everyone on the crew who wants a script gets one from the crafts service guy, to the driver to whomever. I feel that if they have enough interest to read the script, they are more attentive to what's happening on the set. They might see something that someone else is not going to notice and say, "Wait a minute, that's wrong," or they might pull the script supervisor aside and say, "Such and such has happened in the background. Did you see it?"*

In a sense, Marshall's value is that he is familiar with everybody's job, he understands making films, and he knows the script backwards and forwards. If the picture is running behind, (which is always a problem in making films), he is a person that I often consult because he is up on every sequence that's been filmed to date. He knows, for instance, where a scene can be cut without throwing the picture out of whack in the editing room.

A first assistant director can't do it because he isn't always able to observe the filming in its entirety. This isn't true as much in working on a soundstage where the assistant director's attention is focused primarily on the set—as working on location where his attention is down the block trying to control traffic and unable to keep track of what happened through the sequence. Instead, he's watching the crowd to make sure that nobody is sticking their head out the window or doing something obscene that goes undetected until the rushes, when all of a sudden there's some guy who's got a donkey hat on through the whole sequence.

STUDENT: *How about directors? They must know the script better than anyone else.*

HASHIMOTO: *Top directors usually know where they're at in terms of the filming, but with first-time directors, it's often enough that they just get through the day. I say this in jest somewhat unfairly, but there is a lot of pressure when you come out onto the set the first time. If it's a big film, you're looking at 100 to 150 people all waiting for the director's every word. The whole system is set up on a pyramid and everyone looks up to the top for direction. Add a director who doesn't direct, and that's when problems arise.*

STUDENT: *I understand what you're saying but the crew can't just barge in, take over and direct the picture by committee.*

HASHIMOTO: *No, but after you get a few years under your belt, you learn what kind of balance has to be maintained. An experienced script supervisor like Marshall is able to gauge when it's appropriate to offer suggestions. He can assess the director's temperament. Sometimes I think you have to take a couple of classes in psychology to work in this business. Within a few days of working with a director, an experienced script supervisor automatically knows how far to go with a director in terms of suggestion.*

You have to realize that when working with a first-time director, there are usually four people who are very influential in guiding him on the set. These are the assistant director, the production manager, the cameraman and the script supervisor. Once the filming commences, the ability of the assistant director, production manager and cameraman to help the director lessens. They're now too busy working on their own areas of concern. Ultimately, the only person the director can rely on is the script supervisor. The script supervisor is the one crew member who can remain conscious of the film as a whole.

STUDENT: *It really doesn't seem to me that being in tune is going to make all that much difference in the long run.*

HASHIMOTO: *Sure it does. Take matching, for instance. People don't understand the value of matching until they go into the editing room and start to put together a sequence. Suddenly, the editor can't cut to a crucial close-up because the action hasn't been matched. The only choice might be cutting away to an insert and then back into the master. When I worked as an assistant director, I heard constantly that because of a time element, espe-*

cially evident in television, a director or actor didn't want to be bothered with matching. What they didn't really understand is that where costs escalate unbelievably is in post-production. And it's not only matching, but other areas as well.

When it comes to timing, Marshall's input in the past has carried a lot of weight. Often, in the early part of pre-production, most production companies want the script timed to determine how long the film will be before final editing. The idea is that if you know a script is long, you push to cut some things out as soon as possible to save money. If you can determine this early, the options for correcting the problem are greater. There are far more choices about which scenes to eliminate without hurting the script. The worst thing is getting a three-hour movie on the first cut. Cutting the first half-hour out is pretty easy. Cutting the next half-hour is rough. Unless it's a powerhouse movie, most theatres don't want any more than two hours in the final cut. With the previews, titles and credits, they want ten minutes to clear out the theatre and get the next group in. Because Marshall has worked with so many different actors and directors over his 30 years in the industry, about a week into shooting, he can assess accurately how long a script will run if nothing is cut.

STUDENT: *Why after a week?*

HASHIMOTO: *It takes about a week to see how the actors work. If you work with a Hepburn, for example, there is a tendency to draw things out and more dramatic pauses. If you work with someone like George C. Scott, the tempo is different. His actions and dialogue are more concise. No two actors work the same. It's amazing how Marshall's time estimation is accurate within a few minutes of the actual time filmed.*

STUDENT: *So far, you've mentioned matching and timing. How else do you depend on the script supervisor?*

HASHIMOTO: *Another area that can be helpful to me, here again because script supervisors know their scripts so well, is when problems occur. Say you've got to report to location in a new city like Saugus or some place where the maps are all confused. What happens a lot of times, especially in television, is that an actor doesn't get to the set in time. Then we all scramble to find something to shoot while we're waiting for this person to show up. That's when the production manager, assistant director, director and the script supervisor sit down and plan some kind of attack. We try to pick scenes that can be shot in Saugus with the actors on hand. This is the kind of help I would seek from the script supervisor.*

STUDENT: *Why do you consider the script supervisor a good person to consult?*

HASHIMOTO: Again, this comes back to what I said before about the script supervisor being a person always on top of things. By breaking down their scripts, they sometimes know them better than anyone. In television, for instance, one thing I find to be distracting is what I call a rainbow script. A rainbow script is where each rewrite comes in on a different color paper. On some of the jobs I've done in the past, I was lucky when they finished a show, if I still had a white page in my script. After completing a 14-hour shooting day, it's hard to take those revisions home, break them down and then read over the sequence in context. Sometimes all I had time for was checking for changes in props, costumes, effects, cast, etc. Script supervisors have to be more conscious of how the rewrites affect the continuity of the film storyline.

STUDENT: And is it the script supervisor's job to draw attention to any changes in the tone of a film?

HASHIMOTO: I don't necessarily say it's their responsibility, but as both a production manager and an assistant director, I found that the really good ones did. If I needed an answer about specifics in the script, generally the script supervisor was the person I would ask.

STUDENT: In what other ways does a script supervisor's performance affect your job?

HASHIMOTO: Given the fact that you don't have a very knowledgable director, it's ideal from my standpoint that the director be advised of his options in terms of coverage. I find that the tendency today, at least in features with the newer directors, is to not cover enough. It's important in scheduling a picture and paying for locations to complete all necessary coverage in each location before moving on to the next. Returning to a location to reshoot is very expensive and difficult. Locations are generally scheduled to be struck under the assumption that retakes or additional filming won't be necessary. I usually hold off until the following morning to make sure that the film comes back from the lab without problems. After that, I tell the painter, decorator and construction people to go back in and restore the location to its original condition.

I've heard a director say, "Gee, I wish I had got a shot of the old lady exiting," or "How come nobody told me the headlights were on?" Minimizing these problems is one way I depend on the script supervisor. Script supervisors shouldn't push their coverage suggestions on the director, but they should make the director aware of possible needs by saying something like, "Do you plan to do this or that?" or in other words, plant the idea in the director's head as if it were his own. This way, the script supervisor doublechecks that, under the time pressures, the director doesn't forget *something that he should have filmed. If there's one facet that everyone working in film business is always confronted with, it's that time is money. When somebody messes up and the crew has to go back to the location and reshoot, there are a lot of very unhappy people. The tendency is to start pointing fingers. If a script supervisor fails to draw attention to obvious coverage holes or in any other way fails to perform the responsibilities of the job, the script supervisor's reputation suffers. When that reputation falls below a certain professional standard, it's difficult commanding the money and jobs desired unless you ride in on the coattails of a big director or actor as a part of their entourage. Here again, we're dealing with the fine line between knowing when to offer a suggestion and when to remain silent.*

STUDENT: When you're in the process of hiring someone, how do you find out if a script supervisor is any good or not?

HASHIMOTO: I share knowledge with other production managers. To an extent, if I know a director that the script supervisor worked for previously, I talk to him about the script supervisor's competence. For salary background, I call the previous employer. This kind of knowledge is pretty open between production people. But generally speaking, the person I really talk to is the editor because more than anyone the editor knows how good a script supervisor is. In fact, I would say that editors have a lot to do with hiring. An editing and directing team usually go hand in hand. This is especially true one they've had a fairly successful movie together. If the script supervisor keeps bad notes, the editor suffers. In the end, the editor might go to the director and squawk, "If you hire that rotten script supervisor back again, I'm not going to cut your movie." Given those options, most directors are going to side with their editors. But in an overall perspective, I believe a good script supervisor is an extension of the whole film. He or she is the person who serves as a source from which everyone working under the director gets information.

Another important subject is the director's preference for projecting overall progress and needed wild-tracking, retakes and coverage. These can be touchy areas if not handled properly. As discussed earlier in this chapter, running significantly over or under the desired running length can result in a substantial problem. Neglecting needed footage and wild-tracks until the end of the shoot also causes avoidable problems. The script supervisor and director should agree on a method to prevent this from happening.

The relationship with the camera and sound operators seems comparatively simple. The camera operator and assistants provide lens, footage, focal length and zoom operation information. The sound mixer informs the script supervisor about audio problems during filming not readily audible without headphones. In return, the script supervisor provides scene, take and print numbers. If a long scene is coming up, the script supervisor warns the others about the need to reload. Either at the end of the day's filming or throughout the day, the script supervisor should check that the sound, camera and continuity reports all share the same print numbers.

Editors are a little trickier. Since an editor rarely comes onto the set, a good understanding must exist between an editor and the script supervisor. Continuity notes are the editor's essential contact with the director, the cameraman and the film itself. If the continuity notes or forms are unsatisfactory, the editor ultimately suffers. These matters should be discussed during preproduction meetings to limit the margin of error.

Another crew member important to consult is the assistant director. Script supervisors frequently rely on the assistant director for help. The assistant director arranges for a desk and a chair for the script supervisor when filming on a stage. When shooting on location, the assistant director tells the script supervisor where to leave the case of extra supplies and personal belongings. In exchange, the script supervisor provides the assistant director with the daily reports.

The daily continuity report form should be okayed in advance. The assistant director may have a special form; otherwise, the script supervisor can use one of his or her own. The following is a commercially available form used by many script supervisors.

SCRIPT SUPERVISOR'S DAILY REPORT

PRODUCTION CO.   TITLE

CAMERA   DIRECTOR

A.D.   SCRIPT

		SCENE		SET
DAY				
DATE				
CALL				
SHOT				
MEAL				
SHOT				
MEAL				
SHOT				
WRAP				

	PAGES	SCENES	ADDED	RETAKE	MINUTES	SET UPS	WILD
TODAY							
BEFORE							
TOTAL							
SCRIPT			ADDED SCENE #				
LEFT			RETAKE SCENE #				

REMARKS:

ENTERPRISE STATIONERS 7401 SUNSET L.A. CA. 90046 (213) 876-3533

The next custom-designed form offers an alternative way to present the same information.

Daily Production Report

WORKING TITLE _____   FIRST SHOT _____

DIRECTOR _____   LUNCH _____

PRODUCTION NUMBER _____   FIRST SHOT P.M. _____

DAY _____ DATE _____   FINISH _____

TOTAL SCENES	SCENE NUMBERS COVERED:
TOTAL PAGES	
TOTAL SET-UPS	SCENE NUMBERS SHOT:
TOTAL CREDITED TIME	
SOUND TRACKS	
RETAKES	

	SCENES	PAGES		SET-UPS	CREDITED TIME	RETAKES	ADDED SCENES	FOOTAGE
TOTAL IN SCRIPT			TOTAL TODAY					
TOTAL TODAY								
TOTAL PREVIOUSLY			TOTAL PREVIOUSLY					
TOTAL TO DATE								
TOTAL TO BE COVERED			TOTAL TO DATE					

REMARKS:

SCRIPT SUPERVISOR _____

After selecting the forms, the script supervisor should arrange with the assistant director the best method of turning in the forms daily. This should be settled in pre-production meetings. If the script supervisor waits until later, the assistant director will probably be too busy with more pressing problems.

A third form should be used for the script supervisor's personal records. This duplicates the information on the assistant director's form. Additional columns simplify record keeping of cumulative set-ups, credited time and page counts. If the form is filled out throughout each step of the day's events, running lists are updated automatically.

Daily Production Report

Working Title: _____

Production #: _____

Shooting Day: _____ Date: _____

Script Super.: _____

Start: _____

Lunch: _____

1st Shot: _____

Finish: _____

Scene #s Covered: _____ Pages: _____

	SCENES	PAGES
Total In Script		
Previously shot		
Total Today		
Total To Date		
To Be Covered		

	SET-UPS	CREDIT TIME	RETAKES	ADDED SCENES	FOOTAGE
Today					
Previous					
To Date					

REMARKS:

Set-ups	Scene	Prints	Time	Credit Time

The majority of working relationships aren't firmly established until the filming begins. Still, the more the script supervisor can accomplish during the pre-production meetings, the better. At least, learn the crew members' names and functions.

Learning Everyone's Names and Functions

Learning everyone's name and function beforehand simply lessens a script supervisor's worries during the initial days of filming. The advantage of being able to address people by name is obvious, especially on a full-scale feature where the crew list may number 100 people. After receiving a cast and crew contact sheet, the script supervisor should memorize as much as seems reasonable.

One crew member in particular whose job directly affects the script supervisor is the still photographer. On most union shoots the script supervisor is not permitted to take instant pictures. Instead, the still photographer has to be asked to shoot such pictures. A good relationship with the still photographer is crucial as it is with other crew members.

Eliciting Help from Crew Members

Sometimes, asking the help of fellow crew members cuts corners. Individual projects dictate which crew members are the most useful to approach. Many script supervisors ask the prop master and costume designer for copies of their plots. These pre-prepared breakdowns often save considerable time. Many script supervisors reciprocate by furnishing one-line breakdowns. A third swap with the production manager often proves the most useful.

Studying the Production Board and Shooting Schedule

Although there is no need for a script supervisor to become an expert in preparing a shooting schedule, a simple understanding is helpful. The production manager breaks down the film's proposed shots into narrow strips of color-coded cardboard. Each strip includes the date a shot is scheduled to be filmed, the characters involved in the shot, the location, the time of day and various physical requirements necessary to film it. These strips are then placed in shooting order into a specially designed holder called a *production board*.

The following is a portion of a typical production board. From the information included on the production board, the script supervisor can double-check the one-liners for accuracy, obtain up-to-date information regarding revisions and gain a better perspective on scheduling.

	13D	13E	14	7	73	15	15A	16	11	10A	3B	10	25	27	28
BREAKDOWN SHEET No.	13D	13E	14	7	73	15	15A	16	11	10A	3B	10	25	27	28
LOCATION OR STUDIO	L	L	L	L	L	L	L	L	L	L	L	L	L	L	L
DAY OR NIGHT	D	D	D	D	N	D	D	D	D	D	D	D	D	D	D
SCRIPT PAGES	1 4/8	6/8	4/8	3/8	5/8	1 3/8	2/8	3/8	1 3/8	1 3/2	4/8	4/8	1/8	3/8	

PROD. No. 507
TITLE AIRPLANE MOVIE
PRODUCER R. Howell
DIRECTOR T. Howell
ASST. DIRECTOR John Grier

Column titles:

1. EXT. AIR-TO-AIR OVER DESERT
2. EXT. AIR-TO-AIR OVER DESERT
3. EXT. AIR-TO-AIR OVER MOUNTAIN
4. EXT. GROUND-TO-AIR AIRPORT
5. EXT. AIR-TO-GROUND AIRPORT RUNWAY
6. EXT. DESERT
7. EXT. DESERT
8. EXT. DESERT
9. INT. AIRPORT OFFICE
10. INT. OFFICE RECPT.
11. INT. OFFICE RECPT.
12. EXT. OFFICE BLDG
13. EXT. AIRPORT ROAD
14. INT. HANGAR
15. EXT. HANGAR

COST	CHARACTER / PLAYER No.	13D	13E	14	7	73	15	15A	16	11	10A	3B	10	25	27	28
1	SID (PILOT DOUBLE)	D	1/D	1/D		D				1	1	1	1			
2	CAROL										2	2				
3	MICHELLE													3		
4	CONRAD													4	4	4
5	MR. STANLEY															
6	ESTES									6						
7	MECHANIC															
8	GRAHAM LIVINGSTON															
9	DAVID (PILOT DOUBLE)	D	9/D				D	9/D	9							
10	PILOT #1															
11	PILOT #2															
12	HITCHHIKER															

SPECIAL EFFECTS	EFX	13D	13E	14	7	73	15	15A	16	11	10A	3B	10	25	27	28
DOG	D															
ATMOSPHERE	X							X								
VAN	V															
BMW	C													C		
BLIMP	B	B	B	B	B	B										
RED PLANE	RP	RP	RP				RP	RP	(RP)							RP
WHITE PLANE	WP	WP	WP	WP		WP										

SCENES	13D	13E	14	7	73	15	15A	16	11	10A	3B	10	25	27	28
	161-172	177-179	183, 185, 187	32	248	188-190, 196		191-, 197, 199	54-57	53	108	52	78-80	85	86-88

Scene descriptions (by column):

1. Red plane flies close by white plane
2. White plane follows red plane
3. White plane flies all alone
4. Blimp in air over show
5. Stunt landing of white plane
6. Ground-to-air red plane low over desert
7. Crash stunt
8. People rush to help after crash
9. Sid tells Estes the plan
10. Sid flirts with Carol
11. Sid flirts with Carol w/ bandages
12. Sid enters office
13. Michelle speaks w/ Conrad about plane
14. Conrad enters hangar
15. Conrad makes adjustment

A shooting schedule is generally arranged in the best possible order to minimize costs and maximize convenience. Scenes taking place in the same locations are shot together no matter when they appear in the story. Scene 53 is shot at the same time as scene 108 simply because they both take place in the airport office reception area. Sid's scenes are confined to two days so he won't be on payroll longer than necessary. If two sequences require expensive specialized equipment, they are shot consecutively in order to limit rental costs. Day one, two and three require the use of two planes. Day one's flying also requires a blimp. Although flying takes place over numerous locations, the rental cost of the blimp and plane far exceed the expense of moving to nearby locations. Unfortunately, minimizing costs also means that screenplays are rarely shot in continuity, a consequence which greatly affects the script supervisor's work during the shoot.

Attending Rehearsals

Although attending rehearsals is optional, it's a good idea to go. Most script supervisors find not only that they can aid the director, but they can also ease their own jobs. Observing the actors pacing during read-throughs helps to predict more accurate timings. During blocking rehearsals, the script supervisor makes preliminary notes of the actors' movements to remind the director when the scene is filmed. A director who is primarily concerned with an actor's motivations will appreciate having a helper during rehearsal recording details that may be forgotten.

Often many important dialogue changes are made during rehearsals which are helpful to know in advance. A script supervisor makes points with the assistant directors by informing them of costume, set, personnel or other changes as they occur in rehearsals. Finally, the contact with the various performers and the director helps to familiarize the script supervisor with their working methods and the subtleties of the script.

Before filming commences, the script supervisor receives a limited time to prepare. The more the script supervisor accomplishes during the preparation period, the easier it will be to perform continuity duties later on. Taking advantage of pre-production meetings, preparing the working script and organizing equipment are three effective ways to prepare. Once these have been completed, the script supervisor is ready for the shoot.

Chapter Three

The Shoot

Maintaining continuity during the shoot brings together all the theory and preparation outlined so far in this book. The script supervisor's equipment is put to use. All the breakdowns compiled during preproduction serve as the basis for continuity decisions. The effectiveness of the scripting systems and working relationships are tested. Most important, the theories of continuity are applied. With this foundation, the script supervisor should be ready to take complete responsibility for preserving continuity. The first step is to recognize what's going on.

RECOGNIZING CINEMATIC TECHNIQUES

Conscientious script supervisors try to accomplish as much of their jobs as possible without burdening other busy crew members with needless questions. Inexperienced script supervisors may have difficulty recognizing cinematic techniques on their own. A sound understanding starts with the director's coverage approach.

Learning How The Film Material Will Be Covered

The collection of shots filmed to represent the action of a scene or *coverage* is probably the most complicated concept involved in filmmaking. Entire books have been written about how directors and cinematographers visually conceive of screen stories, the manner in which each sequence of the story is shot, and even the very basic question of how many shots are needed to construct the scene. Since script supervisors don't make artistic decisions about coverage, we'll limit this discussion to the script supervisor's immediate authority—helping the director determine if enough coverage has been shot to edit each scene effectively.

77

One method of providing enough material is the *master shot/pick-up approach*. A *master shot* contains most of the action in a scene in one continous take. When a master breaks up before completion, it can be "picked-up" before the break and continued to the end, using the same camera angle. This way, the company doesn't have to spend forever trying to film the master in one complete take. *Pick-ups* can also be used to cover mistakes in the master by using an alternate camera angle.

While a master shot is being filmed, careful notes must be taken to indicate where the master goes wrong. Flubbed lines, continuity mistakes, bad camera moves, awkward moments and the like, all should be noted. If after finishing a sequence, the director forgot to shoot the troublesome area, the problem should be pointed out to him by the script supervisor. An extra shot covering the overlap is needed for a smooth cut. The script supervisor should ask, for instance, "do you think we have adequate coverage for the part where Joe forgot his line during the master?" All needed coverage should be completed before striking the set and moving on to the next location. The new angle may emphasize a different portion of the action. Say, for instance, that the director shoots a wide master of the last 20 yards of a marathon race in which the winner crosses the finish line followed closely by ten other runners. A closer view captures the runner's expression as he breaks the ribbon. The script supervisor should anticipate where the director intends to cut in the close shot so that the action at the transition point of both views will match.

Morris Abrams offers advice about coverage:

> The trick in coverage is to grasp the number of camera set-ups that the sequence, story, budget and schedule allows. You're not going to get the same coverage on an 18-day schedule as you get on a 60-day shoot. No way. And it may be that some scenes will play better with camera moves and zooms, forgetting coverage. If it is a complicated scene with a lot of moves and you have no protection, you might want to spot the places where the camera moves the most violently or quickly, and say to the director, "In case anything goes wrong with the camera moves forcing you to cut them out, do you think you need a cutaway to the girl's reaction so that you can play the line over her?" I'll lay you a bet that what I just said is Greek to some of you unless you've had editing experience. Yet, such a cutaway could be a lifesaver in the editing process. The same applies to censorable lines, (that is, in straight-laced nations). These lines can't be dropped when there is no cutaway. But, I must say to you, it's like the end of a football game. The final score is the payoff.

The *protection shot* he mentioned is another type of coverage approach designed to avoid retakes.

Sometimes undetected problems necessitate re-filming a scene.

These are called *retakes*. The quality of exposed film can't be guaranteed until after developing. If a set has to be reconstructed, retakes are very expensive. In order to avoid excessive retakes, many directors use a *protection shot approach.*

A protection shot is an extra angle that the director doesn't intend to use unless a problem arises with the preferred one. The complicated camera move in the Abrams example appeared to work at the time of filming. When the film was developed, it might have turned out that half-way through the scene, the subject goes out of focus briefly. By filming a protection shot with the identical action during the tricky part, the editor was provided with material to cut away to.

A *cut-to-cut approach* uses far less film footage, but requires an exceptional visual sense from the director. Before filming starts, the director carefully plans every shot in advance. When the director walks onto the set, each shot is filmed one by one closely following the director's plan. This is possible because the director has such a clear idea of what he wants that he can say, "I only need a shot of her little finger at this point." The script supervisor should concentrate on the transition points. An occasional master or partial master may be shot for protection.

Most other systems of coverage are either a combination of these three or a variation. Although this adds up to infinite possibilities, all directors use the same techniques to implement their individual systems. The majority of all coverage is comprised of static and moving shots.

Static Shots

A script supervisor must recognize the size of a static shot and the angle from which it is taken. The names used to describe shots are often used incorrectly. Many filmmakers, for example, use the terms "close-up" and "close-shot" interchangeably, while in actuality, they are entirely different shots. Others use nicknames for shots such as "gurgle" to describe a close-up of a head, since the cut off point severs the throat, or "2T's" instead of medium close shot (for obvious anatomical reasons). The script supervisor should use the most precise term available on the continuity notes.

May Wale Brown, a script supervisor, tells an interesting anecdote illustrating this problem. May was shooting a scene with Barbara Stanwyck in which Barbara Stanwyck ran an elephant farm. During one shot, the actress stood next to an elephant. May asked the camera operator, "How close a shot is this on Miss Stanwyck?" The camera operator answered, "It's a close two-shot—Miss Stanwyck and the elephant." Rest assured that May didn't record close two-shot in the report.

PETER BOGDANOVICH INTERVIEW

Peter Bogdanovich has directed a handful of first-rate, quality features in the last 10 years. Among the titles are *Paper Moon, The Last Picture Show, What's Up Doc?, Saint Jack* and *They All Laughed.* Directing is usually more demanding than any other job on a feature, and Peter Bogdanovich has definite ideas on what kind of crew support helps him best to fulfill his directoral obligations.

STUDENT: Peter, what do you expect of the script supervisor?

BOGDANOVICH: I've given up expecting anything.

STUDENT: You mean you've had bad ones?

BOGDANOVICH: Oh, I haven't had a great one. I could use a good script supervisor, but lately I've had a tough time. Actually, I think it's the director's fault, because there's been a decline in good directors. In the old days, directors knew more about cutting and camera placement, and just about everything. As the directors have stopped knowing about those things, there has been less demand for the script supervisors knowing them. If the director doesn't know, why should they? He's making the big money. The loss of craft in the movies is amazing. The last 20 years have been horrendous. Movies were far better made in the '20s than they are today. In fact, in about 1928, movies were, visually speaking, just about at the top. It's been downhill ever since. Between 1922 and 1929, when sound came in, they had really learned how to make pictures—they knew how to tell stories visually. I'm not one of these people who think sound is bad. I think it's wonderful, but what happened is that it got easier for the director and they got lazy. The care that was required to tell a story visually slowly disappeared. Finally, today, when people run into a problem in conveying the story, they just say, "We'll cover it with a line." But the thing is, you really have to grab an audience's attention to get them to listen to something about plot. They never really give such a damn about that. The point is that, over the past 50 years, movies have become more and more what Hitchcock referred to as "Pictures of people talking." You have two actors and they're perfectly good. You put them in a two-shot and let them talk for two, three, four pages. If they're good and the dialogue is good, they have a good conversation and that's fine. But if you are trying to tell a story visually, you've got to know where to put the camera and where to cut. It's very much like a series of notes in a symphony. When you're telling a story visually, in my opinion, that's when you're making pictures.

STUDENT: What's your biggest complaint about script supervisors?

BOGDANOVICH: I don't like them to talk to me about their job. They come over and ask me questions. I say, "If you don't know, why waste my time?" Of course, the problem is that I have the cutting in my head, which throws script supervisors unless you quite literally sit down and show them exactly what you're shooting. The one thing you don't have is time, and that's the only thing you need. It's a terrible bind you're always in, and it really is. I don't mean to be dramatic, but it's really a little bit like war, sometimes more than a little bit. You just haven't got the time to explain yourself constantly to the people who are supposed to be helping you. The director hasn't really got the time to help them. When I come in in the morning and tell the script supervisor, "Look, here's what we're going to do today—I'm going to be here, then here, then here—there's 12 to 14 set- ups." They have no problem. But that requires time you just don't have, so I start shooting and then they don't know where the shots go.

I learned to direct from talking to a lot of the older directors. Among them was Mrs. Ulmer's wonderful husband, Edgar, who spent very valuable time telling me how to cut corners. I spoke to John Ford and to Leo McCarey, Fritz Lang, Howard Hawks, Alfred Hitchcock. Most of them are gone now, but one thing I learned, and I learned practically everything from them, was not to shoot coverage—which means I cut in the camera, and that is very tough on script supervisors. They refer to my shooting as a jigsaw puzzle and they end up with slates like 14XYZ-F because they just don't know where it's supposed to go.

While we were shooting The Last Picture Show, *there was a sequence in which Jeff Bridges and Tim Bottoms have an argument. As the scene starts, they walk around a car yelling and end up having a fight. It's long—about four to five minutes, about six pages in the script, and we didn't shoot any coverage. I'd rehearsed it like a play. We had done it several times. Not too often, but enough so that they knew it pretty well. Now, there were about 30 set-ups in that sequence, and I was able to jump in at any point and shoot out-of-sequence because the actors knew where we were. I'd say, "O.K. we're over on this side of the car now, so let's do the beginning and* the end." We could do that because the actors knew the whole thing. We never covered it. In fact, the sequence was one of the easiest to put together. Just cut off the slates and cut when I said cut. The script supervisor and the cameraman came up to me long-faced and sort of ashen, and said, "Well, aren't you going to shoot a master?" and I answered, "What do you mean?" "Well," they said, "aren't you going to get back and show the whole car and then get them going around it?" I said, "What for?" "So that you know where you are . . ." "I know where I am."

I really didn't know what they were talking about. Bob Surtees, the cameraman who had won about five Oscars, thought I was completely out of my mind. "What if you get into trouble and you want to cut back to show where they are?" I said, "But I'm never going to cut to a long shot of the car. Where would I go to a wide shot of the car? In the middle?" Well, we didn't need it because I know where I was going to cut. I knew the movement and it was not a problem. I've done that on all my pictures, and it's hell on the script supervisor because they are not used to working that way. They are used to having, particularly today, a master shot, over-shoulders, close-ups, and they usually play the whole scene each time.

Maybe you've got a four-page scene between two people, Shirley and me. There's a master-shot of us talking from over there, and maybe there's another master that's a little bit wider, and there's an over-shoulder on me, and then there's a close-up on Shirley and one on me. And for each angle we play the whole four pages each time. Frankly, I think that's a horrible experience for the actor. If I have to say an important line like, "I love you," which may be tough to say, and I've got to say it for a long shot, for a two-shot, for the over the shoulder shot, and now finally they get to the close-up—the one I hope they're going to use (every actor hopes you'll use the close-up)—and by this time I don't "love you" anymore, I don't even like you. What I prefer to do if I can is to try to shoot the angle for only the lines I need in that angle. Since I only shoot it in the angle I'm going to use, the actor only has to say it for one angle. He may have to say it 20 times, perhaps, but not in six angles.

When I was working as a feature writer for Esquire, I watched a famous director shooting on a distant location. He shot three different masters on every scene. I saw him doing three different two-shots, five over-shoulders, numerous close-ups. People said to me afterwards, "That picture took a long time to shoot, they must have had trouble with the locations." I thought, "Trouble with the locations? The trouble was that the director was shooting every conceivable angle." People ask why movies take so long to shoot. Well, the longer they take, the more likely it is that the director doesn't know what he wants. If you walk on the set and you know what you want—there is a scene of five pages and you know you need eight set-ups—what's the big deal? You shoot the eight set-ups and move on.

STUDENT: *Before you get too pressured, did you ever sit down in pre-production and try to explain how you work?*

BOGDANOVICH: *I always try to explain to everybody, but no one ever thinks I mean it. "Look, I cut in the camera. I don't cover. I don't explain. You'll have to keep up with me because I haven't got time and I don't know until I come on the set exactly how it's going to go."*

I do plan it out before going on the set, but usually just before that particular scene. Maybe on the way to the location. Then when I arrive there's so many things to worry about. First is getting the actors so they feel like acting. And that takes some doing. That often takes you most of the day. I confess to having some impatience with most crews just going in, but the feeling comes because I feel they don't work hard enough and I don't feel they care enough. I don't mind if somebody's not good enough. But I do mind if they don't care.

A lot of union crews don't care. We made a picture in Singapore and I had maybe 12 people who had never worked on a movie before. The camera-man and a couple of his assistants—that was about it. The rest of the crew were all Oriental volunteers and none of them had ever been near a picture before, but they were all wonderful and I loved them. They made a hundred mistakes, but they cared.

STUDENT: *As you think about the problems you've had with script super-visors, would most of these have been solved if they had followed you around during the blocking of the scenes?*

BOGDAONOVICH: *That would help.*

STUDENT: *What else would help?*

BOGDAONOVICH: *More knowledge of the craft. For instance, you always run into a lot of problems about the 180 degree line. Now, there's a rule that's made to be broken. A least three times on every picture the script supervisor will come over and say we've just crossed the line. I usually say, "I know," but they usually persist and we both end up irritated—which is most frustrating to script supervisors because this is one time when they know they're right. As you know, there are tricks you can do with the cross-ing of the line that are every effective visually. We had a tricky shot in The Last Picture Show for a scene between Cybill Shepherd and Ellen Burstyn. There was a mirror involved and as Ellen turned to go one way, we cut and she was literally going the opposite way in screen direction. The script su-pervisor came running up to tell me we were jumping the line and I said, "Don't worry. It'll cut." He said, "It won't cut. It's a complete mismatch and it's a jump; she's going the wrong way. How can you say it'll cut?" I said,*

"We're cutting on movement. It'll work. Please, let's just shoot it." I didn't know how to explain exactly, but Howard Hawks once told me, "Always cut on movement." When you're cutting on a move, you can get away with almost anything. If you look for that shot in The Last Picture Show *you probably won't even notice the cut because it's absolutely smooth. It doesn't jump because the movement takes the eye, and it's a direct reverse, which is sometimes a very exciting cut and you don't quite know why.*

STUDENT: *Do you think the script supervisor was wrong to mention it to you?*

BOGDANOVICH: *No, he was right to mention it, but he went on and on about it. Let's face it. A director can be nuts, and it's considered a tremendous ego trip to direct a movie. A lot of directors go out there and yell at everybody and boss them around. OK, I still think the crew should give the director the benefit of the doubt. I've made a couple of good pictures, and I've made a couple of bad pictures. I've been around for a few years and I've picked up a few things. If I say, "Let's put the camera here. OK, we got that now? Quick, put it over there," the crew inevitably starts saying, "What's he doing?" Usually, they don't really know what he's doing, but instead of getting bored and griping, there are a few who say, "What the hell, this is kind of interesting."*

Now a script supervisor should be a very important person on the set, very important to the director and to every department. A good script supervisor can be invaluable—like a great shortstop. It can be, and ideally should be a key position on the team, a challenging and, eventually, even a most rewarding one.

I know which hand the cigarette was in,
but the question is which head.

CLOSEUP of Harry James in United Artists' *Carnegie Hall*.

CLOSE SHOT of Louis Hayward in United Artists' *Pirates of Capri*.

EXTREME CLOSEUP of Michael Goldstein in *Green Fields*.

INSERT of the chess game from the original *Black Cat* starring Bela Lugosi and Boris Karloff.

Generally speaking, a *close two-shot* and a *tight two-shot* refer to the same image size. Both include the heads and shoulders of two people. A *medium close shot* also captures the heads and shoulders of two people, but the term could also refer to a comparably sized shot of one person or subject.

As mentioned before, *close-ups* and *close shots* are often confused. A close shot highlights only one portion of the action by excluding the surrounding detail. A shoulder up view of a person is one example. If shoulders up is a close shot, then the head only is a close-up. A close-up reveals more detail than a close shot.

Extreme close-ups and *inserts* are closer still. When a shot of a face is a close-up, a shot of the scar on his nose is an extreme close-up. An extreme close-up is sometimes known as a *big close-up*. Inserts, on the other hand, usually refer to written or printed legend seen in large detail. Both terms can be applied interchangeably to a full screen shot of an important prop or detail.

The subtle distinction between *full shots* and *long shots* is also often lost. Technically speaking, a full shot includes all the action in the scene as opposed to a long shot which views the full subject in focus but not the background. Both are commonly used to establish a location before cutting to closer shots. For this reason, they are sometimes known as *establishing shots*.

MEDIUM SHOT of Hedy Lamarr in United Artists' *Strange Woman.*

MEDIUM TWO-SHOT of Robert Clark with "The Man From Planet X."

FULL SHOT of the New York Philharmonic Orchestra in *Carnegie Hall.*

LONG SHOT of Louis Hayward, Zachary Scott, and Diana Lynn in *Ruthless.*

Medium shots perform the same establishing function for television as full shots and long shots do for feature films. The subject and the background of a medium shot are in focus, but not the surrounding locale. A medium shot captures less facial expression than a closer shot while retaining the broader physical gestures.

This partial list of static shots doesn't include the many possible combinations such as; *extreme long shot* or *medium full shot,* nor does it include camera angles. A medium shot, for example, can be shot from a *low angle, high angle, side angle, wide angle, point-of-view* or *reverse angle.* Unless otherwise stated, a shot is presumed to be *eye level.*

High, low and side angles describe the direction from which cameras aim toward subjects. A camera mounted above a card table angling down toward gamblers seated around a table is referred to as high angle. The opposite view, looking up to the top of the Hollywood sign, is a low angle. A profile of the hero's beer belly is filmed from a side angle.

A wide angle differs from side, high and low angles in that the term describes the camera's field of view rather than the direction in which the camera is angled. A wide angle view includes a wide area of the set. Wide angles capture most of the action at once.

LOW ANGLE of Leopold Stokowski in United Artists' *Carnegie Hall.*

HIGH ANGLE of Gene Igleseus in Universal's *Naked Dawn.*

SIDE ANGLE of Betta St. John in *Naked Dawn.*

WIDE ANGLE of *Detour* featuring Tom Neal at the piano.

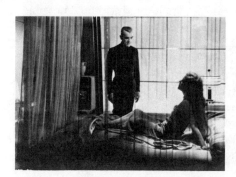

P.O.V. through the curtains to Boris Karloff and Jaqueline Welles in Universal's original *Black Cat.*

P.O.V. of Sidney Greenstreet and Lucille Bremer in *Ruthless.* This shot is both an over-the-shoulder p.o.v. and mirror p.o.v.

The term, point-of-view, refers to any angle designated by a specific viewpoint. Common examples include a view of the body from the killer's eyes, the group below from a pilot's vantage point or a shot through a car windshield. A *racking-shot* is the point-of-view past one subject to another, such as an *over-the-shoulder shot.*

The final term, reverse angle, is another relative term. It originally was reserved for the complete 180-degree opposite camera angle from a previous angle. The definition has since broadened to include any corresponding angle to an established camera direction. If a two-shot of Jack and Jill favors Jack, the reverse favors Jill.

Static camera shots are named by their image, size and angles. Full shots, long shots, medium shots, tight two-shots, close shots, close-ups, extreme close-ups and inserts refer to the size of the image being filmed. Variations are achieved by combining aspects of more than one shot, such as medium close shots, extreme long shots and medium full shots. Camera angles refer to the direction from which the camera angles toward the subject. These include low angle, high angle, side angle and the most common, eye level. Other camera angles don't necessarily define any specific size or angle, such as point-of-view or reverse shots. A script supervisor can determine the size and angle of static shots easily by listening to conversation between the director and cinematographer, or by looking through the camera lens. The composition of moving shots, on the other hand, is harder to recognize.

Moving Shots

Many different angles and image sizes can be included within one camera move. Since the script supervisor will not have the luxury of looking through the camera lens during a moving shot, the script supervisor will have to imagine the composition by understanding basic camera moves. These moves fit into two groups: first, those where the camera remains basically in one spot or *zooms, pans, tilts* and *focus alterations;* and second, those where the camera travels or *dolly moves, hand-held* camera moves and movements made possible by *specialized camera mounts.*

A zoom shot simulates a camera move by using a specialized lens which is capable of varying its *focal length.* The focal length is the distance from the optical center of the lens to the film surface when the lens is focused on a distant object. This distance determines the *field of view.* A short length results in a wide angle view while a long length results in a narrow view. If the lens is adjusted during the process of filming, the adjustment gives the impression that the camera is moving away or towards the subject. These moves are called *zoom out* and *zoom in* respectively.

Sometimes the focus of a shot is changed without altering the framing. Say, for example, that two people share a frame. One stands in the background in focus while the other stands in the foreground out of focus. Shifting the focus from the background character or the foreground character or visa versa is called a *focus pull, racking* or *rack shot.*

Pans and tilts occur when the camera pivots to follow the action. Pans follow the subject from one side to the other while tilts follow a subject up or down. Combining the two results is a diagonal move. All are used to enhance the screen story.

Simple pans follow movement from one place to the next. A horse thief bravely walking toward the gallows might best be covered with a slow pan. Other simple types include *exit* and *entrance pans.* These are frequently used whenever the subject walks toward the door in one shot and away from the exit in the next shot.

A slightly more complicated pan directs the audience's attention by varying the image size within one continuous camera move. In a *medium to close pan,* the camera pans with a general subject first and then pivots over to a specific detail. An example might be a medium shot panning with a detective as he walks from the background towards a table in the foreground and remaining on a bloody knife atop the table after he passes. In the opposite move, a *medium to full pan,* an uneasy looking starlette walks side by side between two burly men in a tight three-shot near the camera while the camera pans to a full shot of a mob of adoring fans.

Revelation pans and *pay-off pans* accomplish the same effect as the medium to close pan, but don't necessarily alter the image size. The revelation pan occurs when the camera moves across an area and holds on an important detail. The pay-off pan follows a subject without holding specifically to that subject so that the camera can hold on a different subject, permitting the first to move out of the frame. Either of these camera moves could be applied to the detective example, depending on what type of effect was desired.

The possibilities are endless. The *reaction pan* technique provides an alternative to direct cutting. While the main action is happening, the camera pans to capture the reaction from a second subject. In a *subjective pan,* the camera approximates the look of a subject scanning an area—such as a criminal eyeing jewelry or a closed-circuit television camera searching for intruders. A *reverse pan* occurs when the camera moves in one direction, then pans in the other direction within the same shot. A camera move that jerks between two subjects in one shot causing a blur of images in between is called a *flash pan, whip pan* or *swish pan.* When the same technique is used at the end of one scene and the beginning of the next, bridging the transition, it is referred to as a *transition flash pan.* The list goes on and on.

The same uses for zooms, tilts and pans can be applied to moving shots where the camera actually travels. A mobile platform with four wheels on which the camera is mounted is known as a *dolly,* and allows the camera to move in all directions. It can move closer to the subject being filmed in a continuous motion or *dolly in. Dolly out* means the camera travels away from the subject. Both cause the image size to change during the shot. In a dolly out move, the image alters from a relatively close shot to a longer one. In a dolly in shot, the image changes from a relatively longer shot to a closer one.

Dolly with are the words used to describe a camera move toward, away or alongside the subject. As long as the camera travels at the same speed as the subject, the image size remains constant. *Trucking, tracking* and *traveling* refer to the same move.

Additional moves are defined by the camera mount. *Handheld cameras* can follow a subject anywhere the camera operator is free to move. *Car mounted* cameras obviously travel in the same path as the car. The same goes for *wing mounted cameras.* Subjective shots such as *helmet mounted cameras* are used for motorcyclists and skydivers. *Crane mounts* permit relatively high angle to lower angle views with the corresponding horizontal, vertical and diagonal movements.

A script supervisor should be able to recognize the composition in each shot of a film or video project. Image size and angle of static shots are easily identified. In addition to the camera angle and image size, the script supervisor should pinpoint the camera move technique in moving shots. Just as picture coverage requires identification, so does audio coverage.

Audio Coverage

Individual sound recordings referred to as *sound tracks* provide coverage in the same manner as static and moving shots. Various tracks are combined to comprise a completed sound sequence. For convenience, most sound editors regard sound as falling into one of three categories—*dialogue, effects* or *music.*

Most dialogue tracks are synchronous, but not all. Any sound track recorded at the same time as the picture is referred to as *synchronous* or *in sync.* These require no special identification by the script supervisor because they are numbered with the picture.

Non-synchronous tracks do require further ·identification. A scene that is recorded without sound should be identified as *M. O. S.,* ("mit out sound"), or *SIL,* (silent). Sometimes a clear track is not possible due to noise problems. A rough recording known as a *cue track* or *scratch track* is recorded anyway. This rough track will be used as a reference for replacing or *dubbing* in a better track later. Most companies record off-camera dialogue and narration, called *voice-overs,* "wild." *Wild tracks* are recordings made completely independent from filming or videotaping. Wild tracks are also used for covering effects.

Most people think of doorbells, telephone rings, footsteps and the like when they hear the term, sound effects. There are several other types of effects used in filmmaking as well. *Walla* or unscripted background noises are recorded to give the impression of a specific location. Cafe walla of clattering dishes and chatting patrons, for instance, would be used to provide the atmosphere of a restaurant scene. *Presence* and *roomtone* are recordings of ambient sound in a given local. Combining or *mixing* these with other soundtracks achieves the desired effect. For instance, a voice-over track might be mixed with an office presence track so that the voice-over sounds as if it were recorded in the office. A second example would be recording dialogue in a hospital waiting room separate from patient walla so that two clean tracks can be mixed to appropriate balance. A script supervisor should be able to distinguish between the various types of effects.

Unlike dialogue and effects tracks, nearly all music sound tracks are recorded in pre-production or post-production instead of production. Sometimes a singer or musician will perform to a tape of pre-recorded music, called a *playback.* [see page 254] But otherwise, music tracks are added to the film after principal photography is completed. Script supervisors rarely deal with recording music tracks.

The first step in recognizing film and sound components is to understand the director's coverage approach. A master shot/pick-up technique, a series of complicated moving shots with protection, a cut-to-cut approach or a combination of all three are the most common systems. No matter which method is employed, various static and moving shots together with music, dialogue and effects sound tracks are used to provide the necessary coverage. Once the script supervisor has identified the shot or sound track, the next step is to enter a description into the continuity records.

RECORDING CONTINUITY NOTES

A script supervisor should keep complete, accurate records of each shot and sound track being filmed or taped. These records will prove invaluable to the editor. The descriptions and printing instructions serve as guidelines for assembling the tape or film footage. Editors depend on continuity notes to provide the crucial link between the set and the editing room. The first two areas of responsibility are numbering and lining the script.

Numbering the Script

Script supervisors number the shots before every camera *set-up*. Significant changes in camera operation, focal length, lens or lighting constitute new camera set-ups. The script supervisor assigns each set-up a different *scene number* or *slate number,* (which may or may not correspond with the scene numbers in the script). Often, the numbers are only used as a point of reference because there are more camera set-ups shot than scenes in the script. After selecting the number, the script supervisor gives each single attempt to photograph the action or *take* a separate number. All this will become clearer as numbering requirements are further explained.

One method of numbering scenes is called the *consecutive numbering system.* Although ineffective, some companies still require the script supervisor to use this system. The first shot is assigned number 1, the second shot 2, the third shot 3 and so on until all the filming is complete. Most companies prefer a second type of numbering system.

The *master pick-up numbering system* has many advantages over the consecutive numbering system. With this method, the script supervisor assigns to the amster shot a number as clsoe as possible to the scene number found in the script. Pick-ups or protection shots are given the same number but followed by letters. A medium-full shot of a conversation between a man and a woman at a restaurant, for instance, is numbered 231. A clsoe-up of the man during the same conversation is 231A while the reverse close-up of the woman, is 231B. An insert of the menu is 231C if there is no number in the script already reserved for it. This numbering system can also be applied to a cut-to-cut coverage approach by assigning each shot of a sequence a different letter following the same scene number. A master pick-up numbering system enables an editor to make immediate assumptions about the shot by merely looking at the number.

Sometimes a scene is filmed that is not included in the script. Many script supervisors assign to the added scene whatever nearby number is available. Say, for instance, that the script's restaurant sequence covers the numbers 230–240. The script supervisor has used 230, 231, 231A, 231B, 231C, 232, 232A and 233. This leaves 234, 235, 236, 237, 238, 239 and 240 free for added scenes in the restaurant. Other script supervisors add a prefix such as X to the nearest scene number to distinguish it from the others. This tells the editor where the added shot falls into the story. Scene X237, for instance, falls between 236 and 237. Assigning a number way out of proportion is a similar solution. If there are only 500 scenes in the script and the script supervisor assigns 801, then the scene is obviously added.

Walla, presence, roomtone and other effects are also number-coded. Preceding all wild track numbers with the letters W.T. identifies them as wild tracks. Voice-overs in particular should be assigned a W.T. number so the editor won't search for non-existing film.

Assume now, that a hypothetical script supervisor is well acquainted with film terminology and has observed the filming. The next step is to record what has transpired into the continuity script. The standard system used by nearly all script supervisors is known as *lining the script*.

Lining the Script

Script lining is a combination of symbols, abbreviations and short descriptions designed to present relevant information in a concise format. Copies of this information are given to the editor after completing each day's shooting. The originals are kept in the continuity script as reference material for further filming. The following continuity notes come from the pre-title sequence of American International Pictures' feature, *Return to Macon County*.

Return to Macon County opens with an action sequence which immediately sets the tone of the picture. The events described reflect the original continuity records, although many changes have been made for the purposes of this book. The example presents a particularly good composite of continuity duties because the director covered the scenes in a completely different manner than was indicated in the script. He used a typical master shot/pick-up approach with many complicated moving shots and protection pick-ups. His coverage provided the editors with ample choices of how to assemble the footage. Complete continuity records were mandatory to prevent the editor from being swamped with endless unidentified footage.

First thing in the morning, the script supervisor walks onto the set ready for work. Since the preparation week was used wisely, most of the day's continuity requirements can be determined by matching the shooting schedule to the one-liners. In our example the schedule allots three days to film the pre-title sequence. These are shooting days 20, 21 and 22. The entire pre-title sequence occurs during fictional day one. No other scenes which occur on day one have been filmed yet, so the script supervisor doesn't have to worry about matching elements such as costumes, props, sets and dialogue to scenes outside of the sequence. The script supervisor needs to be concerned only with internal discrepancies.

Since everyone else on the crew is likely to lose either their schedule or tuck it safely away, never to look at it again, the script supervisor assumes the role of the set's authority on the schedule. Prior to each day's filming, the script supervisor should review the scenes planned. For shooting day 20, the schedule reads as follows:

PROD. NO. 1670 — **SCHEDULE** DATE 1|2

DIRECTOR Compton   UNIT MANAGER J. Doe   ASST. DIR. Smith

DAY AND DATE	SET OR LOCATION SCENE NUMBERS	WHERE LOCATED	CAST WORKING
shooting day #20 1|27	opening chevy scenes 1,2,3,4,5,6,7,8,9, 11,12,13,14,15	bus from Studio 6:00 AM	Bo Harley Stunt driver
	lunch	—	—
	complete above scenes	same	Bo Harley Stunt driver
Standby	inserts	same	Harley

Comparing the schedule to the one-liners gives the script supervisor a better idea of the director's intention.

MACON ONE LINERS

SC #	LOCATION/SET	DESCRIPTION	CAST	TIME
1.	Ext. Access Rd.	Est. pan from cow to Chevy	(Bo, Harley)	D1
2.	Ext. Access Rd.	Harley adjusts engine	Harley	D1
3.	Int. Chevy	Bo in driver's seat	Bo	D1
4.	Ext. Access Rd.	Bo's pov of Harley fixing engine	Harley	D1
5.	Ext. Access Rd.	Bo shoots car toward Harley	Bo, Harley	D1
6.	Int. Chevy	Bo & Harley begin to speed test car	Bo, Harley	D1
7.	Ext. Chevy	wheels spin	--	D1
8.	Int. Chevy	Bo shifts gears	Bo, Harley	D1
9.	Int. Chevy	Harley grins as checks RPM	Harley	D1
10.	Insert	tachometer & v.o.	(Bo, Harley)	D1
11.	Ext. Highway	car rockets off	(Bo, Harley)	D1
12.	Int. Chevy	Harley & Bo discuss 1/4 mark	Bo, Harley	D1
13.	Ext. Highway	car zooms by pole	(Bo, Harley)	D1
14.	Int. Chevy	Bo & Harley discuss results	Bo, Harley	D1
15.	Int. Chevy	Close of happy Bo	Bo	D1
16.	Ext. Highway	Chevy zooming in and out of traffic	(Bo, Harley, & misc. drivers)	D1
17.	Ext. Highway	Mercury cruising	Boy, Girl	D1
18.	Ext. Highway	Chevy passes truck	Bo, Harley	D1
19.	Ext. Highway	Chevy shoots up to Mercury	Bo, Harley, Boy, Girl	D1
20.	Int. Mercury	Boy & Girl notice Chevy	Boy, Girl	D1
21.	Ext. Highway	Chevy moves alongside Merc.	Boy, Girl, Bo, Harley	D1

Scheduled — On Standby — Scheduled

It's obvious that the director wants to start with the Chevy alone before moving onto the other scenes of the pre-title sequence.

Next, our script supervisor reviews the costume and prop requirements. During day one, the only costumes indicated in the script are the character's initial costumes. As far as props go, the only props that travel from one shot to another are the car tools and stopwatch. Of course, our script supervisor realizes that there may be many changes discovered during the filming, but it still helps to know beforehand as much as possible.

After arriving on the set, the script supervisor's first step is to find out which scene the director wants to tackle first. This may or may not correspond with the shooting schedule. A shooting schedule could be running over, it may rain, an actor could come down with a cold or any number of variables may change the proposed schedule. Today, there have been no schedule changes, so the director decides to start with the opening scene. Our script supervisor can now assign a number to the first scene.

As soon as the appropriate scene number is chosen, the script supervisor announces it to the crew in a loud voice. The script supervisor makes certain that both the camera and sound teams hear the number clearly. If the number is followed by a letter, the script supervisor uses a letter code to help ensure that everyone hears the same letter. While announcing 237A, for instance, the script supervisor might say, "This is scene 237 Apple, take 1."

COMMON LETTER CODES

LETTER	SHIRLEY	CAROL	FCC STANDARD
A	APPLE	APPLE	ALPHA
B	BOSTON	BAKER	BRAVO
C	CHICAGO	CHARLIE	CHARLIE
D	DENVER	DAVID	DELTA
E	ENGLAND	EDWARD	ECHO
F	'FRISCO	FRANK	FOXTROT
G	GEORGE	GEORGE	GOLF
H	HARRY	HARRY	HOTEL
I	(skip)	(skip)	INDIA
J	JOHN	JERRY	JULIETTE
K	KABBIBLE	KANSAS	KILO
L	LOVE	LARRY	LIMA
M	MARY	MARY	MIKE
N	NO	NANCY	NOVEMBER
O	(skip)	(skip)	OSCAR
P	PETER	PAUL	POPPA
Q	QUEBEC	QUESTION	QUEBEC
R	READY	RANDY	ROMEO
S	SUGAR	SALLY	SIERRA
T	THOMAS	TOM	TANGO
U	UNDER	UNLESS	UNIFORM
V	VERY	VICKY	VICTOR
W	WINDOW	WHITE	WHISKEY
X	XEROX	XEROX	X-RAY
Y	YOUNG	YARD	YANKEE
Z	ZEBRA	ZOO	ZULU

In our case, the first shot is slate scene 1, take 1. Our script supervisor announces the number as early as possible so that all departments can enter it into their respective reports. This way, there should be no problem in keeping consistent numbers between the continuity, sound and camera records.

Next, the crew continues preparing for the first shot. While the camera crew sets up the shot, the script supervisor diagrams the scene's playing area. Included in the diagram are props and set dressing as well as camera positions. Since the camera moves in scene 1, its travel path is indicated on the diagram along with the relevant camera operation information on the diagram. If part of the shot has to be duplicated, the script supervisor knows that the diagram will make it possible. At this time, the script supervisor also finds out the camera roll number, sound roll number and the lens information.

For slate scene 1, the director selects a right to left establishing pan. It starts on a cow in a field before moving past a nearby tree to a Chevy parked on the access road. The zoom goes from 25mm on the cow to 70mm on the tree and ends with 100mm on the Chevy. The scene is being shot without sound, but according to the script, the car engine should rev. Obviously, a wild track will have to be recorded. Possibly, field presence also will be needed. The script supervisor lists needed wild tracks.

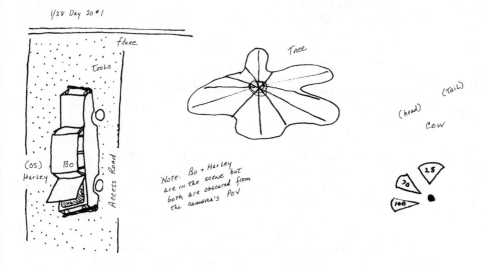

Through observation and subtle eavesdropping, the script supervisor gets a pretty clear idea of the set-up. A diagram is drawn. Our script supervisor double checks the image sizes and camera angles at the beginning and the end of the move by looking through the viewfinder while the set is being lit. The middle of the shot has to be imagined. Next, the script supervisor gets into position as close to the camera as possible for the truest view of the action just before the actors take their places.

When the actors walk onto the set, a description of their costumes is quickly recorded.

Bo C#1 (DAY 1)
    red windbreaker zipped 1/2 way
       sleeves pushed up 3/4 to elbows
    faded straight-leg blue jeans (no belt)
    drk. blue T. shirt with collar + open placket
    white with navy trim tennis shoes
    drk. blue socks
    wallet in back rt. pocket
    James Dean hairstyle

Harley C#1 (DAY 1)
    straight-leg blue jeans rolled at cuff
    dirty white T-shirt—cigarettes rolled into
       left sleeve
    brown braided leather belt
    uncombed hair
    gold colored watch on left wrist w/ 1" metal
       band
    brown loafer styled shoes
    brown socks

At the same time, the script supervisor can check the costume for discrepancies. This is the first shot of the sequence, so there are obviously none. Notice that the script supervisor includes hairstyles and jewelry on the list. Three separate lists would be too impractical, given the time restraints of both recording the information and finding it again when necessary. The composite list can be filed away into the production script either on the back of the previous page or in a tabbed section of the script, leaving the script supervisor to deal with an uncluttered script page.

After the actors take their places, the director holds a *run-through* or rehearsal of the camera and actor action without filming. The script supervisor takes preliminary notes, matching the blocking to the dialogue. Unlike camera movements which are for the most part set during the rehersals and set-up, the actors may change their blocking from take to take. Dialogue in particular is often altered slightly each time the scene is performed. The script supervisor must sense which alterations are worth recording in the preliminary notes. On the first shot, this decision is already made for the script supervisor. Both actors play incidental parts during scene 1. Harley is obscured by the car hood while Bo sits inside the car, hardly visable from the camera's point-of-view. The scene is also being shot MOS which means the script supervisor's main concern will be camera moves.

During rehearsals, the second assistant camera operator readies the slate. *Slate, numberboard* and *clapperboard* are all names for a board or chalkboard attached to a hinged pair of sticks called *clapsticks*. Clapsticks are used to synchronize film footage with sound tracks. By clapping the sticks together, the *sound* the clap can be aligned with the *image* of the clap so that all subsequent images match their corresponding sounds. Keeping the clapper open while filming indicates that the scene is being shot MOS. An upside-down slate appearing at the end of the take is referred to as a *tailslate* or *endslate*. Chalked onto the slate, (or labeled with tape), are the scene number, take number, camera roll, and either sound roll or the letters MOS and other identifying information. A hand waved in front of the lens or *handslate* is used on occasion to save time and still differentiate between takes. The script supervisor should double-check slate information for accuracy *before* the second assistant camera operator holds it in front of the camera.

The procedure at this point runs as follows: The assistant director instructs the camera operator to start the camera. The second assistant cameraman holds up the slate in front of the lens. The assistant director waits for the sound mixer to call out "Speed!" which means that the film is rolling at the correct rate. The assistant director gives the command, "Slate!" or "Mark it!". The second assistant camera operator normally slams the clapsticks together, and then quickly clears the set, but since the first shot is MOS, the sticks remain open. The director calls out "Action!", and the scene commences.

The script supervisor's job now really begins. First, the scene must be timed. The script supervisor starts the stopwatch when the scene seems to start, rather than when the director hollers "Action!". There may be several seconds of pause before the scene starts, or there may even be actor warm-up on the head of the scene. The scene may end before the director calls "Cut!". The script supervisor should also sense the actual ending. No matter how long the filming continues past the end of the scene, the script supervisor should never speak until the director's "Cut!".

In our example, extra footage is required for the FADE IN. A *fade in* is an *optical effect* where each frame of the film receives progressively more exposure, so the film makes a gradual transition from black to normal exposure. During a *fade out* optical effect, the film receives less exposure, resulting in the opposite effect. A *dissolve, lap dissolve* or *cross dissolve* combines the two effects for a crossfade of images. Other opticals include *wipes* where a scene enters the edge of the screen and pushes another off the screen. *Split screens* consist of more than one scene sharing a screen. All of these film opticals are created in the lab, and not on the set. The script supervisor only needs to ensure that there is enough extra footage shot at the beginning or end for the optical to be possible. This extra footage should not be included in the script supervisor's time estimation.

While a scene runs, the script supervisor mainly records continuity observations. Since there is seldom enough time to record every detail of the action and dialogue, the script supervisor must be selective. Only the most significant details which may affect the continuity merit attention.

Continuing with our example, because the scene is silent and the camera moves have already been noted during the setup, the script supervisor watches for coverage. Coverage records are noted by drawing a vertical line on the script page through the shot. The beginning of each line is labeled by a circle shot number. The bottom is indicated by a short horizontal line which clearly marks the end of the shot. Some script supervisors write a short shot description near the circled number for convenience. Any other markings are added to the script text as the script supervisor sees fit.

Next, the same information is transferred into the editorial notes on the opposite side of the script page. A script supervisor should transfer as much as possible before filming. Obviously, information such as the scene number, camera and sound roll numbers, take number and shooting date can be entered onto the form at any time. Even part of the action can be described early, so the script supervisor can concentrate on watching continuity details during the shoot. However, since the action applies to all the takes, the description doesn't have to be completed until striking the camera set-up. The results of each take, on the other hand, must be noted before moving on.

Some script supervisors don't bother filling in lens information. Many years ago, editors felt that cutting from one lens to another caused an unacceptable change in depth of field. Having the lens numbers in the continuity records helped these editors set guidelines for cutting. Since this is no longer the prevalent attitude among today's editors, recording lens information is optional. Our thorough script supervisor dedides to include the lens information. Besides, if anything goes wrong with a lens, this lens information will help determine which is the faulty piece of equipment.

For the first take, the continuity notes appear as follows:

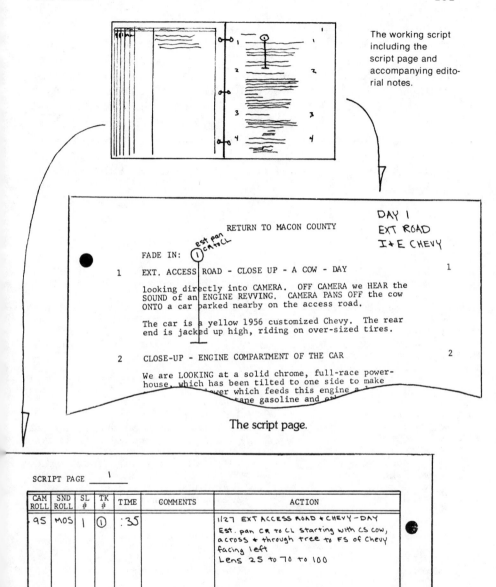

The working script including the script page and accompanying editorial notes.

RETURN TO MACON COUNTY

DAY 1
EXT ROAD
I + E CHEVY

est pan
CR to CL

FADE IN:

1 EXT. ACCESS ROAD - CLOSE UP - A COW - DAY   1

looking directly into CAMERA. OFF CAMERA we HEAR the
SOUND of an ENGINE REVVING. CAMERA PANS OFF the cow
ONTO a car parked nearby on the access road.

The car is a yellow 1956 customized Chevy. The rear
end is jacked up high, riding on over-sized tires.

2 CLOSE-UP - ENGINE COMPARTMENT OF THE CAR   2

We are LOOKING at a solid chrome, full-race powerhouse, which has been tilted to one side to make
_____ wer which feeds this engine _ _
_____ tane gasoline and _

The script page.

SCRIPT PAGE	1					
CAM ROLL	SND ROLL	SL #	TK #	TIME	COMMENTS	ACTION
95	MOS	1	①	:35		1/27 EXT ACCESS ROAD + CHEVY -DAY
						Est. pan CR to CL starting with CS cow, across + through tree to FS of Chevy facing left
						Lens 25 to 70 to 100

Editorial chart on the opposite side.

On the right side of the editorial form is a short description using abbreviations for shot sizes and camera direction. The records on the left side indicate that the take timed out 35 seconds, excluding fade-in time. The director decides to print take one, and the script supervisor circles the number. Any editor knows that only the circled takes are printed on 35mm films. Although it's cheaper to print all 16mm takes, the preferred takes are still distinguished by circling the take number. These abbreviations and symbols save the script supervisor considerable time on the set.

The following is a list of abbreviations used most frequently in marking continuity scripts:

COMMON ABBREVIATIONS

WA	wide angle		CR	camera right
LA	low angle		CL	camera left
HA	high angle		BG	background
			FG	foreground
MCU	medium close-up		CRBG	camera right background
CU	close-up		CRFG	camera right foreground
CS	close shot		CLBG	camera left background
ECU	extreme close-up		CLFG	camera left foreground
BCU	big close-up		FR	frame right
FS	full shot		FL	frame left
LS	long shot		UF	upper frame
MS	medium shot		LF	lower frame
EST	establishing			
POV	point-of-view		NG	no good
			NGA	take no good due to action
SYNC	synchronous sound		NGC	take no good due to camera
DIAL	dialogue		NGDial	take no good due to dialogue
MOS	without sound		NGDir	take no good due to direction
SIL	without sound		NGS	take no good due to sound
WT	wild track		INCPL	take incomplete
WL	wild line		CMPL	take complete
VO	voice-over		H	hold
CT	cue track			
PB	playback		O SH	over shoulder
			OS	-⌈over shoulder ⌊off screen
PU	pickup			
R	retake		OFF S	off screen
TV	for tv version		OC	on camera

The list includes descriptions, numbering codes and take results. Although many other abbreviations for the same terms are possible, these are the most common.

If a script supervisor uses instant photographs for matching, the ideal time to have the stills taken is after the first take. Set details are often altered up until the very moment of filming, or even after the first take. In our *Return to Macon County* example, confusion arose whether or not to have a flare behind the Chevy on the shoulder of the road. The director decided to film another take with the flare and canceled printing take 1. The script supervisor makes small marks through the circle on take 1 to indicate it is no longer a print. When the second take is completed, the results are added to the chart.

SCRIPT PAGE ___1___						
CAM ROLL	SND ROLL	SL #	TK #	TIME	COMMENTS	ACTION
95	MOS	1	①②	:35 :35	without flare with flare	1/27 **EXT** ACCESS ROAD + CHEVY —DAY Est. pan CR to CL starting with CS cow, across + through tree to FS of chevy facing left Lens 25 to 70 to 100

Satisfied, the director moves on to the second camera set-up.

The second shot is far more complicated because it involves intricate camera and actor blocking in addition to synchronous sound. Its action overlaps the tail end of the first shot from the 180 degree reverse angle.

The camera is mounted on the back left passenger window, angling into the car to Bo in the driver's seat. After a beat, the camera pans camera right past Bo to include the front windshield where we see Harley in the background closing the car hood. Dialogue line 1 and 2 are exchanged. At this point, the action varies from the script. Harley first walks around the car camera right and then climbs in. Harley delivers dialogue line 5 before Bo accelerates the car forward.

Numbering this second shot is tricky. The action covers neither script scene 1 nor script scene 2, yet it overlaps both. The second shot could either be used as a protection shot or an alternate view of the opening sequence. Since both the numbers 1 and 2 are needed for the other shots, the second shot has to be numbered something else. The script supervisor chooses the number 1A.

Script lining systems help distinguish between covered and uncovered action. A straight vertical line indicates action clearly visible in a shot. When the line is squiggled or broken the action described in the script is either unclear or not covered. Whenever possible, variations in the action such as dialogue changes are noted in the briefest form possible. Major deviations are entered into the editorial notes on the opposite page.

In example shot 1A, the vertical line begins where Harley fixes the engine. On the first page, all of the action is clearly seen except for the engine details.

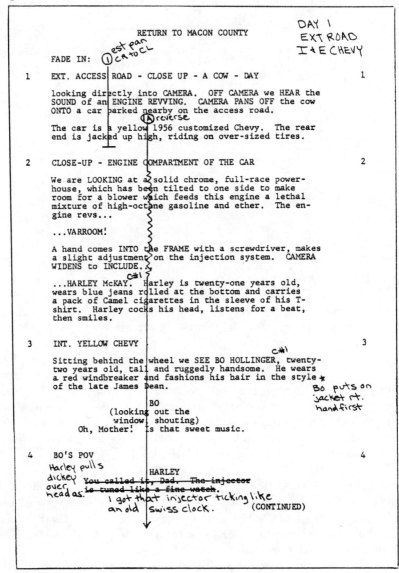

An arrow is drawn at the end of the page to indicate that the shot continues on the next page.

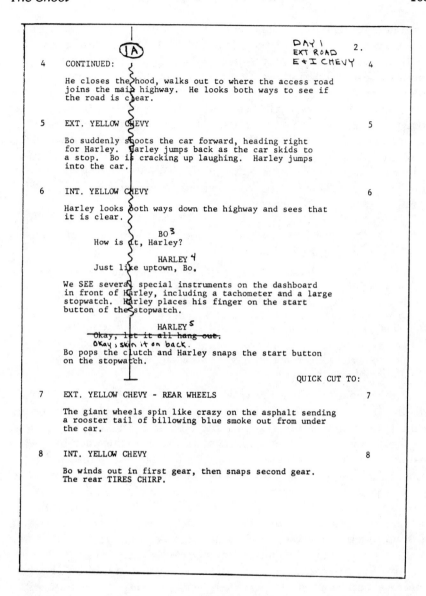

DAY 1
EXT ROAD   2.
E + I CHEVY   4

4   CONTINUED: 4

He closes the hood, walks out to where the access road
joins the main highway. He looks both ways to see if
the road is clear.

5   EXT. YELLOW CHEVY   5

Bo suddenly shoots the car forward, heading right
for Harley. Harley jumps back as the car skids to
a stop. Bo is cracking up laughing. Harley jumps
into the car.

6   INT. YELLOW CHEVY   6

Harley looks both ways down the highway and sees that
it is clear.

                         BO 3
             How is it, Harley?

                         HARLEY 4
             Just like uptown, Bo.

We SEE several special instruments on the dashboard
in front of Harley, including a tachometer and a large
stopwatch. Harley places his finger on the start
button of the stopwatch.

                         HARLEY 5
             ~~Okay, let it all hang out.~~
             Okay, skin it on back.
Bo pops the clutch and Harley snaps the start button
on the stopwatch.

                                         QUICK CUT TO:

7   EXT. YELLOW CHEVY - REAR WHEELS   7

The giant wheels spin like crazy on the asphalt sending
a rooster tail of billowing blue smoke out from under
the car.

8   INT. YELLOW CHEVY   8

Bo winds out in first gear, then snaps second gear.
The rear TIRES CHIRP.

The script supervisor again labels the next page's script line with a circled slate number. This time, the line should be drawn up to the top of the page to show that it is a continuation. A short horizontal line marks the end of the shot.

The editorial records for scene 1A provide a more typical example of script notation than the records for scene 1. Except for the car flare problem, scene 1 was captured in one take right off the bat. Scene 1A required several takes. More detailed notation was necessary to record the take results.

A take that is not circled can either be *NG* or *HOLD*. NG means that the take was no good, and not to be printed. Hold means the director likes the take, but prefers to print a better version. If problems arise after developing the preferred take, the held take will be printed. When no takes are held, an editor may even try to salvage a piece of the NG take. A script supervisor should record specific information about NG takes for this reason.

Academy Award winning editor and now a Vice President of Feature Production at Universal, Verna Fields, agrees about the importance of indicating why a take is NG.

> I would hate to think of trying to cut a picture without the help of a good script supervisor's notes. I have always found that the lined script is a tremendous advantage to me as well as the notes of why takes were not printed. If I need to print a piece of "B" negative, I depend totally on the script supervisor's notes on how long it ran, how good it was and for what reason it was not printed. There are many other little hints and notes in a script supervisor's notes that are time-saving and helpful to the editor.

All NG takes are either *complete* or *incomplete*. A complete take runs all the way through the desired action, without stopping. An incomplete take breaks before reaching the end. If the take is incomplete, the script supervisor should pinpoint the specific line of dialogue or action where the shot goes wrong. Whether a shot is incomplete or complete, the script supervisor should say why the take is unacceptable.

Reasons for not printing a take are usually generalized into five categories. Many takes are not good due to problems involving the action or *NGA*. An actor who opens the door with his right hand when he's supposed to use his left, or a dancer who trips are two examples. Action ruined due to stumbled or incorrect dialogue can be further identified as *NGDial*. Errors due to camera action are *NGC*. These include camera jams, improper focus, jerky moves or any number of camera related problems. When the director decides to alter a performance, the previous takes can be cited as *NGDir*. This director may prefer more energy or a different reaction. A sound machinery malfunction or unwanted noise, such as an airplane overhead, may cause a take to be *NG* due to sound or *NGS*. These five reasons are the most common, although other continuity discrepancies such as costume errors, missing props, lights blowing out, set improperly dressed and other physical details could also be involved.

Sometimes printed takes require explanations in the same manner as NG takes. Most editors assume that circled takes are complete unless they are labeled otherwise. When an incomplete take is printed, the script supervisor should pinpoint which portion of the action is useable.

Going back to our *Return to Macon County* scene 1A example, the completed editorial notes appear as follows:

SCRIPT PAGE ____1____

CAM ROLL	SND ROLL	SL #	TK #	TIME	COMMENTS	ACTION
95	MOS	1	①	:35	without flare	1127 EXT ACCESS ROAD & CHEVY - DAY Est. pan CR to CL starting with CS cow, across & through tree to FS of Chevy facing left Lens 25 to 70 to 100
			②	:35	with flare	
95	41	1A				1127 EXT ACCESS ROAD & INT CHEVY - DAY Reverse angle of SC #1. Camera mounted on back left passenger window. Pans CL to CR over Bo in FG driver's seat & out windshield to Harley in BG. Business different than script. DIAL 1-2. Harley climbs in car. DIAL 5. Car zooms forward (neutral) Lens 25

Notice that because scene 1A was shot with sync sound, the sound roll number is included in addition to the camera roll. Also, portions of the action are pinpointed to the dialogue.

During the first take, the performance wasn't exactly what the director wanted. Harley didn't walk close enough to the car when he crossed from the hood to the passenger seat. He inadverently walked out of frame. Although the take could be used in a pinch, the director requested a second take. The director tells the script supervisor to "Put it on hold . . .", and the script supervisor writes down "NGA compl." Afterwards, she notes, "awk. cross". The second take was incomplete because Harley fumbled his last line. Since the performance was good until the flub, the director decided to print it anyway. The script supervisor writes "incpl. NGDial, good to DIAL 5". The camera jams during the third take, rendering the take useless. The script supervisor writes "NGC (jam) incompl." The last take is perfect, so the script supervisor circles it.

The rest of the day's continuity can be found over the following four script pages:

SCRIPT PAGE ___1___

CAM ROLL	SND ROLL	SL #	TK #	TIME	COMMENTS	ACTION
95	MOS	1	① ②	:35 :35	without flare with flare	1127 EXT ACCESS ROAD + CHEVY—DAY Est. pan CR to CL starting with CS cow, across + through tree to FS of Chevy facing left Lens 25 to 70 to 100
95	41	1A	H1 ② 3 ④	:43 :37 :10 :43	compl. n.g.a. awk. cross incpl. n.g.d. good to DIAL 5 n.g.C. (jam)	1127 EXT ACCESS ROAD + INT CHEVY—DAY Reverse angle of sc#1. Camera mounted on back left passenger window. Pans CL to CR over Bo in FG driver's seat + out windshield to Harley in BG. Business different than script. DIAL 1-2. Harley climbs in car. DIAL 5. Car zooms forward (neutral). Lens 25
96	41	2	1 ②	:35 :38	incmpl. n.g. cam	1127 EXT ACCESS ROAD + CHEVY—DAY Start close on engine from left fender angling down. Dolly round CL + widen to include Harley working on engine. DIAL 1-2. Harley crosses to junction Lens 235 to 60
96	41	2A	H1 ②	:20 :20	compl. hold second sticks	1127 INT CHEVY ON ACCESS ROAD—DAY CS Bo in car facing CR. DIAL 1-2. Bo watches cross. Reaction as shoots forward. Lens 50
96	41	2C	H1 ②	:15 :28	incpl. hold without cross	1127 INT CHEVY ON ACCESS ROAD—DAY CS reverse of #2A. Harley from straight on as he pulls the dickey over head + closes hood. DIAL 1-2. Bo = V.O. Cross away to junction. Reaction as car (+ cam) shoot toward him. Lens 30
96	41	2B	①	:30	3 takes on same sticks	1127 HOOD COMPARTMENT CHEVY—DAY Motor. Right hand enters frame holding screwdriver. Adjustment. Pressure guage goes up. Cleans motor. Ends on motor alone. Lens 50

RETURN TO MACON COUNTY

DAY 1
EXT ROAD
I + E CHEVY

FADE IN: ①est pan CR to CL

1   EXT. ACCESS ROAD - CLOSE UP - A COW - DAY   1   ⓦⓣ X100

looking directly into CAMERA. OFF CAMERA we HEAR the
SOUND of an ENGINE REVVING. CAMERA PANS OFF the cow
ONTO a car parked nearby on the access road.
⑴ⓐ reverse
The car is a yellow 1956 customized Chevy. The rear
end is jacked up high, riding on over-sized tires.

2   CLOSE-UP - ENGINE COMPARTMENT OF THE CAR   2
② ②ⓑ cs Harley's hand + motor

We are LOOKING at a solid chrome, full-race powerhouse, which has been tilted to one side to make
room for a blower which feeds this engine a lethal
mixture of high-octane gasoline and ether. The engine revs...

...VARROOM!

A hand comes INTO the FRAME with a screwdriver, makes
a slight adjustment on the injection system. CAMERA
WIDENS to INCLUDE...   ②ⓒ cs Harley
c#1
...HARLEY McKAY. Harley is twenty-one years old,
wears blue jeans rolled at the bottom and carries
a pack of Camel cigarettes in the sleeve of his T-
shirt. Harley cocks his head, listens for a beat,
then smiles.

3   INT. YELLOW CHEVY   3
cs BO ②ⓐ
c#1
Sitting behind the wheel we SEE BO HOLLINGER, twenty-
two years old, tall and ruggedly handsome. He wears
a red windbreaker and fashions his hair in the style ✱
of the late James Dean.   Bo puts on jacket rt. hand first

BO[1]
(looking out the
window, shouting)
Oh, Mother! Is that sweet music.

4   BO'S POV   4
Harley pulls
dickey   HARLEY[2]
over   ~~You called it, Dad. The injector~~
head as: ~~is tuned like a fine watch.~~
              I got that injector ticking like
              an old swiss clock.   (CONTINUED)

SCRIPT PAGE __2__

CAM ROLL	SND ROLL	SL #	TK #	TIME	COMMENTS	ACTION
96	41	5	1	:00	no roll	1/27 EXT ACCESS ROAD + CHEVY –DAY overlaps SC#2 Dolly master following Chevy as it turns + takes of CR to CL just after hood is closed onto the road. Harley chases alongside car, then jumps inside. Car takes off down road with both passengers. Lens 40
96	41		2	:45	compl. n.g.c.	
97	41		③	:45		
97	41	6	①	1:20	fair	1/27 INT CHEVY – DAY Two-shot of Bo + Harley from straight on inside Chevy going all through script scene 15 + mastering DIAL 3-18. Lens 35
97	42		2	:50	incpl. n.g. dir.	
98	42	'/	③	2:45	2 takes with hand claps	
98	42	6A	H1	1:20	roll out	1/27 INT CHEVY –DAY CU Harley from front, center of wind-shield. DIAL 3-18. Bo = V.O. Lens 75
99	42		②	1:30		
99	42	6B	①	1:30		1/27 INT CHEVY DAY CU Bo from front. DIAL 3-18. Harley = V.O. Lens 75
100	42	6C	1	:00	no roll	1/27 INT CHEVY – DAY reverse of #6 Two-shot of Bo + Harley from rear of Chevy covering DIAL 3-18. Lens 35
100	42		2	:00	camera jam	
101	42		③	1:30		
100	MOS	10A	①	:10		1/27 INSERT Harley clicks button on stopwatch Lens 100

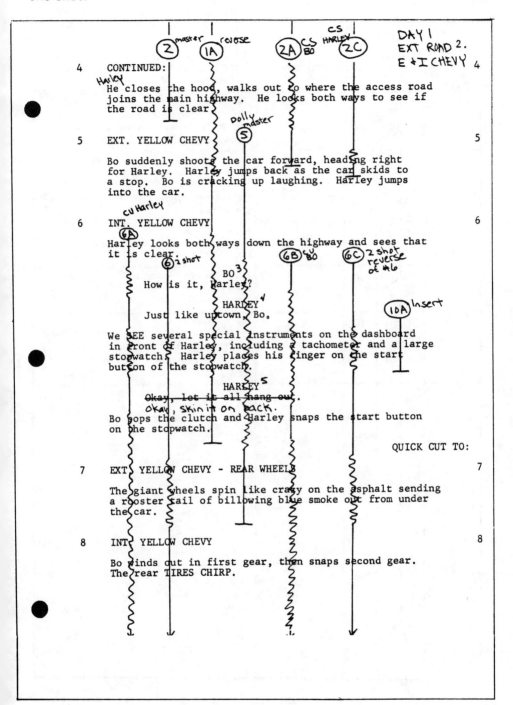

DAY 1
EXT ROAD 2.
E & I CHEVY 4

② master reverse ①A ②A CS BO ②C CS HARLEY

4   CONTINUED:
Harley
He closes the hood, walks out to where the access road
joins the main highway. He looks both ways to see if
the road is clear

5   EXT. YELLOW CHEVY
Dolly master ⑤

Bo suddenly shoots the car forward, heading right
for Harley. Harley jumps back as the car skids to
a stop. Bo is cracking up laughing. Harley jumps
into the car.

cu Harley
6   INT. YELLOW CHEVY
⑥A

Harley looks both ways down the highway and sees that
it is clear.
⑥ 2 shot   ⑥B cu BO   ⑥C 2 shot reverse of #6

                BO
        How is it, Harley?

                HARLEY
        Just like uptown, Bo.
                                            ⑩A Insert

We SEE several special instruments on the dashboard
in front of Harley, including a tachometer and a large
stopwatch. Harley places his finger on the start
button of the stopwatch.

                HARLEY
        ~~Okay, let it all hang out.~~
        Okay, skin it on back.
Bo pops the clutch and Harley snaps the start button
on the stopwatch.

                                    QUICK CUT TO:

7   EXT. YELLOW CHEVY - REAR WHEELS

The giant wheels spin like crazy on the asphalt sending
a rooster tail of billowing blue smoke out from under
the car.

8   INT. YELLOW CHEVY

Bo winds out in first gear, then snaps second gear.
The rear TIRES CHIRP.

SCRIPT PAGE __3__

CAM ROLL	SND ROLL	SL #	TK #	TIME	COMMENTS	ACTION
101	43	11	①	:22		1127 EXT CHEVY ON HIGHWAY – DAY Runby of Chevy CR to CL High angle undercranking 20 FPS Lens 60 to 250
			②	:20		
101	43	11A	①	:10		1127 EXT CHEVY ON HIGHWAY – DAY Same runby of Chevy CR to CL as #11 only low angle from high hat . zooms by + over yellow line. Undercranking 20 FPS Lens 28
100	MOS	10	①	:10		1/27 INSERT Tachometer needle nears red Lens 100
100	MOS	10B	①	:10		1127 INSERT Harley's hand flips switch Lens 100
100	MOS	10C	①	:10		1127 INSERT Harley's hand flips switch from driver's position . To be used in drag sequence. WT 110 = same as WT 100 Lens 100

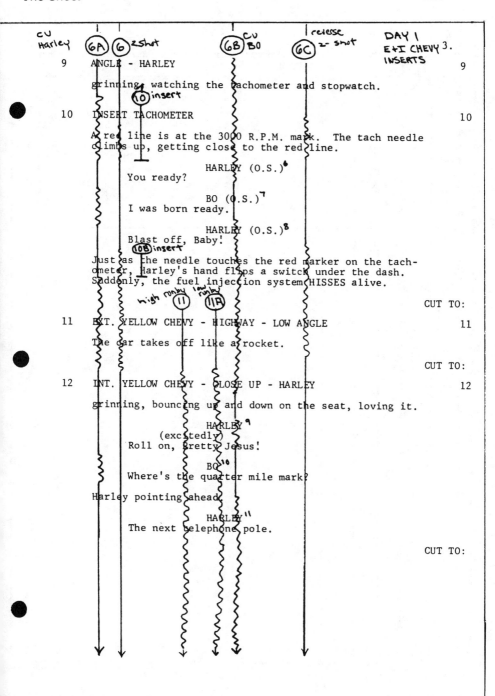

CU
Harley
6A 6 2shot   6B CU   6C release
                        BO   2-shot   DAY 1
                                                     E+I CHEVY 3.
                                                     INSERTS

9   ANGLE - HARLEY   9

grinning, watching the tachometer and stopwatch.

10 insert

10   INSERT TACHOMETER   10

A red line is at the 3000 R.P.M. mark. The tach needle
climbs up, getting close to the red line.

                    HARLEY (O.S.)[6]
     You ready?

                    BO (O.S.)[7]
     I was born ready.

                    HARLEY (O.S.)[8]
     Blast off, Baby!

10B insert

Just as the needle touches the red marker on the tachometer, Harley's hand flips a switch under the dash.
Suddenly, the fuel injection system HISSES alive.

high runby   low runby
         11   11A   CUT TO:

11   EXT. YELLOW CHEVY - HIGHWAY - LOW ANGLE   11

The car takes off like a rocket.

                                                     CUT TO:

12   INT. YELLOW CHEVY - CLOSE UP - HARLEY   12

grinning, bouncing up and down on the seat, loving it.

                    HARLEY[9]
                  (excitedly)
     Roll on, pretty Jesus!

                    BO[10]
     Where's the quarter mile mark?

Harley pointing ahead.

                    HARLEY[11]
     The next telephone pole.

                                                     CUT TO:

SCRIPT PAGE ___4___

CAM ROLL	SND ROLL	SL #	TK #	TIME	COMMENTS	ACTION
101	43	13	①	:45		1127 EXT CHEVY ON HWY HILL - DAY Runby of Chevy passing the mark over the hill CR to CL high angle panning Lens 75
101 100	43 43	13A	1 ②	:15 :45	incpl. n.g.a.	1127 EXT CHEVY ON HWY HILL - DAY Runby of Chevy passing the mark over the hill CR TO CL. Same as #13 only low & stationary. Lens 60 to 250

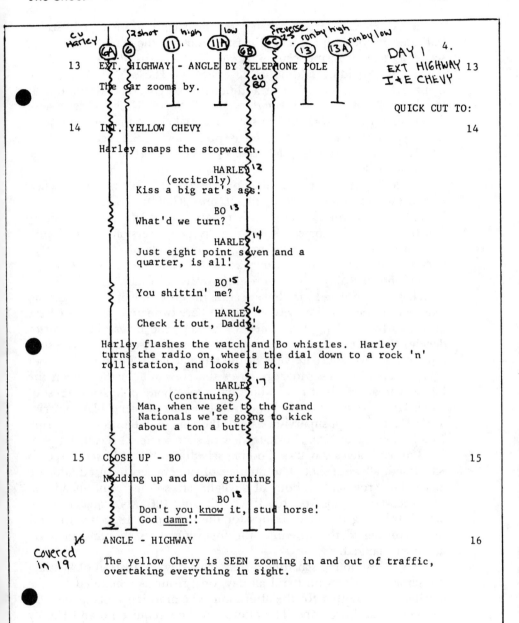

cu Harley   5-2 shot   high   low   reverse   2s runby high   runby low

(6A) (6) (11) (11A) (6B) (6C) (13) (13A)

DAY 1   4.

13   EXT. HIGHWAY - ANGLE BY TELEPHONE POLE

The car zooms by.

cu BO

EXT HIGHWAY 13
I+E CHEVY

QUICK CUT TO:

14   INT. YELLOW CHEVY   14

Harley snaps the stopwatch.

                    HARLEY 12
               (excitedly)
          Kiss a big rat's ass!

                    BO 13
          What'd we turn?

                    HARLEY 14
          Just eight point seven and a
          quarter, is all!

                    BO 15
          You shittin' me?

                    HARLEY 16
          Check it out, Daddy!

Harley flashes the watch and Bo whistles. Harley
turns the radio on, wheels the dial down to a rock 'n'
roll station, and looks at Bo.

                    HARLEY 17
               (continuing)
          Man, when we get to the Grand
          Nationals we're going to kick
          about a ton a butts.

15   CLOSE UP - BO   15

Nodding up and down grinning

                    BO 18
          Don't you <u>know</u> it, stud horse!
          God <u>damn</u>!!

16   ANGLE - HIGHWAY   16

Covered
in 19

The yellow Chevy is SEEN zooming in and out of traffic,
overtaking everything in sight.

Scenes 2 and 6 serve as masters for the balance of the first 14 scenes indicated in the script. Scene 2 masters most of the action from script scene 1 through script scene 4. Scene 2B serves as a pick-up for the master by providing additional coverage for Harley's engine adjustment. Scenes 2A and 2C offer additional close coverage. Scene 6 masters from script scene 6 through scene 15. Scene 6C is the reverse of 6. Scenes 6A and 6B cover the same material as the master, only from closer point of views. Scene 6B focuses on Bo while 6A focuses on Harley. These views can be cut together to make a complete representation of the action.

Scene 5 serves a similar function to scene 1A. It overlaps the tail-end of the preceding shots, 2, 2A, 2B and 2C. The action of the overlapping sections differ, but the discrepancy poses no continuity problem because the editor can select the preferred version. Scene 5 provides a clearer view of what is happening physically than the more selective views of 2 and 6. Scenes 2 and 6 display more detailed information and probably more interesting coverage visually.

Having completed the above scenes, the crew moves down the road to a new location. Script scenes 11 and 13 are two run-bys of the Chevy on a nearby rural highway lined with telephone poles. The director decides to shoot both at once, so the script supervisor assigns the slate number, 11. An alternate view of the same action is given the number 11A. Afterwards, the director moves the crew still further down the highway to a stretch of road which has a telephone pole at the crest of a hill. Here, he plans to re-shoot the latter part of scene 11A or script scene 13. The script supervisor assigns the same number as in the script, 13 for convenience. An alternate view of slate scene 13 is called 13A.

This completes day 20's shooting schedule. Of the 14 script scenes scheduled, all were shot. The number of camera set-ups used adds up to 15. The crew had an hour of daylight left, so they went ahead and shot the standby inserts. 10, 10A, 10B and 10C were quickly completed, bringing the total set-ups for the day up to 19. Since the day ran according to the schedule, the following day's shooting plan remains unchanged.

Day 21's shooting schedule differs from day 20. Instead of keeping the same two actors on hand all day, one group is scheduled for the morning and another for the afternoon. The morning shots involve Bo and Harley and two cops. The afternoon shots require Bo and Harley again, but this time the Boy and the Girl are called. The stunt will be attempted only if time permits.

DAY AND DATE	SET OR LOCATION SCENE NUMBERS	WHERE LOCATED	CAST WORKING
Shooting Day #21	Sign chase 33, 34, 35	bus from studio 6:00 AM	Bo Harley 2 cops
1|28	Sign chase 31, 32	Same	Bo Harley 2 stunt drivers
	chicken race 17-27	bus from studio 10:00 AM	Boy Girl Bo Harley 2 stunt drivers
	lunch	—	—
	chicken race finish 17-27	same	Boy Girl Bo Harley 2 stunt drivers
Stand by	truck stunt 28, 29	S/B afternoon	+ 3rd stunt driver girl double

PROD. NO. 1670   SCHEDULE   DATE 1\|2
DIRECTOR Compton   UNIT MANAGER J Doe   ASST. DIR. Smith

The next four pages of the pre-title sequence illustrate the difference in complexity between shooting day 20 and 21. The example is lined using a second scripting style. Obviously, there are innumerable methods. Two are rarely used although they do have their individual advantages. One describes the shot composition vertically along the line while the other indicates where each take ends by a horizontal mark.

22.

54   EXT. OLYMPIC DIVISION HEADQUARTERS - ESTABLISH -   54
       DAY (STOCK)

                                (55) MC HONDO

55   INT. S.W.A.T.-E.C.EROOM - DAY   55

    Hondo has a piece of paper in hand as he faces Deacon,
    Street, Luca and T.J.

                     HONDO
          Police intelligence has come up
          with some information that could
          fit... money's being spread around
          on the street. Someone's
          recruiting expensive guns. And it
          could be they're being recruited
          to break Wilson and Moore out.

                     STREET
          Trying to bust them out of jail
          would be a tough way to go.

                     HONDO
              (nodding in
               agreement)
          Too tough...
              (thinking)
          ... but they're not going to risk
          letting those two sit around behind
          bars for very long, either.

                     DEACON
          I had the feeling they might have
          given you something yesterday --
          before Bridges showed up.

                     HONDO
          Yeah.
              (beat; then)
          So that leaves the arraignment,
          tomorrow.
              (beat; then)
          Deacon, I want blueprints of
          Division Five Courthouse. McCabe,
          Luca, get a complete, detailed set
          of street maps -- including traffic
          signal patterns between here and
          the courthouse.
              (he is already
              leaving, putting
              on his hat)
          Let's go.

    All exit fast.

In comparison, the alternate style used in the following pages is
quite common. Here, a dotted line indicates uncovered action rather
than the squiggled line used in the previous pages.

21.

52   CONTINUED: (2)   52

                              STREET
                         (grimaces)
                    Diane's something else. Special.

                              HONDO
                    Agreed.

                              STREET
                    I don't think she wants to marry
                    me.
                         (off Hondo's look)
                    Because I'm a cop -- a special kind
                    of cop.

          Hondo nods his head in understanding.

53   INT. HOUSE - NIGHT   (53)   53

          Peterson sprawls, shirt off, an open can of beer in
          his hand, looking at a picture magazine. Simon is
          with Bridges, who is business-suited, his hat in hand.

                              BRIDGES
                    It's okay. They've calmed down
                    for now. But they won't stand still
                    for any prison time.

                              SIMON
                         (thoughtfully)
                    What's chances of making bail?

                              BRIDGES
                         (thoughtfully)
                    The arraignment's day after tomorrow,
                    Division Five. No chance of bail,
                    they're cold on a Murder One. I'm
                    the best money can buy, but there's
                    no way I can get them off.

                              SIMON
                         (beat; then)
                    Okay, then we'll bust 'em out. At
                    the arraignment. Division Five.

          Simon reaches for a phone as Peggy strolls in -- in
          her negligee.

                              PEGGY
                    Hey. It's nearly midnight.
                    Doesn't anyone around here ever
                    go to bed?

          Simon ignores her as he starts to dial a number.

Obviously, a script supervisor shouldn't use both systems at the same
time, but for the sake of showing script lining techniques, we are illustrating each style.

SCRIPT PAGE __5__

CAM ROLL	SND ROLL	SL #	TK #	TIME	COMMENTS	ACTION
A104 B105	44	19	①	1:30	Director is wild about cam. B	1/28 EXT HIGHWAY + BOTH CARS-DAY Mercury travels alone CR to CL, then Chevy pulls up to Mercury, follows for short distance CAM A: high panning Lens 120 to 250 CAM B: low stationary Lens 50
106 107	MOS	20	#1 ②	3:00 3:30	incpl. "not wild"	1/28 INT MERCURY from EXT - DAY Master of int. Mercury mounted on hood including partial view of Chevy alongside in center lane (engine wild track to be added) Lens 20
108	45	20A	①	3:30		1/28 INT MERCURY - DAY Close 2-shot from straight on of Boy + Girl (Chevy not in P.O.V.) DIAL 19-27 Lens 75
A109 B110	45	20B	①	3:20		1/28 INT CHEVY - DAY Inside Chevy taking Bo + Harley through DIAL 21-24 + action script scenes 20-27. CAM A: Bo + Harley straight on. Lens 75 CAM B: Full 2-shot mounted on Chevy covering entire interior of Chevy from left side. Mercury traveling CR to CL in view through window. Lens 35
111	45	20C	①	3:15		1/28 INT MERCURY - DAY Close 2-shot favoring Girl DIAL 19-25 Lens 100
112	46	20D	①	3:15		1/28 INT CHEVY - DAY Close 2-shot (closer than #20B cam. A) of Bo + Harley DIAL 21-24 Lens 100
112	cue track 46	19A	①	:30		1/28 EXT HIGHWAY + BOTH CARS - DAY Stationary FS of cars whizzing by on highway. First Mercury followed by Chevy CR to CL Lens 35

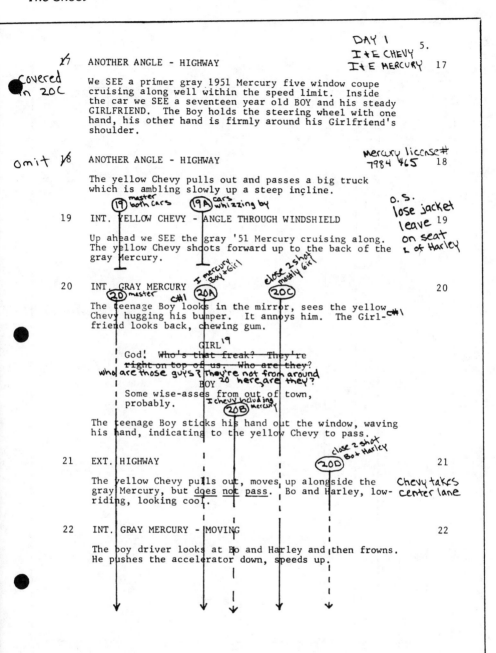

DAY 1
I + E CHEVY 5.
I + E MERCURY 17

~~17~~ ANOTHER ANGLE - HIGHWAY

Covered in 20C

We SEE a primer gray 1951 Mercury five window coupe
cruising along well within the speed limit. Inside
the car we SEE a seventeen year old BOY and his steady
GIRLFRIEND. The Boy holds the steering wheel with one
hand, his other hand is firmly around his Girlfriend's
shoulder.

omit ~~18~~ ANOTHER ANGLE - HIGHWAY

Mercury license #
7984 465 18

The yellow Chevy pulls out and passes a big truck
which is ambling slowly up a steep incline.

(19) master both cars   (19A) cars whizzing by

19 INT. YELLOW CHEVY - ANGLE THROUGH WINDSHIELD

O.S.
lose jacket
leave 19
on seat
L of Harley

Up ahead we SEE the gray '51 Mercury cruising along.
The yellow Chevy shoots forward up to the back of the
gray Mercury.

I mercury Boy + Girl   close 2 shot mostly Girl

20 INT. GRAY MERCURY   20
(20) master C#1   (20A)   (20C)

The teenage Boy looks in the mirror, sees the yellow
Chevy hugging his bumper. It annoys him. The Girl- C#1
friend looks back, chewing gum.

GIRL 19
~~God! Who's that freak? They're~~
~~right on top of us. Who are they?~~
who are those guys? They're not from around
BOY 20   here, are they?
Some wise-asses from out of town,
probably. I chevy including
(20B) mercury

The teenage Boy sticks his hand out the window, waving
his hand, indicating to the yellow Chevy to pass.

close 2 shot Bo + Harley

21 EXT. HIGHWAY   (20D)   21

The yellow Chevy pulls out, moves up alongside the   Chevy takes
gray Mercury, but does not pass. Bo and Harley, low- center lane
riding, looking cool.

22 INT. GRAY MERCURY - MOVING   22

The boy driver looks at Bo and Harley and then frowns.
He pushes the accelerator down, speeds up.

SCRIPT PAGE ___6___

CAM ROLL	SND ROLL	SL #	TK #	TIME	COMMENTS	ACTION

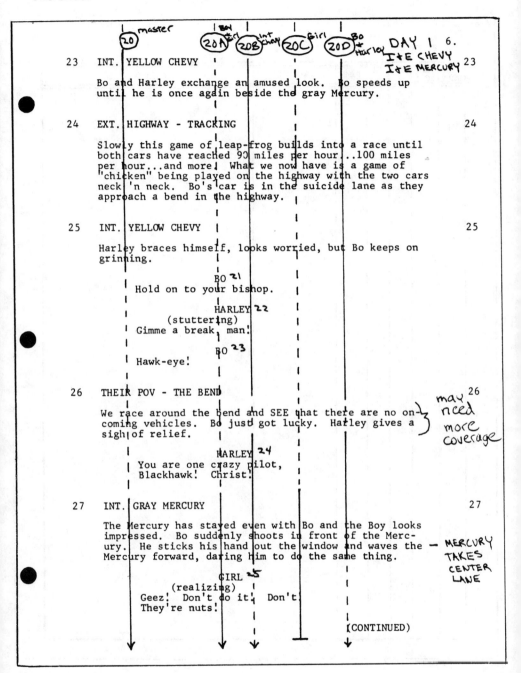

① master
②⓪ ②⓪A [BOY] ②⓪B [int. chevy] ②⓪C [Girl] ②⓪D [Bo + Harley]

DAY 1 6.
I & E CHEVY
I & E MERCURY

23   INT. YELLOW CHEVY   23

Bo and Harley exchange an amused look. Bo speeds up
until he is once again beside the gray Mercury.

24   EXT. HIGHWAY - TRACKING   24

Slowly this game of leap-frog builds into a race until
both cars have reached 90 miles per hour...100 miles
per hour...and more! What we now have is a game of
"chicken" being played on the highway with the two cars
neck 'n neck. Bo's car is in the suicide lane as they
approach a bend in the highway.

25   INT. YELLOW CHEVY   25

Harley braces himself, looks worried, but Bo keeps on
grinning.

                    BO 21
          Hold on to your bishop.

                    HARLEY 22
                (stuttering)
          Gimme a break, man!

                    BO 23
          Hawk-eye!

26   THEIR POV - THE BEND   26

We race around the bend and SEE that there are no on-   may
coming vehicles. Bo just got lucky. Harley gives a }   need
sigh of relief.   more
                                                           coverage
                    HARLEY 24
          You are one crazy pilot,
          Blackhawk! Christ!

27   INT. GRAY MERCURY   27

The Mercury has stayed even with Bo and the Boy looks
impressed. Bo suddenly shoots in front of the Mercury. He sticks his hand out the window and waves the   — MERCURY
Mercury forward, daring him to do the same thing.   TAKES
                                                         CENTER
                    GIRL 25   LANE
                (realizing)
          Geez! Don't do it! Don't!
          They're nuts!

                                              (CONTINUED)

SCRIPT PAGE 7

CAM ROLL	SND ROLL	SL #	TK #	TIME	COMMENTS	ACTION

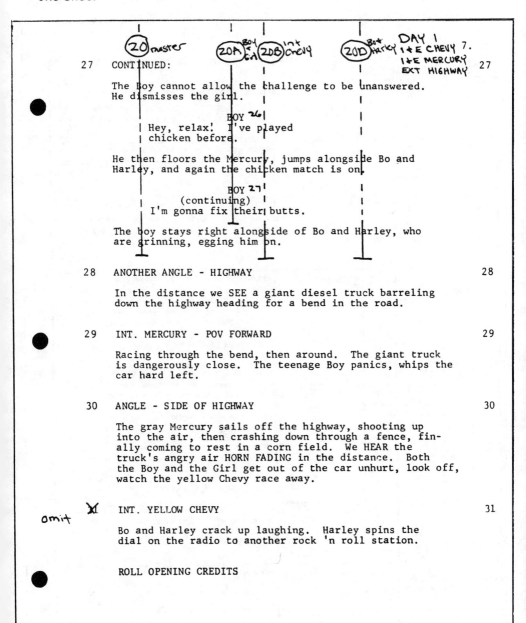

27 CONTINUED: 27

The Boy cannot allow the challenge to be unanswered.
He dismisses the girl.

                    BOY 26
            Hey, relax! I've played
            chicken before.

He then floors the Mercury, jumps alongside Bo and
Harley, and again the chicken match is on.

                    BOY 27
                (continuing)
            I'm gonna fix their butts.

The Boy stays right alongside of Bo and Harley, who
are grinning, egging him on.

28 ANOTHER ANGLE - HIGHWAY   28

In the distance we SEE a giant diesel truck barreling
down the highway heading for a bend in the road.

29 INT. MERCURY - POV FORWARD   29

Racing through the bend, then around. The giant truck
is dangerously close. The teenage Boy panics, whips the
car hard left.

30 ANGLE - SIDE OF HIGHWAY   30

The gray Mercury sails off the highway, shooting up
into the air, then crashing down through a fence, finally coming to rest in a corn field. We HEAR the
truck's angry air HORN FADING in the distance. Both
the Boy and the Girl get out of the car unhurt, look off,
watch the yellow Chevy race away.

omit 31 INT. YELLOW CHEVY   31

Bo and Harley crack up laughing. Harley spins the
dial on the radio to another rock 'n roll station.

        ROLL OPENING CREDITS

SCRIPT PAGE __8__

CAM ROLL	SND ROLL	SL #	TK #	TIME	COMMENTS	ACTION
102	44	34	①	:22		1128 EXT HWY (SIGN STRETCH) - DAY
			2	:10	incmpl. n.g.c.	Wide of police car chasing Chevy CR to
			③	:20		CL. Chevy speeds up, losing cops. Lens 35
102	44	34A	①	:15		1128 EXT HWY (SIGN STRETCH) - DAY High angle police car in pursuit of chevy. Enters from BGCR, continues toward camera & exits FBCR Lens 35
102	44	34B	1	:15	cmpl. n.g. a+c	1128 EXT HWY + 2ND SIGN - DAY
			2	:15	cmpl. n.g. a.	Low angle police car run by alone CR to CL panning along. Hold on
			③	:15	tail slate	second sign as cops pass. Lens 75
102	44 cue track	33	1	:42	cmpl. n.g.a.	1128 EXT HWY + 1ST SIGN - DAY Wide master patrol car with driver waits
			②	:42		behind sign facing CL. Other cop stands behind car, zipping pants as Chevy flies by CR to CL. Cop jumps into car. Cam pans with car as zooms off onto hwy CL Lens 20
102 .102 103	44 cue track	33A	1	:20	incmpl. n.g.c.	1128 EXT HWY + 1ST SIGN - DAY MS cop stands behind cop car zipping pants,
			2	:42	cmpl. n.g.c.	sees Chevy zip by CR to CL. Cam pans with cop as runs to car & jumps in.
			③	:42		Car zooms off onto highway CL Lens 50
103	44	33B	①	:41		1128 EXT HWY + 1ST SIGN - DAY MS driver as Chevy zooms by CR to CL. Driver reacts as second cop jumps into car. Driver steers off onto hwy CR to CL Lens 125 to 50
103	44	32	1	:00	no roll	1128 EXT HWY (PRIOR TO SIGN STRETCH) - DAY Wide Chevy as passes car in light
			②	:20		traffic nearly clipping L. rear bumper. Chevy travels CR to CL. Lens 35
A103 B104	44	35	①	:35	good for cam A only	1128 EXT HWY + 2ND SIGN - DAY CAM A - Stationary wide behind sign of
			②	:35		Chevy facing CL. After cops pass, Chevy hangs u-turn onto road and zooms off CL to CR. Lens 50
					director loves B	CAM B - Wide view from road side. Cops pass CL to CR, then Chevy comes out hanging u-turn & takes off CR to CL Lens 50.

DAY 1 -DAY 2
EXT HIGHWAY.

32   EXT. THE HIGHWAY - VARIOUS ANGLES -DAY 1   32
      (32) runby
      The yellow Chevy racing along the highway, zooming in
      and out of traffic anad passing everything in sight.

33   EXT. HIGHWAY - A BILLBOARD SIGN   33
      (33) master   (33A) fours policeman outside (33B) fours driver
      A state police car is hiding inconspicuously behind
      the sign. One POLICEMAN is by the rear fender of the
      patrol car taking a leak. We HEAR the SOUND of the
      YELLOW CHEVY approaching. The officer reacts, zipping
      himself up hurriedly, dashing to the car where the dri-
      ver, also aware of the oncoming car, has started the
      engine. The yellow Chevy flies by erupting with loud
      ROCK 'N ROLL MUSIC and laughter. The police car spins
      out onto the highway in pursuit.

34   EXT. HIGHWAY - WIDE ANGLE   34
      (34) wide   (34A) high   (34B) low by sign
      The police car is desperately trying to catch the
      speeding yellow Chevy, but it's no match for the street
      racer, which eludes them by skillfully maneuvering the
      tight bends in the highway.

35   ANOTHER ANGLE - HIGHWAY   35
      (35) 2 cam
      The police car approaches with its SIREN WAILING, red
      lights blinking on and off. As the police car passes
      CAMERA, we HOLD on another billboard. The yellow Chevy
      eases out from behind this billboard and dashes off in
      the opposite direction.

                                                          CUT TO:

36   EXT. HIGHWAY - VARIOUS ANGLES   USE stock shots in   36
thru   addition to following: thru
41   A MONTAGE SHOWING a passing of time.   41

      A) LONG SHOT — DAY 2   sequence = 22 seconds

   C#1   The yellow Chevy racing along the highway. We SEE
   C#2   a young girl alone hitchhiking by the side of the
          road. Bg zips by, then slams on the brakes and
          skids to a stop. He backs up stopping near the
   C#1   girl. Just then two boys run out from the bushes
   C#1   nearby. The girl gets into the car and the boys
          are about to follow but the yellow Chevy takes
          off leaving them by the side of the road.

      C#2 Harley (also in car)
                                            (CONTINUED)

The scenes scheduled for the morning of day 21 are shot in a different order than listed on the shooting schedule. The director starts with scene 34, and two pick-ups, 34A and 34B. Scene 34 captures the police car chasing after the Chevy, camera right to camera left. Scene 34A switches the directional pattern as the police car enters the frame from camera right in the background, and continues in pursuit of the Chevy toward the camera and out of frame camera right.

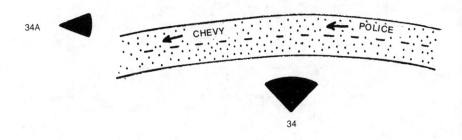

Scene 34B picks up the police car a moment later traveling camera left to right after the Chevy has cleared out of sight.

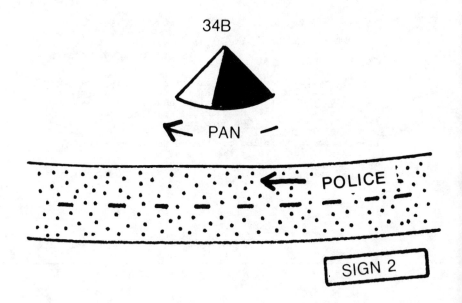

Next, the crew moves to a nearby location where scenes 33, 33A, and 33B are shot. All three provide coverage of the cops waiting behind a sign when they spot the Chevy speeding by camera right to camera left. They hop into their police car, and take off toward the Chevy.

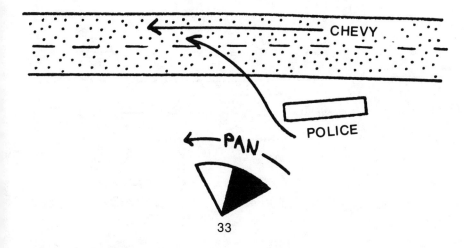

33

After completing script scene 33, scene 32 is shot on a slightly more populated stretch of road. Scene 32 involves a third driver as the Chevy races past a third car, camera right to camera left.

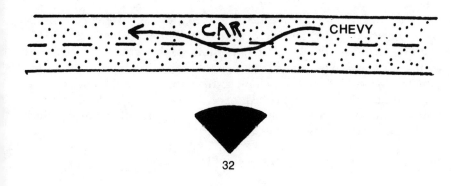

32

The crew returns to the first location to film scene 35. The reason 35 wasn't shot at the same time as 33, 33A and 33B is because two cameras are required to cover the tricky stunt. Just as the police car sails by camera left to camera right, the Chevy peels off camera right to left.

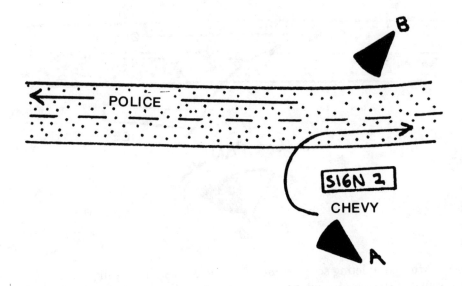

The script supervisor draws these diagrams on the backside of the previous script page and in the margins to check for direction consistency. After finishing at 11:30, the assistant director realizes that there isn't enough time to shoot the main stunts. He releases the stand-by stunt crew. Together, the assistant director and the director decide to squeeze in scene 19, a simple run-by requiring two cameras before lunch.

After lunch, filming continues with the Chevy and Mercury "chicken race" scenes 20, 20A, 20B, 20C and 20D. Although scene 20 doesn't master any of the dialogue, it covers more of the total action than any of the pick-ups. The cars in all views either travel in a right to left direction or in a neutral direction, so the script supervisor doesn't feel it's necessary to diagram the sequence. Before wrapping for the day, the director goes back to film a pick-up of scene 19 and 19A which again uses a right to left pattern.

The remainder of the pre-title sequence is scheduled for filming day 22. The entire day is devoted to the chicken and crash stunts. Compared to the two previous shooting days, this may seem sparse, but stunts are very time-consuming.

PROD. NO. 1670   SCHEDULE   DATE 1/29 R

DIRECTOR Compton   UNIT MANAGER J Doe   ASST. DIR. Smith

DAY AND DATE	SET OR LOCATION SCENE NUMBERS	WHERE LOCATED	CAST WORKING
Shooting day #22 1/29	Chicken stunt 28, 29	bus from studio 6:00 AM Bus #1	Boy Girl Harley Bo Stunt truck driver Stunt Mercury driver Girl double
	Crash set up	bus from studio 6:00 AM Bus #2	2'nd unit stunt team
	lunch	—	—
	Crash stunt. 30	bus from studio 2:00	Boy Girl stunt driver S/B Girl double

To save time, the assistant director arranges for the second unit to set-up the crash stunt while the first unit films the chicken stunt.

The continuity records for day 22 are presented in a third style:

page 7

1/29 SL#28 1 - :15 cmpl n.g.s. 2 - :15 cmpl n.g.a. ③ - :15	SC 28,29 EXT HWY BEND FROM INT MERCURY - DAY master view from out Mercury windshield o. sh. of Boy + Girl. Truck approaches as Mercury + Chevy race through bend. Boy panics + whips car left. Cam Roll 113 Lens 20 Sound Roll 47
1/29 SL#28A ① - :20 preferable but may have c. probl. ② - :20 protection	SC 28 EXT HWY BEND W/TRUCK, CHEVY + MERC - DAY FS mounted on front of Mercury including hood, truck approaching + Chevy on CR. Mercury whips left. Cam Roll 113 Lens 20 Sound Roll 47
1/29 SL#29 (STUNT DOUBLE) ① - :15	SC 29 EXT HWY BEND W/TRUCK, CHEVY, + MERC-DAY wide of Mercury in F.G. traveling CR to CL, Truck in FG. traveling CL to CR, + Chevy in B.G. traveling CR to CL. All meet at bend where Mercury swerves toward cam infront of truck Cam Roll 113 Lens 35 Sound Roll 47
1/29 SL#29A ① - :15 cmpl. director wants more fear 2 - :15 cmpl. n.g. dir. ③ - :15	SC 29 INT MERCURY - DAY CU Boy's reaction as panics from front Cam Roll 113 Lens 50 Sound Roll 47
1/29 SL#30 (STUNT DOUBLE) ① - :20	SC 30 EXT HIGHWAY STUNT - DAY Stunt accident where Mercury flies over embank- ment CL to CR + crashes through fense, 32 FPS CAM A - high panning Lens 250 CAM B - low stationary near fense Lens 120 cue track A cam roll 113 B cam roll 214 Sound Roll # 47
1/29 SL#30C 1 - :08 no roll #2 - :10 "so so" compl. ③ - :10	SC 30 EXT HIGHWAY FIELD - DAY MS Boy helps girl out of car after crash - passenger side with car facing A. Cam Roll 113 Lens 75 Sound Roll 47
1/29 SL#28B (STUNT DOUBLE) ① - :15	SC 28,29 EXT HWY BEND W/TRUCK, CHEVY, + MERC-DAY low angle FS of truck moving toward cam. CL to CR, Mercury swerves off road infront of truck CR to CL Cam Roll 114 Lens 20 Sound Roll 47
1/29 SL#28C (STUNT DOUBLE) 1 - :08 false start ② - :15 ③ - :15 ④ - :15	SC 28,29 EXT HWY BEND W/TRUCK, CHEVY, + MERC-DAY FS alongside truck moving away from cam while Mercury + Chevy approach. Mercury swerves off road CL to CR infront of truck Cam Roll 114 Lens 35 Sound Roll 47

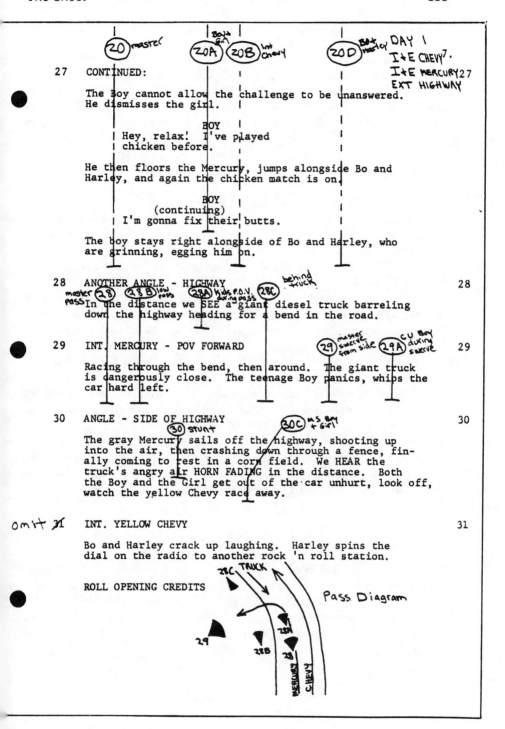

20 *master* 20A *Boys cu* 20B *Int chevy* 20D *Bo+Harley* DAY
I+E CHEVY
I+E MERCURY 27
EXT HIGHWAY

27   CONTINUED:

The Boy cannot allow the challenge to be unanswered.
He dismisses the girl.

                 BOY
   Hey, relax! I've played
   chicken before.

He then floors the Mercury, jumps alongside Bo and
Harley, and again the chicken match is on.

                 BOY
         (continuing)
   I'm gonna fix their butts.

The boy stays right alongside of Bo and Harley, who
are grinning, egging him on.

28   ANOTHER ANGLE - HIGHWAY   28

master 28   28B *low pass*   28A *kids P.O.V. during pass*   28C *behind truck*

pass In the distance we SEE a giant diesel truck barreling
down the highway heading for a bend in the road.

29   INT. MERCURY - POV FORWARD   29

29 *master swerve from side*   29A *CU Boy during swerve*

Racing through the bend, then around. The giant truck
is dangerously close. The teenage Boy panics, whips the
car hard left.

30   ANGLE - SIDE OF HIGHWAY   30

30 *stunt*   30C *MS Boy + Girl*

The gray Mercury sails off the highway, shooting up
into the air, then crashing down through a fence, finally coming to rest in a corn field. We HEAR the
truck's angry air HORN FADING in the distance. Both
the Boy and the Girl get out of the car unhurt, look off,
watch the yellow Chevy race away.

omit 31   INT. YELLOW CHEVY   31

Bo and Harley crack up laughing. Harley spins the
dial on the radio to another rock 'n roll station.

ROLL OPENING CREDITS

28C TRUCK

Pass Diagram

29   28B   28A   29

MERCURY   CHEVY

During the first half of the day, four camera set-ups cover the chicken stunt. These include slate scenes 28, 28A, 29 and 29A. The numbering is not indicative of the master pick-up system. 29 and 29A could be considered further pick-ups except that 28 doesn't really master the scene any better than 28A, 29 or 29A. If anything, 29 masters the scene. The script supervisor had no idea that 29 was going to be filmed after 28 and 28A. Scenes don't always fit conveniently into any numbering system. The script supervisor shouldn't get too wrapped up in the numbering and hold up the filming. As compensation, she leaves her diagram on the script page to help clarify any questions for the editor.

After lunch, the director moves to the crash stunt. He is not very happy with the morning's results, but he knows that his first priority is to capture the crash. Because of the dangerous and expensive nature of the shot, he is only allowed one chance. Using two cameras increases the probability of filming the shot in one take. Fortunately, stunt scene 30 runs smoothly. The director quickly shoots the next scene, 30C, at the wreckage site, replacing the stunt driver and double with the Boy and Girl actors. Afterwards, the director goes back to the morning scene to capture the additional coverage he felt was lacking. He films 28B and 28C.

The preceding three days of filming completes the pre-title sequence. Illustrated over these eight script pages are the most common methods of lining. One uses a squiggled-line to indicate off screen action while the other uses a broken line. Also illustrated are two types of editorial breakdowns which include concise descriptions of image size, angles, camera moves, action and take results. These notes provide the editor with the necessary information to assemble the footage. Continuity notes make up only half of a script supervisor's responsibility to the editor. The other half involves matching.

MATCHING

Throughout this book, recording continuity notes has been handled independently of matching. On the set, however, the script supervisor doesn't have the luxury of separating the two. While filming, the script supervisor carefully watches for both simultaneously. The first group of typical matching problems is matching props and set dressing.

Matching Props and Set Dressing

Sometimes, it's hard to distinguish between props and set dressing—not just for the script supervisor, but for every crew member. A story comes to mind about the time a missing ladder held up a shoot. The ladder was an important detail of the background. Since no one actually picked up or used the ladder, the prop master considered it set dressing. The set dresser insisted that the ladder was a prop and therefore not within set dressing jurisdiction. A stalemate resulted, with both men refusing to get the ladder. Meanwhile, their stubborness disrupted the day's shooting. The assistant director wasn't about to hold up the entire crew until a union arbitration could be arranged so he went to the grip truck for a lighting ladder. Unfortunately, the truck rental-company had stamped their name on all sides of the ladder to prevent theft. Rather than trying to reason with the angry feuders, the assistant director decided it would be quicker to paint the ladder. Just as everyone thought the problem was finally solved, onto the set storms the scenic painter, raising hell.

Problems like this happen all the time. A script supervisor friend jokes about a similar experience she had on location in Lake Tahoe with *Bonanza*. She claimed that she could pinpoint the exact moment when a Mississippi Riverboat paddle streamer became a prop. It happened when the steamer didn't show up the second day on location! A script supervisor can avoid these problems by considering props and set dressing the same.

When keeping track of props and set dressing, observation is the script supervisor's most effective tool. Instant photographs and set diagrams help, but concentrated attention is what really counts. The pre-title sequence of *Return to Macon County* doesn't illustrate the potential problems as clearly as other parts of the script. Interiors usually involve more complicated matching requirements. A coffee-shop scene of *Return To Macon County*, for example, presents a better example.

Toward the end of this coffee-shop scene, a fight breaks out between Bo, Harley and another restaurant customer. With food and furniture flying everywhere, the job of matching the master to the pickups becomes impossible. The scene involves details too numerous for diagrams or memory. The only choice is to use an instant camera. A quick shot of the set before and after, and if possible, mid-scene, enables the master to be reconstructed for a pick-up.

SCRIPT PAGE __16__

CAM ROLL	SND ROLL	SL #	TK #	TIME	COMMENTS	ACTION
175	86	52	①	:30		2/15 INT COFFEE SHOP — DAY FS angled toward door of Bo swinging at Big Man through DIAL 51-53 Bo + Harley throw down $5.00 + exit as Junell + cook look on. Sign business as in script. Exit CR. Lens 35
175	86	52A	①	:30	unconvincing punch but can be covered with insert	2/15 INT COFFEE SHOP - DAY Med. Long behind counter. Cook's P.O.V. of same action as above. Bo swings at Big Man through DIAL 51-53. Bo + Harley throw down money, then sign as Junell looks on. Exit slightly CR. Lens 50
175	MOS	52B	1 ②	:10 :30	n.g.a.	2/15 FIGHT CLOSE-UP — DAY hand held shot of Fat man taking punch. Socks in breath. To be used in reverse print. Lens 25
175	MOS	52C	1 ②	:10 :10	n.g.c.	2/15 FIGHT CLOSEUP — DAY Extreme CU face of fat man sucking in breath. Hand held Lens 25
175	MOS	52D	①	:10	tail slate	2/15 FIGHT CLOSE-UP — DAY Fat head going back. Hand held. Lens 25
175	MOS	52E	①	:15		2/15 FIGHT CLOSE-UP — DAY close on fat man's face on ground as a sign flies into it, then a milkshake. Hand held Lens 25
175	MOS	52F	1 ②	:00 :20	false start	2/15 FIGHT CLOSE-UP — DAY close on Junell watching fight. Stays on cooks face as she leaves frame R. Hand held. Lens 50

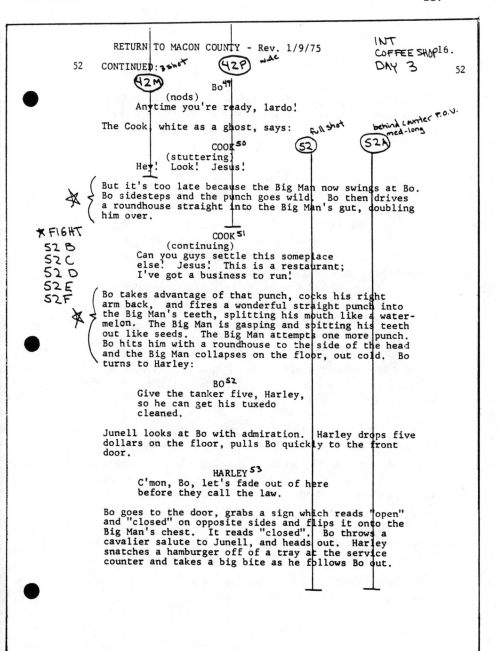

RETURN TO MACON COUNTY - Rev. 1/9/75

INT
COFFEE SHOP 16.
DAY 3

52   CONTINUED: 2 shot   42P wide   52

42M   Bo 49
            (nods)
    Anytime you're ready, lardo!

The Cook, white as a ghost, says: full shot   behind counter P.O.V.
                                                                med-long

                    COOK 50   52   52A
                (stuttering)
    Hey! Look! Jesus!

But it's too late because the Big Man now swings at Bo.
Bo sidesteps and the punch goes wild. Bo then drives
a roundhouse straight into the Big Man's gut, doubling
him over.

                    COOK 51
                (continuing)
    Can you guys settle this someplace
    else! Jesus! This is a restaurant;
    I've got a business to run!

★ FIGHT
52 B
52 C
52 D
52 E
52 F

Bo takes advantage of that punch, cocks his right
arm back, and fires a wonderful straight punch into
the Big Man's teeth, splitting his mouth like a water-
melon. The Big Man is gasping and spitting his teeth
out like seeds. The Big Man attempts one more punch.
Bo hits him with a roundhouse to the side of the head
and the Big Man collapses on the floor, out cold. Bo
turns to Harley:

                    BO 52
    Give the tanker five, Harley,
    so he can get his tuxedo
    cleaned.

Junell looks at Bo with admiration. Harley drops five
dollars on the floor, pulls Bo quickly to the front
door.

                    HARLEY 53
    C'mon, Bo, let's fade out of here
    before they call the law.

Bo goes to the door, grabs a sign which reads "open"
and "closed" on opposite sides and flips it onto the
Big Man's chest. It reads "closed". Bo throws a
cavalier salute to Junell, and heads out. Harley
snatches a hamburger off of a tray at the service
counter and takes a big bite as he follows Bo out.

LESLIE MARTINSON INTERVIEW

Like Morris Abrams, Leslie Martinson also started his motion picture/television career as a script supervisor. After scripting more than 25 features including *Easter Parade, Command Decision, Summer Stock, Monty Stratton Story, The Pirate, Ambush* and others, Leslie moved on to directing. With 27 years of directing experience, it's safe to say that Leslie Martinson has exposed as much Eastman Kodak Negative as any living director. The great classic filmmakers would have to live another 25 years to catch up because there has hardly been a week that Leslie has stopped directing in one phase of filmmaking from multimillion dollar films to episodic television. Of his 20 films and hundreds of teleplays, perhaps the most well-known include *PT 109, Fathom, Mrs. Pollifax, Spy, Lad, A Dog, Batman Movie, For Those Who Think Young,* and in television, from *Maverick* to *Dallas.* It's interesting to see how his attitude differs so dramatically from that of Peter Bogdanovich.

MARTINSON: I was a script supervisor at MGM for seven years before I became a director. Prior to that, I worked in the production office. Many young men who want to get into the business have come to me to ask what is the best step to becoming a director. Invariably, it's not the assistant director who is in the better position. There is no person on the set more qualified to make the jump to director than a well-qualified script supervisor. That is, no one is more qualified assuming that they grow and learn and study. When the mechanics become secondary, you can begin to concentrate on words and people, which is really where directing is at.

In the early days, the days of great luxury, a script supervisor was on a film for five or six months. When the director was assigned, the script supervisor was also assigned. I worked as a script supervisor on Judy Garland's last four films. Summer Stock, for instance, ran seven or eight months. At one point in the picture, Judy weighed 98 pounds, and at another, she weighed 144. I would sit in on the rehearsals while all the musical numbers were being done. For a month, I'd get to watch the choreographer do his thing, preproduction and recording the numbers. Finally, the filming would start. So the script supervisor was up on every detail along the way. The script

138

supervisor would see the changes made and would know the contributions. The director never uttered a word if the script supervisor wasn't there. Now, I must say, it was a little different then. The script supervisor didn't have the freedom to make suggestions to the director unless the script supervisor had an unusual relationship with the director. Nowadays, even though the script supervisor isn't assigned until two weeks or so before production, the script supervisor is still in the best position on the set to learn how to direct.

STUDENT: How free do you think the script supervisor is to make suggestions today?

MARTINSON: There is no set rule. You're dealing with personalities. When I'm directing, I expect the script supervisor to come up to me and say, "Hey, Leslie, you're not going to let them play that last scene like that are you? Way over the top?" It all depends on with whom you're working. I will take suggestions from anybody; for example, on two different occasions, a very bright camera operator made excellent suggestions. When I gave the direction to the actors one of them said, "That's a hell of an idea." I answered, "Don't thank me, thank Cliff." You work with a director. I am not infalliable.

I think the fun of the script supervisor's job and the reason why I always enjoyed scripting is trying to make contributions, particularly if the director is one who is receptive to the play of a scene. You see, I don't believe in the auteur theory or the divine right of the director. There have been some of the biggest successes with total autonomy, but for every one success, there are five or ten failures. Maybe seven out of ten directors will shy away from contributions from the crew. Unfortunately, many of these directors won't survive, or if they do, they're going to have lean periods until they learn that it's a team effort.

STUDENT: Even if a director is receptive to contributions, I assume the script supervisor still has to know how to approach the director.

MARTINSON: Sure. It's very important to know when to back away, when to make your point and when to be a little solicitious. It makes for happy scripting. The script supervisor's job is tough enough without worrying about personalities. The day I put that book down, I was happy. Matching, for instance, was torture to me. I just got lost in the scenes. I'll give you a very classic example. Robert Jay Walker was probably the fastest director known. Bob would shoot 115 to 120 set-ups a day. He once shot 121 set-ups before he lost the light on a long summer's day. We used to do only three or four at MGM, and sometimes only one. Keeping up with this kind of pace is not easy for a script supervisor. Or another example: I was working on my second picture with a director named Sam Wood, so we had established a relationship. We were ready to shoot a scene where June Allison holds a baby in her arms when Sam yells, "Hold it!" He turns to me to say, "Leslie, was the baby holding the rattle in the left hand or the right hand?" I started to mumble and look at my notes. I had no idea so I took a calculated risk. I looked up at Sam Wood and I said, "Mr. Wood, was she holding the baby?" Of course, the crew all fell apart. Sometimes with humor you can get out of a bind when you don't have the notes.

STUDENT: What other suggestions can you make about attitude that will help a script supervisor?

MARTINSON: Nothing takes the place of exuding security. You walk out, you're very gracious, and you say, "Hi, my name is Leslie Martinson. I'm your script supervisor. I'm here to help you," or "If there's any particular thing you expect out of the ordinary, I'd be very happy to do it." Just lay it right on the line. People react to a feeling of confidence.

Scripting is hard. You'll get behind. In television, when you're using two cameras, sometimes that pencil is flying. Suddenly the director says to you, "Would you mind reading that offstage line?" There's nothing wrong with saying, "Look, I'm 10 minutes behind now in these notes." A script supervisor doesn't have to be subservient. That's the wrong attitude. Just be positive, and for heaven's sake, be good. You can't be positive if you don't know your job.

STUDENT: Given the limitations on a set, sometimes its hard to be positive about everything. Are there any duties that are more important than others?

MARTINSON: Let me try to capsulize. It's a matter of priorities. Now you'll probably be very surprised to hear what the first priority is because you're going to think that it isn't even in our jurisdiction. There's only one aspect of scripting that can wipe you out, and that's wardrobe. We can get out of every bind in the world—wrong looks, not enough change in size for figure, wrong action, wrong matching—but not wrong wardrobe. You must make your wardrobe notes, get together with the costumer and know your wardrobe breakdown. Sounds silly, but errors in costumes are probably the principal reason for retakes. Whenever a retake is needed for anything other than performance, it is ultimately the responsibility of the script supervisor.

STUDENT: Can you give us any other tips about priorities?

MARTINSON: Yes. You can learn to save yourself time. You know, the script supervisor is the one person who is working almost every minute. While the crew is lighting, the script supervisor is writing notes. Say you're out on location, and it's cold. The wind is blowing the pages, the actors keep going up on their lines, you can't walk around, you're chained to the book and you just want to throw that pencil away. One thing you learn as fast as you can is when to look for matches. It'll help cut down on the time. Try and sense where the cuts are coming. If the director plays a master, you should be able to guess accurately what the coverage is so that you know what has to match. When somebody moves, when they stop, where they stop, on what word he rose, when the center line changed—those are the things you must get.

STUDENT: What about dialogue?

MARTINSON: On long dialogue scenes with two people, watch the words because there's not going to be a match. Many directors don't use their scripts while the camera is rolling. I don't. I'm all involved in watching the shading and listening for the tempo. I don't really hear the substance of the words. What I demand of a script supervisor more than anything is to inform me when the dialogue variations change the substance of a line. I don't wed actors to periods and commas, but sometimes a little word change or an inversion changes the meaning.

So, when you get into big head-to-head scenes or close-ups, you already know when they're going to move. Stay on your dialogue. When the director is blocking a scene with the actors and the actor forgets his line, try and get a sense of when to throw the cue line. Actors are so defensive. That's the nature of the beast. Again, your own sensitivity and awareness will help you in these areas.

STUDENT: When you talk of sensitivity and awareness, I suppose you're also referring to sensing the director's needs?

MARTINSON: Definitely. When I rehearse, I like to feel the hot breath of a script supervisor down my back. When I block a scene, be there. Let your notes go and watch the dialogue. I find that many script supervisors are very weak in this aspect. They're often two lines behind the dialogue when an actor says, "What's the cue?" It's exasperating.

But there is a real priority on good script supervisors. Many are being upped to associate producers and so forth. The stakes are very big. As a matter of fact, I have a daughter who is a sophomore now, majoring in theatre arts. She says she wants to learn all the phases of the business. I'm very seriously thinking of sending her to Shirley Ulmer's class.

Like any other artistic medium, you grow with experience. Once you begin to lose enthusiasm, old age sets in. If you don't continue to love the challenge, then you retrogress. I feel sorry for many of my colleagues who are financially well off but artistically frustrated because they can't get work. In *any form of the arts, one must be totally dedicated to growth and never lose the desire to learn from the old as well as from the new. The hunger to be progressive must be constant, and the awareness that complacency and compromise is deadly.*

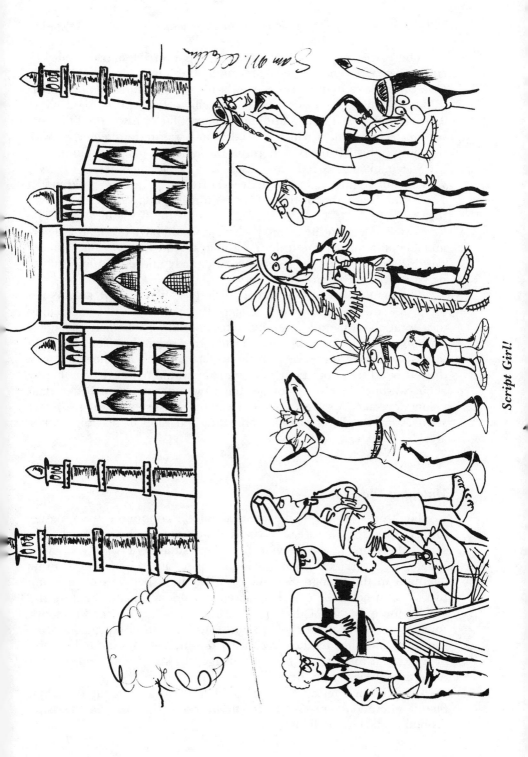

Script Girl!

There are times an editor can cover up a terrible inconsistency by cutting away from the problem area, and other times, when he/she can't. One of Shirley's nightmares was on a film called *Bluebeard.* John Carradine was allowed to exit a house carrying a lamp in his right hand. The exterior wasn't filmed until much later. Shirley discovered that she had neglected to mark which hand the lamp was in. John emerged with the lamp in his left hand. The result was editorial pandemonium.

She managed to redeem herself later while shooting *The Bandit,* with Arthur Kennedy. Arthur arrived in front of a cafe in an old model Ford. The headlights of the car were on as he stopped the car. When they were ready to film the next cut, one of the lights blew out. The location was deep in the country where it would have taken an indeterminable amount of time to locate a bulb for the old machine. Shirley saved the moment by suggesting that Kennedy notice the unlit bulb as he passes the car before going on with the planned action.

The same advice applies to both examples. Watch for details. When the script supervisor knows in advance that the crew will be returning to a location, copious continuity notes should be taken. If the notes turn out to be lacking, admit it. The *Bluebeard* example could have been solved by filming one take with the right hand and another take with the left hand for protection. The company would not have been happy about wasting the extra footage, but it would have been better than risking a retake. A script supervisor can only absorb as many prop and set dressing details as possible, and then move on to matching other areas.

Matching Dialogue

The words spoken by the actors should be continuous from master to pick-ups. If for any reason, the dialogue can't be heard clearly, the sound department will provide the script supervisor with a headset. Whenever a variation occurs, it is the script supervisor's job to draw attention to the change. Sometimes, a variation happens during one pick-up and not another. The discrepancy doesn't matter because the editors use only one of the views during the cut sequence. The script supervisor should draw the director's attention to any problem after each take, and then let the director decide whether to reshoot the scene or leave it. If the director ok's the change, the script supervisor should write the revisions into the continuity script.

Dialogue changes made during rehearsals are handled in two ways. Simple alterations are noted directly on the script page in the same fashion as during the filming.

                    GIRL

God! ~~Who's that freak? They're~~
~~right on top of us. Who are they?~~
who are those guys? They're not from
around here, are they?
                    BOY

Some wise-asses from out of town.

More complicated alterations may require retyping the page or *sides*.
Whenever sides are added, the date is typed on the top of the page to
help distinguish it from the old page.

    RETURN TO MACON COUNTY - Rev. 1/9/75   16.
52   CONTINUED: 52

                    Bo
              (nods)
    Anytime you're ready, lardo!

Most sides are printed on colored paper to further differentiate between obsolete and current pages. Each new revision comes out in a
different color. The script supervisor should file away old pages with a
note indicating the date it became obsolete in case the producer or
director decides to go back to an earlier version. These discarded pages
should be kept until the management gives the script supervisor permission to throw them away.

Matching dialogue also involves watching mouth movements. When
a sound track is recorded before filming as in the case of some musicals, the script supervisor checks that the playback matches the performers' mouths. The same applies to dialogue tracks that are recorded
during pre-production. The mouth movements must be precise, so the
dialogue will match when dubbed later.

Once while working with Louis Hayward in Italy shooting *The Pirates of Capri*, Shirley encountered a matching problem that the crew never
let that poor man forget. One of the leads in the film was Mariella
Lotti, an Italian actress. Since she wasn't proficient in English, her dialogue had to be mouthed. Filming is handled this way often in Italy
where companies are used to dubbing in their sound after the film is
finished. In this instance, Mariella was supposed to greet Hayward with
the line, "The Count of Amalfi, I presume." There was no way to make
her pronounce the *O* in Count, which afforded all except Hayward a
lot of laughs thereafter.

Whether a dialogue track is recorded before filming, added after or recorded simultaneously, the script supervisor should watch for continuity problems. When variations occur, the script supervisor should point them out to the director who will either accept them or reshoot the scene. The same applies to matching blocking.

Matching Blocking

The script supervisor should match actor movement, or *blocking,* from shot to shot in the same manner as dialogue. Not all variations need to be pointed out to the director. If a director has a well-defined plan of coverage, it may not be necessary to duplicate the master action in the pick-ups. Many directors, for instance, prefer to use close-ups in the edited film more often than master shots except at the beginning or ending of a sequence. If this is the case, a script supervisor can make continuity judgments accordingly. During a conversation between two people, the script supervisor should devote more attention to matching over-the-shoulder shots to each other rather than over-shoulder shots to the master.

Selecting the blocking of one camera angle over another doesn't work for all scenes. Movements such as rising and sitting must overlap from one shot to the next for a smoother cut. Repetitious action should match as closely as possible in all camera angles. Take the example of two people at a table sipping coffee. Unless each sip is pinpointed in the script and duplicated during every new camera angle, the result is disastrous. The actor's hands may appear to jerk up and down the frame senselessly in the cut version. At the end of one sip, the cup is lowered only to be at the actor's lips again immediately following when one shot cuts to the next. Mistakes of this sort create severe limitations during editing.

Matching blocking also involves directional continuity. Using our *Return to Macon County* pre-title sequence example, directional continuity is consistent through both the chicken race and the cop chase. The Mercury and Chevy travel in the same direction. The truck approaches the two cars by moving in the opposite direction. When the Chevy loses the cops, the Chevy changes direction on camera as it pulls out from behind the second sign and then travels off in the opposite direction.

Space continuity depends on the camera's relationship with the action. Drawing an action line takes care of some of the more obvious problems, but changes in the direction an actor looks require special attention. The script supervisor, with the aid of the camera operator, pinpoints eye movements to specific sections of the script. *The Return to Macon County* director didn't ok any deviations, so all eye positions match throughout the sequence.

While a friend was shooting a courtroom scene, she had three masters. One from the back of the courtroom, another from behind the Judge, and a third from behind the Jury. When the camera operator asked this script supervisor which way the Judge should look toward the Defendant, the script supervisor for once could say, "Anyway he wants to." The Judge's look would match one of the three masters no matter which direction he looked. This is one of those rare situations when a script supervisor can't be wrong.

Even though the *Return to Macon County* example is relatively simple from a matching standpoint, the script supervisor should pay careful attention to the rhythm of each cut. Generally speaking, ordinary movie viewers are less likely to notice small details than errors in the rhythm of an action. A prop appearing in one shot but missing in the next usually causes less of a disturbance than if Harley slowly sauntered up to the Chevy only to hop rapidly into the passenger seat. Changes in the rhythm of an action are hard to disguise by clever editing. An attentive script supervisor will guard against them.

Script supervisor, Marshall Schlom, explains his past experience in matching blocking on a feature entitled *The Bad News Bears*.

> One of my most difficult assignments was *The Bad News Bears*. We had seven or eight weeks of baseball. We had to shoot bits and pieces of over twenty baseball games. We didn't have the time, luxury and money to film in sequence, and we had to be prepared to shoot the scripted portions of each game completely out of continuity. After two weeks of pre-production rehearsal, it was evident what I needed to do to be prepared for the largest jigsaw puzzle I had ever helped put together. After conferring with Michael Ritchie, the director, I spent one entire weekend diagramming each of the games to be photographed, complete with copius notes and sketches, so that at any given time, whenever the camera was placed to photograph any particular piece, every other shot for any game in the script could be photographed at the same time, and I could advise each department what to prepare for. I knew which of our Bears was where, what position they were playing for each game (some of them switched positions from game to game), who the opposition was and where their players were, which way the ball had to be pitched, hit, fielded and thrown, who and how many were in the dugouts and who were on base, who were our background atmosphere in the bleachers and what they should be wearing, what the scoreboard had to read, where the background bicycles and cars were parked, and a hundred other things which pertain to continuity! It took a great deal of concentration on my part and coordination with Jack Roe, our assistant director, to make sure no mistakes were made and to avoid costly retakes. I hope my contribution as the script supervisor showed in the cutting room and on the screen.

From broad movements to subtle eye placements, blocking of action should be continuous from shot to shot. Coverage styles dictate which shots need to match exactly and which are more flexible. While drawing an action line ensures directional continuity automatically, pinpointing the action to specific moments depends on detailed notes. At the same time as matching blocking, the script supervisor must continue matching other areas.

Matching Costumes

There is no flexibility in matching costumes. An editor cannot cut around costume inconsistencies. Fortunately, scenes with few characters are easier to keep track of. Discrepancies in multicharacter scenes often get lost in the shuffle. The script supervisor still must pay careful attention to costume detail on the set.

Costume continuity in the *Return to Macon County* example was easy to preserve because the scenes never involved more than four characters. The initial costumes of Bo and Harley were described as soon as they appeared including jewelry and accessories. The same was done for the Boy and Girl as well as for the two cops. When variations occurred, they were also described. Harley pulls the dickie over his head during script scene 4 and wears it throughout the rest of the sequence. Bo puts on his red windbreaker during script scene 3 with his right hand first only to remove it later off-camera during the time lapse before script scene 19. The only costume matching the script supervisor had to watch was whether the windbreaker and dickie were supposed to be on or off at any designated point of the sequence. The rest was obvious.

Other examples are not so predictable. A script supervisor friend was filming in front of a saloon. A gang of cowboys came running out, jumped on their horses and rode off before the sheriff arrived. Naturally, all the cowboys were wearing cowboy hats. A few days later, an interior saloon brawl was shot. As soon as the fight started, all the cowboys lost their hats. In order to match the exterior which had already been shot, the cowboys had to find their hats quickly and slam them on their heads before running out. These are the hazards of shooting out of sequence. Similar hazards can be extended to matching make-up and hairstyles.

Matching Make-up and Hairstyles

The technique for matching make-up and hairstyles parallels that of matching costumes. Initial descriptions are made when the characters first appear. Any variations from the first appearance are pinpointed to specific moments in the script. A braid of hair, for example, may start over the left shoulder. All following shots have the braid over the left shoulder until we see the character flip it over to the right, or until there is a time lapse. Story changes, such as shaving a beard, also set the continuity requirements for all scenes that follow. The problems of matching make-up, hairstyles and costumes are all directly related to sequencing.

Sometimes production techniques create additional work for continuity. The script supervisor on a horror movie called *Mind Over Murder* encountered an interesting matching problem while shooting a rather complicated sequence. Throughout the film, the leading lady had recurring visions which always began with everything around her coming to a standstill. During one particular vision, the leading lady was crossing a street when everything suddenly stopped. Achieving the desired effect required shooting a master of the leading lady as she crossed at different camera speeds. Eventually, the rest of the action was filmed in front of projected scenery. [see process shots page 261] The script supervisor noticed that the leading lady's long hair was blowing in the wind during the master shot. The hairdresser had to be reminded to have a fan on the set for the later shots so that the leading lady's hair would continue to appear windblown.

Matching make-up, hairstyles, costumes, blocking, dialogue, props and set dressing, all involve countless details. A combination of careful observation and selective notes help the script supervisor keep track of these details. Similar attention must be paid to matching cinematic techniques.

Matching Cinematic Techniques

Matching cinematic techniques is the script supervisor's easiest job. No matter how a scene is covered, the shots provided must vary in image sizes and angles. Nothing is more boring that cutting together a series of close-ups without visual variety. Although script supervisors rarely encounter this problem with professional filmmakers, an inexperienced director may need a reminder. Even a veteran director sometimes likes to be told the last shot in the preceding sequence or the first shot in the following sequence.

In any of the matching types mentioned, the script supervisor may observe potential or even definite problems in continuity that the director chooses to ignore. If this happens, the script supervisor should not argue, but instead make a note for the editor. A simple note such as "Sally's exit the wrong way was okayed by the director" alerts the editor. It also protects the script supervisor from any blame. The script supervisor's job only goes as far as bringing the director's attention to the problems.

Throughout the filming of a motion picture, a script supervisor is busy keeping detailed records and watching that each shot flows smoothly to the next. This is not where the job ends. A script supervisor also traces a film's progress.

TRACING OVERALL PROGRESS

One of the main duties assigned to the script supervisor is keeping track of a film's overall progress. This responsibility overlaps the assistant director's job; however, many of the assistant director's judgments are based on information received from the script supervisor. Their combined efforts help the management and director project how close the picture is to completion, whether a film is on schedule, the efficiency of the crew and the estimated running time of the film shot. A script supervisor can easily expedite the process by using the daily reports and running lists set up during the preparation week.

Running List of Sound and Picture Coverage

A running list of sound and picture coverage needs should be updated daily, and it should include only those scenes which have already been filmed. Obviously, all scenes that haven't been filmed still need to be covered, but these do not appear on the list. The list should be limited to pick-ups that the director has requested, wild tracks, and any coverage that the script supervisor suggests.

A script supervisor may notice an area of the story that doesn't seem adequately covered. Since the script supervisor usually knows the script better than anyone except the director, it's only natural for a producer or director to ask the script supervisor for an opinion about the coverage before moving on to a new location. A carefully thought-out suggestion can be very useful.

Using our *Return to Macon County* example, there are several areas the script supervisor questions. Since these suggestions are subjective, they should be made only upon request. First, the script supervisor suggests that the director consider adding two pick-ups during the Mercury crash. A close-up of the terrified expression on the driver's face would enhance the immediate danger. The director may also want a close reaction shot of the truck driver. Although neither of these areas are covered in the footage shot, they are a matter of taste. Other suggestions might fill an important gap in the story.

On one film Carol worked, the main character strains to control his anger as he encounters a devastating experience. Unfortunately, the depth of his anger is never revealed to the audience. In order for the rest of the story to make sense, the audience must understand that this unresolved rage is the motivation for what follows. When the producer asked the script supervisor's opinion regarding the problem, the script supervisor suggested adding a short visual where the character blows up as he is leaving. The director and producer took the suggestion, and the added shot filled in the missing gap.

The sound department may have its own list of coverage requirements. These could include walla, presence, sound effects, narration or
off screen dialogue, music and any other non-synchronous sound tracks.
Some will be recorded in post-production while others need to be recorded on the set. The script supervisor should keep a running list of
all sound needs, especially where actors are needed, so the actors won't
be accidentally dismissed.

Over the three days of filming the *Return to Macon County* pretitle
sequence, various wild tracks needs are listed. Only WTX100, a non-
sync engine revving track, was recorded. WTX100 will also double as
WTX110, another engine revving track. Many other engine noise and
presence tracks may still be required to cover the scenes which were
shot MOS. Certainly, switch clicks for the inserts are possibilities. Music
for the Chevy radio will undoubtedly be recorded in post-production,
but the script supervisor lists it anyway, just in case.

Once all the possibilities are listed, the script supervisor confers
with the sound department. The sound mixer usually removes those tracks
not necessary to record on the set from the list. The mixer might add
other wild tracks that the script supervisor missed. Updating this list
periodically helps keep track of the sound department's progress.

Running lists of both sound and picture coverage requirements help
the script supervisor assess a film's progress. This information applies
to scenes which have already been shot. Daily reports, on the other
hand, reflect day-by-day results as well as cumulative progress.

Daily Production Report

After each shooting day, the script supervisor fills out a *daily production report,* and turns it in to the assistant director before the next
day. Some script supervisors turn in the forms in the evening after
shooting while others wait until the next morning. As explained in
Chapter Two, there are several types of forms, but all provide similar
information.

The sample form which appears on page 152 is divided into four
parts. The spaces at the top are for identifying information. This includes the production number assigned by the management, the date,
the shooting day, the film's current title and the script supervisor's name.
Next, the script supervisor fills out the time when the first take is completed, the time lunch begins, the time that the first take after lunch is
completed, and the time that the last take is completed before the wrap
begins. The rest of the form is divided between daily and cumulative
progress.

Daily progress records make a distinction between the script scenes
covered and the scenes actually shot. The script scenes are listed and

Daily Production Report

WORKING TITLE _Return To Macon County_   FIRST SHOT __8:20__

DIRECTOR _Compton_   LUNCH __12:45__

PRODUCTION NUMBER __1670__   FIRST SHOT P.M. __2:15__

DAY __20__   DATE __1127__   FINISH __4:50__

TOTAL SCENES 15	**SCENE NUMBERS COVERED:** 1, 2, 3, 4, 5, 6, 7, 8, 9, 10, 11, 12,
TOTAL PAGES 3 7/8	13, 14, 15
TOTAL SET-UPS 19	**SCENE NUMBERS SHOT:** 1, 1A, 2, 2A, 2C, 2B, 5, 6, 6A, 6B
TOTAL CREDITED TIME 3:50	6C, 11, 11A, 13, 13A, 10A, 10, 10B, 10C
SOUND TRACKS	WT100
RETAKES	—

	SCENES	PAGES		SET-UPS	CREDITED TIME	RETAKES	ADDED SCENES	FOOTAGE
TOTAL IN SCRIPT	267	104 4/8	**TOTAL TODAY**	19	3:50	0	4	2,225
TOTAL TODAY	15	37/8						
TOTAL PREVIOUSLY	174	70	**TOTAL PREVIOUSLY**	228	65:05	2	50	33,075
TOTAL TO DATE	169	73 7/8						
TOTAL TO BE COVERED	98	30 4/8	**TOTAL TO DATE**	247	68:55	2	54	35,350

REMARKS:

10C to be used in drag sequence

WTX100 = same as WTX110

SCRIPT SUPERVISOR __Ulmer__

counted, and the corresponding pages are also added. On shooting day #20, script scenes 1 through 15 were covered. These 15 scenes span over 3⅞ pages. Next, the scenes shot are listed. For the 15 scenes covered, 19 set-ups were shot. This means that four scenes were added. No retakes were shot and only one wild track was recorded.

While listing daily progress, it is very important to distinguish between partial and complete credit. Sometimes only part of a script scene is shot on one day. When this happens, the scene number should appear in the "scenes covered" column followed by the word "part." The total scenes credited should not reflect this part. If, on the other hand, the part completes the coverage, the scene number should be followed with either "final part" or "completion," and the scene should be added to the total credit count. After a scene has been credited, the director may decide to shoot another pick-up. The scene number should again be listed to avoid confusion and labeled "additional coverage." Naturally, the scene should be excluded from the total. The corresponding page-count credit can either be divided between the days or applied to the day of the scene's completion. Credited time is nearly always added as it is shot. The pages, time and scene number of each script scene must only be credited once for the cumulative progress to be accurate.

The bottom of the form is devoted to cumulative progress. The totals from shooting day #20 are added to the previous totals of shooting days #2 through #19. Two of these figures—the page and scene totals—are then subtracted from the totals in the script to indicate how much has yet to be shot. Time totals show if a picture is running long or short. The footage, set-ups, retakes, and added scenes totals are of use to the management for budgetary considerations. The data for filling out this form is compiled by completing the next form.

Daily Production Report for Personal Records

While the daily production form is filled out at the end of the day, most of the script supervisor's personal report is handled throughout the course of shooting. It duplicates the most important information from the editorial notes. If properly executed, the form provides all the data needed to fill in the daily production report.

The following form is a typical example:

Daily Production Report

Working Title: Return To Macon County

Production #: 1670

Shooting Day: 20   Date: 11 27

Script Super.: Shirley Ulmer

Start: 8:20

Lunch: 12:45

1st Shot: 2:15

Finish: 4:50

Scene #s Covered: Pages:

1, 2, 3, 4, 5, 6, 7, 8, 9,   3 7/8
10, 11, 12, 13, 14, 15

	SCENES	PAGES
Total In Script	267	104 1/8
Previously shot	174	70
Total Today	15	3 7/8
Total To Date	169	73 7/8
To Be Covered	98	30 2/8

	SET-UPS	CREDIT TIME	RETAKES	ADDED SCENES	FOOTAGE
Today	19	3:50	0	4	2,275
Previous	228	65:05	2	50	33,075
To Date	247	68:55	2	54	35,350

REMARKS: 10C to be used in drag
sequence

WTX110 = same as WTX100

Set-ups	Scene	Prints	Time	Credit Time
1	1	1, 2	:35	:35
2	1A	3,4 (H1)	:37 :43	—
3	2	2	:38	
4	2A	2 (H1)	:20	:40
5	2C	2 (H1)	:28	
6	2B	1	:30	
7	5	3	:45	
8	6	1, 2	1:20	
9	6A	2 (H1)	1:30	1:30
10	6B	1	1:30	
11	6C	3	1:30	
12	11	1, 2	:21	:20
13	11A	1	:20	
14	13	1	:45	:45
15	13A	2	:45	
16	10A	1	:10	—
17	10	1	:10	—
18	10B	1	:10	—
19	10C	1	:10	—

On the right hand side of the form, each set-up is listed in shooting order. The first set-up, scene #1, is numbered #1; the second set-up, #1A, is numbered #2, and so on in consecutive order. The corresponding page and screen credits are laid out on the left. The script supervisor enters print and timing information into the next two columns. From this information, the script supervisor can determine the credit time.

Credit time refers to the amount of time out of the total time filmed that will be included in the picture after editing. Credit time is also known as *actual time, estimated time* and *picture time.* When a number of camera set-ups cover the same action, only one portion at a time will be put in the picture. The average timing of all the views provides a much more accurate time estimation than adding all the individual times together. During shooting day #20, for instance, set-ups #3 through #7 all overlap. The credit time is the average of these five scenes or about 40 seconds. The same applies to set-ups #8 through #11, #12 and #13, and #15. The inserts—#10, #10A, #10B, and #10C—probably won't add any picture time. Neither will scene #1A which overlaps scenes 1 and 2. The credit time for the day adds up to 3 minutes 50 seconds.

At the end of the day, the cumulative progress blanks at the bottom of the form should be filled in. The previous day's totals are transferred from the preceding form. The only remaining blank is the footage column. On some projects, the script supervisor doesn't have to keep footage records; otherwise, the script supervisor can find the needed data on the camera reports.

Daily Sound and Camera Reports

As discussed in Chapter Two, the sound reports, camera reports and continuity records must all designate the same takes for printing. Throughout the day and after the last shot, the script supervisor should confer with the sound mixer and second assistant cameraman to compare notes. Theoretically, the responsibility of verifying print instructions belongs to all three departments, but somehow the burden always falls on the script supervisor. The script supervisor can either give a list of prints to the sound mixer and the second assistant cameraman, or the script supervisor can check over the camera and sound reports.

The following two forms are typical examples of daily sound and camera reports:

CAMERA REPORT

CFI

CONSOLIDATED FILM INDUSTRIES
959 Seward Street
Hollywood, California 90038
(213) 462-3161

Company: American International Pict.

Address: 9033 Wilshire Bev. Hills

Production: Return to Macon County

Date: 1/29/75   Camera Report No. _____

Director: Compton   Cameraman _____

Magazine No. _____ Roll No. 113

UNLESS OTHERWISE INDICATED ALL DAILIES WILL BE PRINTED AS ONE-LIGHT COLOR   400

CIRCLE ONE: COLOR B & W (A)   CIRCLE ONE: B C D   FILM TYPE 5247

SCENE NO	1 5	2 6	3 7	4 8	DAY OR NIGHT	REMARKS	INT OR EXT
28	30	30	(30)			Day Ext	
28A	(35)	(40)					
29	(30)						
29A	(25)	30	(30)				
30	(45)					32 FPS	
30C	5	20	(20)				

Print: 255'
BNeg: 115'
Short end 30'

No. Cams to Lab. .... Bal. Neg. on Hand ....
Good Footage .... Received ....
N.G. Footage .... Exposed ....
Waste Footage .... On Hand ....
Total Footage .... Emul. No. ....

The Company respectfully points out that as prices are never proportionate to the value of the negative and positives entrusted to it, Customer's films are received, developed, printed and stored by the Company only at the Customer's risk, and the Company does not accept responsibility for any loss or damage to such films from any cause whatsoever. Films delivered to the Owner thereof for the full amount of all risk and possible damage and loss, and the Company holds a lien thereon for the general balance from time to time due to the Company by the Customer, whether in respect to processing, printing, storage charges or otherwise.

51860

FORM NO. 10 (3-74)

SOUND REPORT

PRODUCER	AIP	DATE	1/28
PRODUCTION	1670	ROLL	45
LOCATION	MISC STREETS	SHEET	1
AUDIO		SYNC	

SCENE	TAKE	*	COMMENTS
			CAM ROLL #113
28	1		
	2	N6	plane through end
	(3)		
28A	(1)		
	(2)		
29	(1)		
29A	(1)		
	2	N6	low hum
	(3)		
30	(1)		
30C	1		
	2		
	(3)		
			CAM ROLL #114
31	1		
	2		cam m.slate #1
	3	SM	
	4		
	5		
	6		
	(7)		not recommended
	8		for sound
	(9)		
WT31	(1)		HIGHWAY PRESENCE
38	1	inc	plane through 2nd speech to end
	(2)		
	(3)		
			con't 2nd sheet

* FS-false start   WT-wild track   INC-incomplete   GT-guide track
NG-not good   FX-effects   SM-second marker   ES-end slate

Each represents one roll of film or audiotape. Since sound rolls are considerably longer than camera rolls, there are usually considerably more camera reports than sound reports. Notice that the printed takes are circled on both forms. The camera report differs slightly in that the footage exposed is circled rather than the take number. The take number appears at the top of the column. By glancing over these reports, a script supervisor can easily verify print instructions, camera and sound roll numbers and cumulative footage counts. After completing this task, the script supervisor can move on to the last report.

Daily Editorial Report

The *daily editorial report* duplicates the information in the continuity script. Since the editors don't receive a full continuity script until the end of principal photography, these records allow the editors to begin assembling the daily footage. Editorial reports are turned in before the next day's filming begins.

There are several methods for compiling editorial reports. Some script supervisor's merely photocopy the lined pages and corresponding editorial notes right out of the continuity script. If this is the case, most script supervisors trim off any editorial notes from previous days so that only the notes from the current shooting day are included. Many editors prefer to receive whole pages rather than trimmed pages. Some script supervisors don't photocopy their notes but instead re-write them on a separate form which is turned in with copies of the lined pages.

If the script supervisor opts to rewrite the editorial notes after each day's filming, the same type of form can be used as in the continuity script. A sample form appears on the next page.

DAILY EDITORIAL REPORT

JOB # _____ TITLE _____ DIRECTOR _____

SHOOTING DAY _____ DATE _____ SCRIPT SUPERVISOR _____

SETS/LOCATIONS _____

CAM ROLL	SND ROLL	SL #	TK #	TIME	COMMENTS	ACTION

The only difference between this form and the one in the script is that the former has identifying information printed on the top. Using a form similar to the one in the script simplifies transferring the information from one to the other.

RALPH SCHOENFELD INTERVIEW

Ralph Schoenfeld has been one of the busiest film editors in television for the last 20 years. He has worked extensively in every format from single camera film to three-camera video to six-camera film. His early credits include such series as *Lassie, Beverly Hillbillies, Green Acres* and *Petticoat Junction.* More recently, he has edited episodes from numerous popular television series including *Happy Days, Mrs. Colombo, The Incredible Hulk, Bionic Woman, Six Million Dollar Man, Police Story, Police Woman, Hart to Hart, When the Whistle Blows* and many more. Throughout his interview, Ralph Schoenfeld speaks of the value of a script supervisor to an editor.

SCHOENFELD: Year before last, I had the honor of editing two segments of Centennial *which were like baby features—two-hour movies of the week. On a production of this size, we shot a little over 105,000 feet of film. That means that I relied on the script supervisor to give me a record of everything that was shot so I would know exactly what was on the film. Now, I don't know how much you know about editing film, so I will start at the beginning and if you've heard it before, bear with me.*

When I look at a piece of film, I get it in rolls. Literally in rolls. All I receive with the film is a Xerox copy of the day's shooting telling me the production, the scene and the take. Centennial, *Scene 164, Take 5. That's all I know. It may be a thousand feet. When I edited a courtroom scene in* Centennial, *I had 11,000 feet in 11 reels, of which I had to cut down to 450 feet. The director covered everything in the book. He had a master, then moved his camera a little bit this way, then he went this way and so on. Or a second example: One reel of film may have as many as 20 reels of sound effects with it. Say the scene is a gun fight and there are three gunfighters. The sound editor can't put all the gunfire on one track, so he builds units. He'll put one set down on A track, one on B track and the third on C track. Then, he'll build horses the same way. He may end up with 20 tracks for one reel. I did on a picture called* On The Waterfront. *In order to keep track of all this footage, I need continuity records.*

By looking at the script supervisor's notes, I know what I'm cutting. I have to decide what to cut from what the script supervisor tells me. The more I'm told about a scene, the easier it is for me to know what the director wants out of it. These notes are what I use as my Bible to cut with.

There is a lot of work that goes into the making of a film. It's a tough business. And there are many people involved in the process and everybody works. Like the script supervisor—the script supervisor runs her department and it's essential. If she doesn't do it right, then it takes me twice as long to run mine.

On occasion, I didn't get a lined script right away because the production crew was out shooting in Colorado or Texas or some place. After I saw the dailies, I would mark them myself. I'd have to run literally each piece of film and mark them, so I would know what to cut.

With good script notes, I don't have to fumble along in the editing room. I know by looking at the script where I go from one scene to another scene to a pick-up to a two-shot to a close-up. I know that a scene starts on the Fade In and where it stops. It's all marked and labeled. This is the reason that the script supervisor's notes are so important for an editor. I have difficulty cutting without notes.

STUDENT: How much of the script supervisor's behavior on the set do you have to rely on? Surely matching, for instance, is just as important as labeling individual scenes.

SCHOENFELD: Matching is another big problem that you have to be aware of. When actors are coming from the right, you have to make sure they leave from the same way they came in. Or cigarette smoking—you've established a cigarette in the right hand and the next shot you come back and it's in the left hand. Now, that's difficult to cut. Right? But it happens. Sometimes, if we can, we flop over a scene to correct the mistake. Maybe the script girl didn't remember to write down that an actor was heading right to left. When the crew gets around to shooting the next shot of the sequence, they say, "Oh, yeah, I remember. We were going this way. Sure." And so they shoot it left to right. Then all of a sudden I get the footage and say, "Holy Roller, what do I do now?" The script supervisor has to be the one to say, "Hey, wait a minute. He was heading right to left." It's very important for the script supervisor to make sure the match is right because you know these guys. They're actors and many can be the most difficult people in the world when it comes to remembering where they were at any given time in a scene. They have to be. Without the self-centered quality, they couldn't do their jobs. It's for you to say, "Hold on, he's got to head this way."

Timing is another area. The script supervisor's timings are equally important.

Each picture is figured on a strict, pre-determined time basis. A two-hour movie has to come in at a certain time, an hour movie has to come in at another time, a half-hour movie the same way. This is especially true in television where we are locked into inflexible time slots. That's where the script supervisor's timings are important. Usually, if the script supervisor is good, the timings are pretty accurate. When the script supervisor says that I'm 15 minutes over, I know to go in and start trimming because I have to take out the extra footage. If the script supervisor comes in short by a minute, then I start stretching the film; for instance, I can lengthen run-bys. Instead of bringing the horse in at the bottom of the hill, I bring him in at the top because I was told that I'm a minute short going in.

STUDENT: *It sounds like the script supervisor sure better be right.*

SCHOENFELD: Exactly. I've been where a film was off by four minutes. The script supervisor said, "We're four minutes over, but we're all right. We'll take out a couple of pages." And they cut the pages. All of a sudden, we edit the picture and we're four and a half minutes short. How did that happen? The script supervisor didn't figure her times right.

STUDENT: *Is noting the need for a pick-up important to the editor in the same way?*

SCHOENFELD: You have to watch what goes on, yes. The script supervisor should make sure that the actors are reading lines correctly. If they're not, the script supervisor tells the director. Then he will decide if he wants to reshoot it. You see, he's not always aware of the script. He hasn't been concentrating on the exact wording but instead he's been watching the total performance. The script supervisor is the one who is checking to make sure that the words flow within the balance of the scene. If they fall too far off, then the script supervisor has to bring attention to it by saying, "Bruce, hey, she didn't do this and she didn't do that. Is it okay with you?" And he is likely to say, "Well, maybe we'd better reshoot it because this scene is important and the actors are too far off." Then they go back and make a pick-up. When I get the footage, I disregard the n.g. dialogue and replace it with the pick-up. Having the necessary information on the continuity records makes it much easier for me to determine which take I'm going to use.

STUDENT: *Do you ever get too much information?*

SCHOENFELD: No. You can't get too much. The only thing I would stress is that somebody else is going to read your notes. The editor has to be able to read and understand them. I may have the worst handwriting in the world but don't let the script supervisor. If I look down and say, "What the *hell does this say?"*, then I think, *"Oh, my God, she's awful."* This is very important.

STUDENT: Suppose everything is labeled correctly on your daily continuity notes and that you can read them. Then what?

SCHOENFELD: After we assemble what was shot that day, we run it for dailies to be sure that everything is in sync, the color is good, the focus is in, the performances are right and the sound is clear. The script supervisor usually attends along with the director to know if he likes the performances. If a performance is bad, he can decide to reshoot it. The fault may be due to wardrobe, directing, props or any other factor as well as a performance problem. The director tells the script supervisor, "Make a note that I want to reshoot this." She makes the note and reminds him later that they have to shoot a pick-up or a retake of the scene.

STUDENT: Isn't it the case that sometimes a reading is bad in one take and not in another, and that they wouldn't necessarily have to go back and reshoot the scene?

SCHOENFELD: Sure. A lot of times what happens when a producer or a director watches the dailies is that they get very upset. They're looking at somebody for two minutes. Out of that two minutes, I may use only one line in the finished film; but they're looking at the whole scene and they don't understand why the performance is off. Actually, all that's off is one sentence and the rest is fine. They can't always visualize by looking at the dailies what the finished product will look like.

STUDENT: Is it true that editors can even speed up the pace of a speech?

SCHOENFELD: Oh, yes. That's one reason why there are close-ups and two shots and masters. Because with these choices, I can alter scenes. I can go from a full shot to a close-up and lose 300 feet out of the scene in the process. But if the director didn't give me that close-up to cut away to, then I'm locked in with the complete scene. As long as I am provided with alternatives, the director can change the scene any way he wants to as long as it makes sense dialogue-wise.

STUDENT: What kind of changes are they likely to request?

SCHOENFELD: A lot of times when we run dailies for the director and producer, someone says, "Gee, I think she looked better in this shot." My assistant will make a note so when I get ready to cut the next day, I will review what they have said and try to follow through. Sometimes I can't if it's a matching problem or maybe if the footage just isn't available. When I'm unable to comply, I call and let them know and we pick another alternative.

On other occasions, I've cut the next day's rushes because the producer and the director wanted to see if an actor is good in a scene. They may want to replace him with someone else. By looking at the cut sequence they can make their decision.

STUDENT: *What happens if they like the performance but they want to select another camera angle or a different reading?*

SCHOENFELD: *That's when the takes that are not circled, the out-takes, become significant. Often, we run a show for the director and he says, "On this scene, I know I got a better reading in take 3. Joey didn't fumble the last line," so I'll go back and look at take 3. Since take 3 wasn't printed with the others, I tell my assistant to have the negative girl pull the negative. The sound department does the same. When I get the track and picture back, I examine them and find out that Joey read the line much more clearly. Then I remove the n.g. line and cut the sound and picture of the pick-up in.*

STUDENT: *Why is the date so important?*

SCHOENFELD: *The reason the script supervisor has to record the date is because all negative and sound are stored by the shooting date. Say, for example, a month from now, I rip scene 58 and need a reprint. What I do is put an order into the lab telling them my production number, the scene number, the take and what day the scene was shot. Then they can pull the negative and put it through for a reprint. Without the date, they would have to look through the whole bloody 5,000 feet to find it. Everything is broken down into the date's shooting. Some days 10 pages are shot, some days 20 pages are shot; it depends. But whatever the date is, that information is essential on the script supervisor's log. Then once we have the dailies and everything is good, then we start putting it all together.*

If the footage is bad, we can make it good. If it's good, we can make it excellent. Really. What I like about it is that it's my choice first. I get to do what I want with the film. I decide if I want to go to a full shot or a two-shot. Shall I stay in a close-up longer or shall I overlap because I think she gives a little more expression? For me, it's a good feeling. Every time I see a film that I've done, I feel great. I really do. I say, "Oh, God, I did that." It's because I enjoy what I do. No one else can do it. You're going to feel a sense of accomplishment too when you do a good script. Everybody has their niche. You have a big niche. You are behind the scenes telling a lot of people which way to go, what to do, where the film is. Without you, it would be very tough for me and a lot of people to do our jobs.

The use of continuity, sound and camera reports is the standard method of relaying all the necessary information to management and editor at the end of each shooting day. The universality of terms found on the forms helps organize the material in a way acceptable to the majority of motion picture/television companies. The forms enhance the speed and efficiency at which the job can be executed. The only shortcoming of these forms is that none provides a complete at-a-glance reference to the film's total progress. Although page counts and scene counts present a partial view of progress, the script supervisor can adapt the one-liners for a more informative picture.

Using the One-Liners

The script supervisor's one-liners can be updated as the shoot progresses. Writing the date a scene was shot in the margin permits the script supervisor to check quickly what has been shot and what hasn't. The dates also serve as a checklist. If a day's shooting schedule unexpectedly has to be rearranged due to rain or other unforeseen problems, this reference will come in handy for selecting alternative scenes to shoot. Valuable time will be saved since the one-liners list costume, cast, set and various other requirements needed to make a viable list of options. Even if no unexpected problems arise the script supervisor should always check the one-liners to make sure all scenes are completed before moving on to another location.

Notice that on the first page of the *Return to Macon County* one-liners that appear on the opposite page, helpful notes are written in the margins. In addition to the dates each scene was shot, costume notes are marked whenever a variation occurs that wasn't previously noted during pre-production. These help the script supervisor keep track of changes made during production. The same could be done for set dressing, props, lighting or any other noticeable element which would make a difference in a film's direction or time continuity in the scenes to follow.

To summarize the script supervisor's function during a shoot, a script supervisor is responsible for the care and maintenance of a film's continuity. The job entails a complex combination of duties performed simultaneously under time-pressed conditions. The script supervisor must first recognize the director's coverage system's cinematic techniques. Next, the script supervisor records everything being filmed by numbering and lining the script. At the same time, the script supervisor is in charge of matching to ensure a continuous flow from shot to shot. A final duty is tracing the film's overall progress through the use of running lists, daily reports and one-liners. The script supervisor's effectiveness at performing this job depends on the script supervisor's

		MACON ONE LINERS		
SC #	LOCATION/SET	DESCRIPTION	CAST	TIME
✓1. ^{1/28}	Ext. Access Rd.	Est. pan from cow to Chevy	(Bo, Harley) C#1 C#1	D1
✓2. ^{1/28}	Ext. Access Rd.	Harley adjusts engine	Harley	D1
✓3. ^{1/28}	Int. Chevy	Bo in driver's seat	Bo + windbreaker + dickie	D1
✓4. ^{1/28}	Ext. Access Rd.	Bo's pov of Harley fixing engine	Harley + dickie	D1
✓5. ^{1/28}	Ext. Access Rd.	Bo shoots car toward Harley	Bo, Harley	D1
✓6. ^{1/28}	Int. Chevy	Bo & Harley begin to speed test car	Bo, Harley	D1
✓7. ^{1/28}	Ext. Chevy	wheels spin	--	D1
✓8. ^{1/28}	Int. Chevy	Bo shifts gears	Bo, Harley	D1
✓9. ^{1/31}	Int. Chevy	Harley grins as checks RPM	Harley	D1
✓10. ^{1/29}	Insert	tachometer & v.o.	(Bo, Harley)	D1
✓11. ^{1/29}	Ext. Highway	car rockets off	(Bo, Harley)	D1
✓12. ^{1/28}	Int. Chevy	Harley & Bo discuss 1/4 mark	Bo, Harley	D1
✓13. ^{1/28}	Ext. Highway	car zooms by pole	(Bo, Harley)	D1
✓14. ^{1/28}	Int. Chevy	Bo & Harley discuss results	Bo, Harley	D1
✓15. ^{1/28}	Int. Chevy	Close of happy Bo	Bo	D1
#19 ~~16.~~	Ext. Highway	Chevy zooming in and out of traffic	(Bo, Harley, & misc. drivers)	— time lapse — D1
#20C ~~17.~~	Ext. Highway	Mercury cruising	Boy, Girl C#1 C#1	D1
omit ~~18.~~	Ext. Highway	Chevy passes truck	Bo, Harley jacket off O.S.	D1
✓19. ^{1/29}	Ext. Highway	Chevy shoots up to Mercury	Bo, Harley, Boy, Girl	D1
✓20. ^{1/29}	Int. Mercury	Boy & Girl notice Chevy	Boy, Girl	D1
✓21. ^{1/29}	Ext. Highway	Chevy moves alongside Merc.	Boy, Girl, Bo, Harley	D1
✓22. ^{1/29}	Int. Mercury	Boy speeds up	Boy, Girl	D1
✓23. ^{1/29}	Int. Chevy	Bo speeds up	Bo, Harley	D1
✓24. ^{1/29}	Ext. Highway	leapfrog builds to race	Bo, Harley, Boy, Girl	D1
✓25. ^{1/29}	Int. Chevy	Harley is worried. Bo encourages.	Bo, Harley	D1
✓26. ^{1/29}	Ext. Hwy Bend	POV around corner. clear.	Bo, Harley	D1
✓27. ^{1/29}	Int. Mercury	Mercury pulls into suicide lane	Boy, Girl, (Bo, Harley)	D1

skill at selective observation, and the ability to juggle duties in order to get everything accomplished.

The examples in this chapter have involved feature film production although many of the techniques can easily be transferred to other types of motion picture/television projects. Different production requirements sometimes lead to different continuity demands. The more the script supervisor learns about other specializations, the easier it will be to adapt these scripting skills to other formats.

Chapter Four

Scripting Videotape

Single camera filming comprises the majority of motion picture-television production. Feature films, telefeatures, mini-series and hour drama television series are for the most part shot with one film camera. Still, there are many other information and entertainment formats that use different production techniques.

The following chapter will deal with one of these alternative styles—videotape production. In order to fully understand how videotape procedures affect the script supervisor's job, it's helpful to recognize the basic difference between film and video technology. A script supervisor has to reorient his or her thinking substantially to cross over to the new medium.

VIDEOTAPE FUNDAMENTALS

While film utilizes a light projection system, video relies on a computerized electronic system. A simplistic explanation of the projection system in film production can be made by comparing motion picture photography to still slide photography. A motion picture is made up of a series of still photographs positioned along a strip of film. Each frame of this film is exposed individually in a similar manner to a still slide, only the moving picture camera usually exposes at the rate of 24 frames per second. After the film is developed and printed, the light is projected through the film at the same rate of 24 frames per second.

Unlike film cameras, videotape cameras reproduce images by changing patterns of light into electrical impulses. The lens of the camera focuses light rays onto a *vidicon tube*. During the early days of television, other versions called iconoscope tubes, dissector tubes and orthicon tubes were used, but their functions were similar. A photosensitive element called the *target area* makes up the front portion of the tube. When light rays from the image strike the target area, the target surface becomes electrically charged. Bright portions of the image cause a different intensity of electrical charge than darker spots. All other shading falls in between, depending on the relative brightness or darkness.

At the opposite end of the vidicon tube is a device called an *electron gun* which "sweeps" the target area and breaks down its charges into a varying signal. A black and white video camera includes only one gun; a color camera has three, each of the three sensitive to only one of three primary colors. The electron gun shoots its steady beam of electrons at the target while scanning the entire surface in uniform horizontal lines. The lines along which the gun scans the target surface are referred to as *lines of resolution*. A camera capable of recording more lines of resolution affords a higher quality picture.

As the beam of electrons scans a line on the target, it sets up a current that varies according to the target charge. This current becomes the basis for the *television signal*. These live signals are transmitted either through the air in the form of electromagnetic waves, or through wires to home receivers. The signal is converted back into a scanning beam of electrical charges. When the charge comes in contact with the phosphor coating on the receiver screen, each point of contact glows in differing degrees for a brief moment, depending on the strength of the signal. The combination of all the variously illuminated contacts gives the impression of a complete image.

While transmitting live television signals was achieved in the early '30s, video recording wasn't developed until much later, after the perfecting of audio recording. Audio recording systems convert sound into electrical impulses by monitoring the movements made by sound waves on a vibrating surface. These impulses are recorded magnetically with a fine layer of iron oxide. Audio tape recordings are capable of reproducing the original sound with remarkable clarity as well as capable of being erased and used again.

Video signals are far more complex than audio signals, but the step-by-step process is comparable. First, the sound or image is translated into electrical impulses, and then these electrical signals are recorded onto a strip of plastic backed with a magnetic medium known as *magnetic recording tape*. The sound or image can be reproduced at any time from the recording. A more detailed explanation of the recording process can be understood by discussing the various video recorders.

Helical Scan & Quadraplex VTR Systems

Generally, there are two types of videotape recorders, *helical scan* and *quadraplex.* Quadraplex VTRs are more sophisticated machines which consequently makes them considerably more expensive. Both efficiently store video programs through complex systems of audio and video heads capable of recording a large amount of electrical information onto a relatively small amount of tape.

The term, *helical scan,* is derived from the helical or spiral pattern in which the head makes contact with the tape.

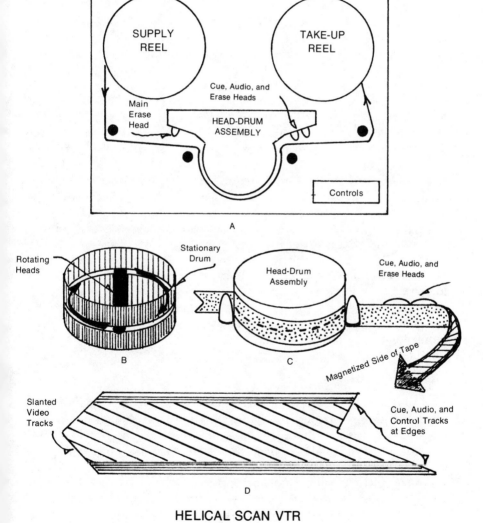

HELICAL SCAN VTR

The tape deck is arranged so that the supply reel is mounted at a different level than the take-up reel, (A). The video heads, on the other hand, spin in a strictly horizontal plane within a stationary head drum. There are usually one or two heads in the drum which protrude from a slit to make contact with the tape, (B). When the tape moves past the head on its way to the take-up reel, it travels either halfway around or all the way around the head in a helical or diagonal path, (C). The resulting electrical messages are recorded onto the magnetic surface of the tape in correspondingly slanted tracks, (D). The audio heads are offset from the video (A). While the video tracks are recorded on the center portion of the videotape, the audio signal is on one or two tracks at the edges of the same tape, (D).

The main difference between the helical scan VTR and the quadraplex on the opposite page lies in the head assemblies. The quadraplex's supply and take-up reels are mounted on the same plane so the tape travels in a uniform horizontal path past the heads, (E). Instead of one or two rotating heads, the quadraplex has four heads mounted in a vertical wheel, (F). When the wheel spins, each head makes contact with the tape in sequence. The tape moves slowly at the same time that the head wheel spins. As the head scans down toward the bottom of the tape, the tape is moving slightly from where the head first contacted the top surface. This results in a very subtle slant of the recorded video tracks, (G). But compared to the helical tracks, the quadraplex tracks appear perpendicular, and as a result the quadraplex VTR is also referred to as a *transverse scan videotape recorder*.

Whether helical scan or quadraplex videotape recorders, the advantages and disadvantages of using videotape over film involves a number of financial concerns, image quality considerations and differing production techniques. The budget and quality considerations won't influence how the script supervisor observes continuity. The differences in production techniques, on the other hand, directly alter the script supervisor's methods. In particular, electronic video editing procedures will have the greatest effect.

Videotape Editing

Compared to film, videotape is immediate. While film requires time for developing, a videotape system is capable of simultaneous monitoring and transmission. By regenerating the video camera signals before they reach the videotape recorder, the signals can be sent to the playback monitor and the recorder at the same time. Mistakes in focus, exposure, picture composition or performance can be viewed on the set as they occur so that all guesswork is eliminated. In fact, most modern video equipment even supplies assemblies and opticals right on the

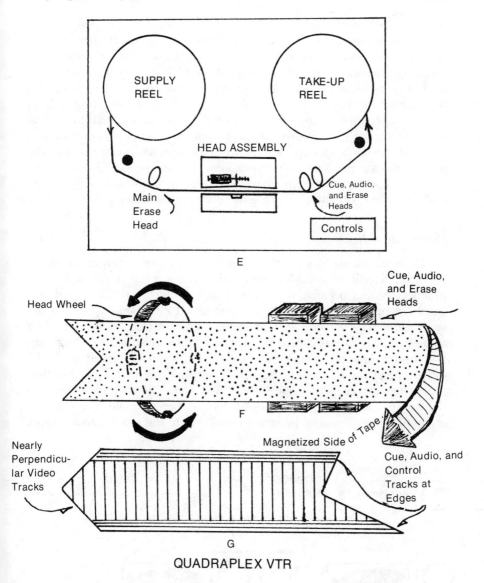

SUPPLY REEL

TAKE-UP REEL

HEAD ASSEMBLY

Main Erase Head

Cue, Audio, and Erase Heads

Controls

E

Head Wheel

Cue, Audio, and Erase Heads

F

Magnetized Side of Tape

Nearly Perpendicular Video Tracks

Cue, Audio, and Control Tracks at Edges

G

QUADRAPLEX VTR

set. These differences make it essential that the script supervisor is acquainted with video editing techniques starting with the distinction between physical and electronic editing.

Physical Editing

Physical editing is the process of actually cutting the videotape and reassembling the pieces to compile a desired sequence. Assembling those pieces without disturbing the electrical synchronization of the picture is a tricky business. In film, distinct divisions between frames provide easy cuts. In video, this is not the case. All the even lines of a complete scanning comprise one *field,* and all the odd lines comprise a second field. These field signals are used to add control pulses to the tape. The two fields together form a complete picture or *frame* which must remain synchronous. By painting developing solution on a magnetic tape and viewing the tape through a specialized microscope, sync tracks are revealed. An improper splice appears as an obvious interruption in the picture during playback. It's impossible to sever the tape between the tracks and still preserve the sync. As a result, physical editing is virtually obsolete, except in the case of repairing damaged tape.

Electronic Editing

Electronic editing was developed as an alternative to physical editing. Most video editors consider electronic editing a far safer and more practical system because the original tape is never cut or erased. Instead, segments of video tape are assembled electronically into a desired sequence by using two or more videotape recorders. This first scene of a sequence is copied from an original videotape recording onto a second videotape or *composite master*. If the next segment is on the same tape as the first, then the tape is simply recued. If it's on another tape, then the reels or cassettes are switched. The second segment is then recorded onto the composite master directly following the first segment. The composite program is built up in the same manner scene

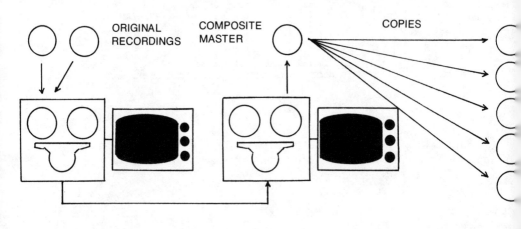

ORIGINAL   COMPOSITE   COPIES
RECORDINGS   MASTER

FIRST GENERATION   SECOND GENERATION   THIRD GENERATION by scene in order, and the process is known as *assembly editing*. When a scene in the sequence can't be added until later, a precisely-timed gap is left in the composite. The missing scene can be inserted into the gap later, which is referred to as an *insert edit*. Both assembly and insert editing usually, unfortunately, cause the tape's picture and audio quality to drop at least one generation each time the tape is copied.

Similar to editing film, electronic video editing requires two steps to maximize picture and sound quality. For film, the editors first assemble the footage by using a positive copy of the film negative, known as workprint. After the workprint is assembled to everyone's satisfaction, the assembly is duplicated by cutting the negative to match the workprint. The video equivalent to cutting a workprint is referred to as *off-line editing* while the equivalent to cutting the negative is referred to as *on-line editing*.

Off-line editing is the process of assembling a working copy of a video program. These working copies are usually an inferior cassette recording (VCR). While taping, VCRs record identical signals in sync with the primary VTRs. Sometimes the masters are transferred later to cassettes, in a procedure referred to as a *dub-down*, before off-line editing. The cassettes are assembled into a composite master. Since the cassettes will never be broadcast, little attention is given to generations lost and picture quality. The off-line cassettes are only used as a guide for on-line editing.

On-line editing or *auto assembly* of a final video program, uses the original tapes. Each cut that appeared in the off-line cassette is duplicated automatically by computer onto the on-line composite master. The resulting on-line master drops only one generation in quality. Because it retains its broadcast quality, the on-line master is often referred to as the *broadcast master*.

Both off-line and on-line editing is made possible by *SMPTE* (Society of Motion Picture and Television Engineers) *time codes*. Time codes are eight digit numbers automatically laid down on the control track of each frame of the tape. Although time code signals are always present on the control track, they are only visible on a playback monitor with a *character generator*. Home television sets don't transmit time codes. Whenever codes are visible they appear across the bottom of the screen.

16 : 20 : 15 . 18
hours   minutes   seconds   frames

The frame numbers change 30 times per second. Hours, minutes, and seconds advance at the same rate as any clock. For simplification, AM and PM distinctions are made by using a 24-hour clock. Noon is called 1200 hours, one o'clock is called 1300 hours, two o'clock is 1400 hours, and so on up to midnight which starts over with twin zero hours. When the off-line editor tells the computer to cut after 16:20:15.18 and resume at 03:20:50.30, the cut is made automatically on the composite master. For on-line editing, the computer reads the time code signal information off of the off-line master and duplicates the cuts onto the broadcast master. Since each frame has its own individual time code, the computer automatically places all cuts between frames to avoid picture interruption.

Audio editing on a videotape recorder is handled electronically as well. Because the audio signal is offset from the video signal, physically editing the audio is imprecise. Electronic editing provides a solution to this dilemma by separating the audio signal from the video signal without disturbing either.

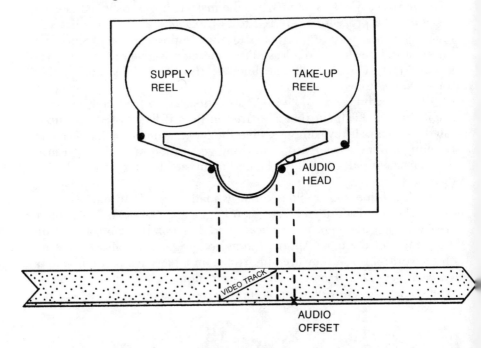

Audio dubbing, a form of electronic audio editing, replaces an old audio signal with a new signal. The original sound is erased as the new sound is recorded in its place. Voice-overs, wild tracks or music for instance, might replace a previous track when the editor is certain that the original won't be needed.

A safer method, referred to as *audio sweetening,* retains the original recording by copying only the desired sounds onto a composite master. Again two videotape recorders are required. The video signal is copied from the first videotape recorder to the second directly. The audio signal goes through an audio-mixer before it is recorded onto the composite master.

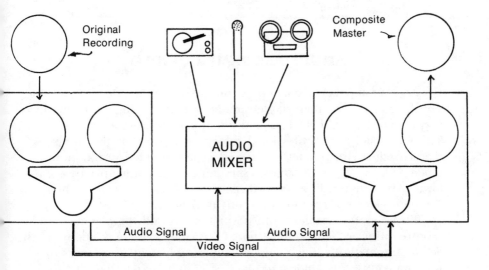

An audio mixer accepts signals from various sources such as microphones, phonographs, audio tape recorders or videotape recorders; and mixes their levels together to a desired balance. An editor can add, subtract or combine music, dialogue and effects.

More often, off-line audio sweetening is executed on quarter-inch audio tape. The audio signals are transferred from the videotape onto quarter-inch audio tape because audio tape allows finer recording. While videotape is usually capable of handling only one or two audio tracks, 8- or 16-track audio tape is common. While transferring the audio signals, time codes are recorded onto one of the quarter-inch tape's audio tracks. Dialogue, music and effects are then mixed on the remaining tracks as the video is played for reference. When the balance is achieved, the audio signals are reduced to two tracks and transferred back to the videotape.

A videotape script supervisor requires a rudimentary knowledge of editing both audio and video tracks. If video programs were edited entirely in post production, this would not be the case. Just as in single camera film production, the script supervisor could merely ensure that the individual shots are compatible for later editing. Because most commercial video programs aren't assembled exclusively in post production, but instead through a combination of production and post production, the video script supervisor has to be well-informed in those editing procedures which occur on the set. These procedures are commonly referred to as *in-camera editing* and they affect the continuity duties, particularly as the script supervisor becomes involved in multiple camera video.

MULTIPLE CAMERA VIDEO

A script supervisor encounters multiple camera videotape production far more often than single camera videotape. Single camera video is very rarely used in professional situations requiring a script supervisor. The majority of professional videotape production, including commercial television, pay television and in-house video programming is taped with two or more cameras simultaneously. For simplicity, the following discussion will focus on three and four camera video—the most common video set-ups used currently in American television.

Three or four cameras are positioned around the playing area to capture differing views of the action. Compatible camera positions match action automatically. Each view usually complements the others by offering a contrasting angle and image size, and by focusing on a different aspect of the action. One camera might be used part of the time for shooting title cards or other graphics. On some tapings, the titles are laid over later in post production by a computer called an *electronic title generator.* Rarely will any one camera remain with its original composition the whole time. During a take, the cameras zoom, tilt, pan and move at the director's discretion. The playing area is for the most part evenly lit so that the action can be seen clearly from all angles. Except in the case of optical effects, only one of the views is selected at any moment to go into the finished program.

The various camera signals are fed into an electronic editing device called a *vision switcher* or *vision mixer.* All camera views are monitored individually so the director can select the best from the monitors. The vision switcher permits only the signal from the selected view to pass to the VTR recording the master program. "On the line," "line feed" and "line copy" are all terms used to describe the master program. The remaining views are either blocked in the switcher or directed to other VTRs referred to as *isolated* or *iso* VTRs. Videotapes recorded on iso are often referred to as *slaves.* Usually, the signal which is recorded onto the master program line is regenerated and sent to the iso as well.

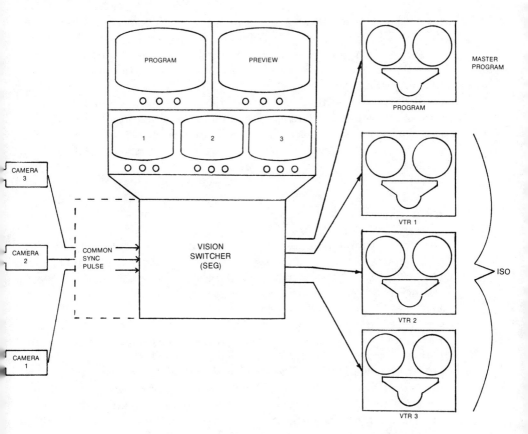

Although each camera signal can be directed to any iso VTR, most often the camera-to-VTR relationship remains consistent throughout a taping. Say, for instance, that camera 1 goes to VTR 1, camera 2 goes to VTR 2 and camera 3 goes to VTR 3. The video reels from camera 1 would be numbered in codes ending with the digit 1 such as 11, 21, 31 and so on. Similarly, camera 2 signals recorded on VTR 2 are numbered 12, 22, 32 and the like while camera 3 signals recorded on VTR 3 are numbered 13, 23, 33, etcetera. The reels recorded on the program VTR are numbered ending in the digit 0 such as 10, 20, 30 and 40. It's obvious which camera was used by reading the reel number.

A less common system codes by the first digit. Camera 1 views recorded on VTR 1 are 101, 102, 103, 104 and 105. Camera 2 views on VTR 2 are 201, 202, 203, 204 and 205. Camera 3 views recorded on VTR 3 are 301, 302, 303, 304 and 305. In this second system, the program tapes are labeled program 1, program 2, program 3 and so on. Again, any editor knows which camera view is on which iso.

A signal recorded on the master program is also recorded on the iso VTRs for protection. Theoretically, one program and two isolated VTRs should be adequate for recording three signals. In the real world, it's safer to record two copies of the program view because defects in the magnetic coating of videotape are common. *Dropout,* for instance, happens when a portion of the iron oxide coating is uneven. This causes a momentary loss of electrical information resulting in an interruption of the picture. *Glitches* are also due to uneven iron oxide which cause problems with the picture such as a flash or a line, usually at edit points. Sometimes glitches occur on the audio only, sometimes the picture only and other times on the control track. A strip of videotape may lose its control track if there is a crinkle or *edge damage. Warped reels* tend to cause edge damage. *Tape curl* results in similar problems. Some tape has even been known to have a 10-foot section with no magnetic coating at all. Although some imperfections cause interruptions that can only be seen on an oscilloscope, the defects affect transmission. The FCC inforces strict standards to ensure quality consistency for broadcasting. Having the second copy of the program view on iso ensures that one will meet specifications.

While taping, the director watches the iso monitors and switches from one view to another as many times as desirable to compile the master program. As long as the three cameras all share common sync pulses, the switcher automatically times the cuts between field signals without picture interruption. The master program can be constructed from as many different views within one continuous take as the director sees fit. The director's selections appear on the program monitor.

One type of vision switcher called a *special effects generator* or *SEG* not only switches between camera signals, but also adds special effects. Although different models vary in which effects are included, certain minimum effects are found on most models. SEGs cut, fade in, fade out, crossfade or "mix," wipe and superimpose. Usually, a screen can be electronically split so that portions of one signal share the screen with portions of another. Split screens come in various patterns. These

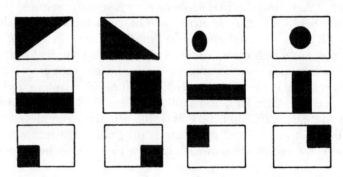

patterns are the most common combinations, although more sophisticated switchers offer many more possibilities.

Sometimes horizontal and vertical controls for split screens are
available making wipes possible in patterns corresponding to the split
screens.

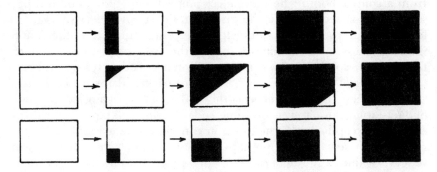

Other functions of the SEG, which script supervisors won't encounter
as often during production, include inserting film or slides into a video
program or combining the dark portions of one signal with the light
portions of another signal to form a composite picture which is known
as *keying*.

Once familiar with electronic video equipment and editing procedures, the script supervisor is ready to take charge of the continuity
records. At this point, generalizing about taping techniques becomes
very difficult. Working conditions change from project to project. A
company may tape audio separate from video on quarter-inch audio
tape with time codes on one track, or a company may tape audio tracks
directly onto the videotape. Most multiple camera video programs edit
in the camera, yet some edit later. While many tape in front of live
audiences, others tape entirely in closed studios. Taping two performances "live" and editing the best from each together is common as is
taping one "live" and one "dress." Of those that tape in front of live
audiences, some tape pick-ups during the performance at the risk of
boring the audience to avoid excess changes of scenery and costumes.
Others wait until the audience leaves before taping pick-ups because
they are afraid of losing fresh audience responses. If three cameras are
used, most often the center camera is a master view while the outside
cameras are crossviews. If four cameras are used, then anything goes.
There could be four close-ups or two close-ups with two masters, or
the cameras could change so often that it's hard to say what the com
bination is at any given time. The only safe generalization is that most
multiple camera video programs do the majority of their taping indoors.

Just as techniques vary, so does the physical relationship between one crew member to another. These variations will directly affect the script supervisor. Unlike film, the script supervisor doesn't always observe the taping from the set. Often, the script supervisor sits at the director's side away from the live action. The director usually works from a control booth where the electronic editing equipment and personnel are located. If this is the case, then the script supervisor watches the action on a set of monitors with time codes. If, on the other hand, the script supervisor remains on the set, then some type of communication with the control booth is necessary for time codes. It's not unheard of that a script supervisor has had to run back and forth to a control truck between takes to retrieve the codes. Then again, some lower budget tapings don't even use time codes during the taping, but this is more the exception than the norm in commercial television.

Given these variations, perhaps the best way to illustrate how a script supervisor lines a multiple camera video program is by using representative samples. The following two examples are designed to illustrate two typical iso shows. The first traces the process of taping one scene from a small-scale industrial training three-camera iso program where no time codes were available. The second presents a popular commercially produced four-camera iso television series.

Industrial Three-Camera Iso Sample

Industrials are video or film programs designed to relay specific information to a restricted audience. Audiences are usually limited to members of large companies or organizations. Since these programs are rarely, if ever, shown to the general public, they are referred to as *in-house*. A program might instruct school teachers about their medical benefit programs. Another might supply the latest developments in plant care to nursery employees. Still others might teach armies about military procedures. A combination of graphics and charts with narration, docudrama, animation, questions and answers, interviews or any other visual presentation of information are all common formats. For our purposes, Interact Learning Systems' training tape for Ford Marketing Institute is an interesting example of an industrial production using three-camera video.

Interact Learning Systems is a top Los Angeles based company specializing in sales and management training. They provide client companies with training packages. In our example, Interact produced a sales training course for Ford Marketing Institute in which 15 to 20 students learn to sell cars. The course was comprised of a four-day multi-media presentation designed to supplement a Ford Marketing Institute handbook of basic selling techniques. The presentation included lectures, audiotapes, overhead projections, posters, graphics and three video segments. It was only in the producing of the video segments that a script supervisor was involved.

All three segments were shot without an audience on a minimal studio set referred throughout the script as a "space stage." The performers play against a clean white cyclorama with a fitted ground roll which gave the impression of empty space. For the most part, scenes involved no other scenery. When sets were used, they were simple and stylized, often cut-outs standing free style. Both the stylized scenery and the costumes were constructed out of bright colors.

The body of the programs is carried by the Spokesman—a brisk, good-humored performer capable of assuming a wide variety of attitudes and characters at any given moment in the story. The spokesman travels freely from location to location on the space stage to interact with other characters. All of these roles are handled by five ensemble players of varying ages and types. They combine into differing relationships with the spokesman as they appear and reappear throughout the programs.

In the following three-page excerpt, the spokesman introduces several basic business principles as he travels through three locations. He makes his opening remarks in front of a white cyclorama. Next, the spokesman walks from the white background where he delivers a line, and then continues over to the lemonade stand. The spokesman and a character called Young Man share a short exchange of dialogue. Once the spokesman has finished his business with the young man, it's off again to the white space for a concluding remark.

The studio was too narrow to accommodate all three sets—the laundromat, the hardware store, and the lemonade stand—at the same time. Instead of shooting the sequence in entirety, it was broken down into three parts. Dividing the sequence was possible because each white background resembled the others regardless of where in the studio it was taped. The opening speech, for instance, was taped on the empty space stage before any other scenery was set. By having the spokesman walk camera left away from where he delivered the opening speech in front of a white background and into the next scene from a white background camera right, a smooth bridge is achieved. The next step of the sequence included the first two locations illustrated in the following diagram:

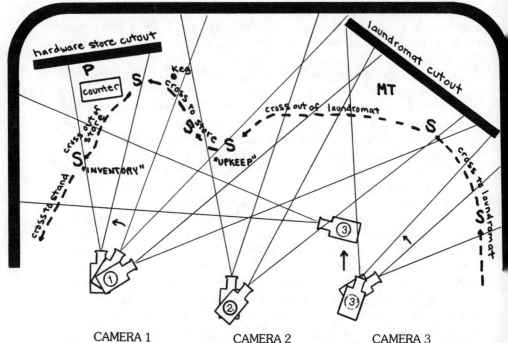

CAMERA 1	CAMERA 2	CAMERA 3
2-shot of MT and S. Pan with S as he enters store. Master store scene with 2-shot.	2-shot favoring MT. Pan with S as he exits laundromat.	MCS of S as he enters laundromat. Pan with S and widen to master laundromat scene. MS of S at end of hardware scene.

The diagram presents a top view of the studio. The spokesman travels camera left along the dotted line into the laundromat set. "MT" represents Mrs. Thorne while "S" refers to the spokesman. Notice that as the spokesman crosses out of the laundromat, he moves in front of the white cyclorama. It isn't until he continues over to the hardware store that he returns to a scenic background. Here, the spokesman shares a scene with "P" or Peterson. As the spokesman leaves the hardware store, he enters another white area.

The second diagram shows how the last portion of the sequence was covered. The hardware store set was shifted from the left to the right side of the studio. The spokesman repeated the action at the end of the first diagram by walking out of the hardware store at approximately the same angle in the second diagram as the first. He then moves

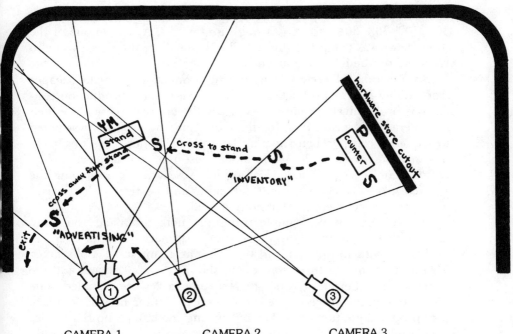

CAMERA 1	CAMERA 2	CAMERA 3
Wide master end of hardware store. Pan with S as he exits. Continue pan CL to lemonade stand. Master 2-shot scene. Pan with S as he exits stand to end.	2-shot favoring YM.	CU of YM at beginning of lemonade stand scene.

over to a white area where he says "inventory" before continuing further camera left to the lemonade stand. Against the lemonade stand background, the spokesman and Young Man, abbreviated "YM," share a scene. After the scene, the spokesman exits to the white background for "advertising" and then out of frame camera left.

To capture the action on tape, three cameras were used simultaneously. The continuity records in our example were altered slightly to help illustrate our points, but they still reflect the actual taping. The three camera signals were fed through an SEG to four videotape recorders. One of the four VTRs recorded the master line feed and three recorded slaves. The signal from camera one was recorded on iso VTR #1 and the corresponding videotapes were numbered 101, 102, 103, 104 and so on. The signal from camera two was recorded from iso line #2 onto slave tapes numbered in the two hundreds such as 201, 202,

203, 204 and so on. Camera three's signal went to slavetapes numbered 301, 302, 303, 304, etcetera through iso line #3. Any time one of the three views was being fed through the master line, the signal was also recorded on the iso simultaneously.

Even with a full crew, editing during production is usually cheaper than editing in post production. For our project, post production editing was prohibitively expensive so nearly the entire project was edited in-camera. This meant that, for the most part, the program was taped in sequence except when shooting later saved money. Inserting pick-ups in post, for example, made more sense than trying to repeat an entire scene. Post production editing was reserved for assembing the selected takes as well as general tightening and perfecting. The script supervisor's notes were used as editing guides.

Notice how on the sample continuity notes on page 185, only camera three was used for the opening speech. Its signal was recorded on both the master and the iso. The script supervisor's notes indicate that camera three was a long shot of the spokesman, and the scene was numbered 1. Notice that no time codes are included. The time codes on this project were laid in after the taping in order to make post production editing possible, but during the taping, no time codes were available. The script supervisor had to devise a system to identify each segment of tape without using time codes. This script supervisor assigned scene and take numbers. Notice that every take is lined unlike film notes where one line represents all takes of the same set-up. The notes at the right margin identify what's on the iso. In our case, the signal from camera three was isolated as well as recorded on the program, while cameras one and two were shut off.

Just as in film, the opposite side of the script page for this project was reserved for editorial notes. The results of the taping were recorded in the same manner as a comparable film form in the scene, take, and time columns. The columns for "in" and "out" refer to time codes and were left blank for now. The scene description applies to the action of the line feed only. By looking at the "cam/reel" column, an editor can determine on which reels the action was recorded.

For our scene #1 example, take #1 was erased or "burned" due to two glitches. Erasing tape during production is rare, but this company knew that the take was unusable. Bad takes are generally saved in case, for some unforeseen reason, they will be needed. Erasing and re-recording over tape increases the likelihood of tape imperfections.

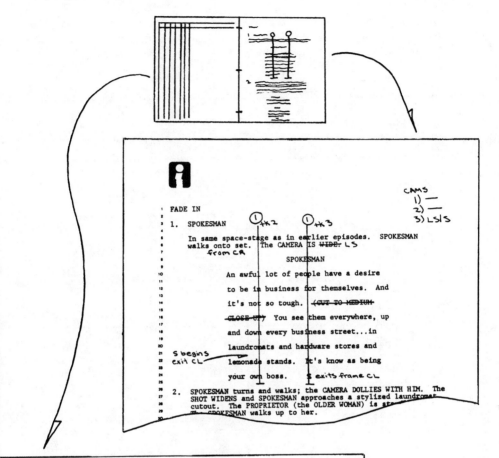

FADE IN

1. SPOKESMAN ① +K 2   ① +K 3

CAMS
1) ‾
2) ‾
3) LS/S

In same space-stage as in earlier episodes. SPOKESMAN
walks onto set. The CAMERA IS ~~WIDE.~~ LS
from CR

SPOKESMAN

An awful lot of people have a desire

to be in business for themselves. And

it's not so tough. ~~(CUT TO MEDIUM~~

~~CLOSE UP)~~ You see them everywhere, up

and down every business street...in

laundromats and hardware stores and

S begins
exit CL   lemonade stands. It's know as being

your own boss. *S exits frame CL*

2. SPOKESMAN turns and walks; the CAMERA DOLLIES WITH HIM. The
SHOT WIDENS and SPOKESMAN approaches a stylized laundromat
cutout. The PROPRIETOR (the OLDER WOMAN) is st...
SPOKESMAN walks up to her.

TITLE _FM 1   segment 8_ page _1_

SCENE	CAM/REEL	IN	OUT	TAKE	TIME	ACTION
1	301			1		n.g. 2 glitches, burned
	P1			②	:25	keep
				③	:26	minimal dropout on line feed. Iso Somewhat cleaner
						2/24 PROGRAM ACTION: LS/Spokesman cam 3 only. Spokesman enters CR. Opening DIAL. in front of white b.g. EXITS CL

The second portion of the sequence was far more complicated than the first because all three cameras were used simultaneously. The master program was assembled by switching between the three signals.

TITLE _FMI segment 8_ page _1_

SCENE	CAM/REEL	IN	OUT	TAKE	TIME	ACTION
1	301 P1			1		n.g. 2 glitches, burned
				②	:25	keep
				③	:26	minimal dropout on line feed. I so Somewhat cleaner 2/24 PROGRAM ACTION : LS/Spokesman cam 3 only. Spokesman enters CR. Opening DIAL. in front of white b.g. Exits CL
2	101 201 301 P1			①	:45	cut to cam 2 at keg business = slightly late. Director wants to cut when S starts cross from inside store
				②	:48	S somewhat dark as he crosses to hardware store, but director prefers this version to pickup 2/24 PROGRAM ACTION: S enters white frame. Cam widens to 2 shot/ S + MT. DIAL. MT writes check, hands it to S. S exits laundromat, holds up check to CAM + says "upkeep" S picks up kegs + wheels them CL to hardware store. DIAL. P writes him a check. S exits store, stops, holds up check to CAM + says "inventory". S exits CL.

Although the editorial form is handled in the same manner as scene one, the lined side requires additional information. The continuity records should reflect the iso. On line 33, for instance, camera view three widened from a medium close shot of the spokesman to a master of the laundromat scene. The continuity notes indicate the change.

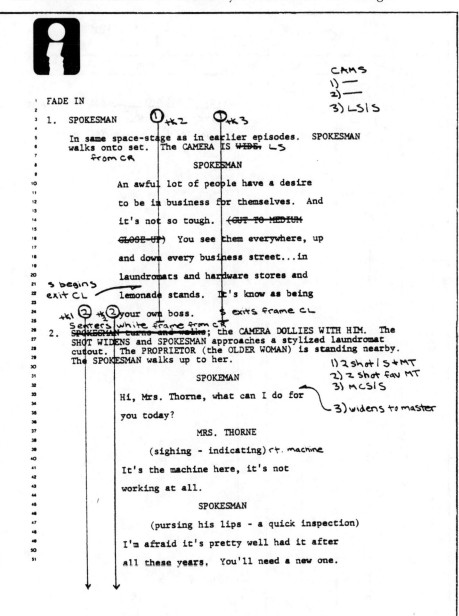

On the next page, camera two switched from a two-shot favoring Mrs. Thorne to a pan following the spokesman's exit toward the laundro-mat. After the spokesman said "upkeep" and began his cross, camera

TITLE __F M 1 segment 8__   page __2__

SCENE	CAM/ REEL	IN	OUT	TAKE	TIME	ACTION
2A	101 201 301 P1			①	:15	2124 PROGRAM ACTION : pickup for scene 2. Cross after check to "inventory." Director prefers 2 to 2A

two shut off. Camera one switched to a two-shot favoring the spokesman on line 25 from a fifty-fifty two-shot. With these notations, the
editor should be able to determine what's on the iso at any given moment.

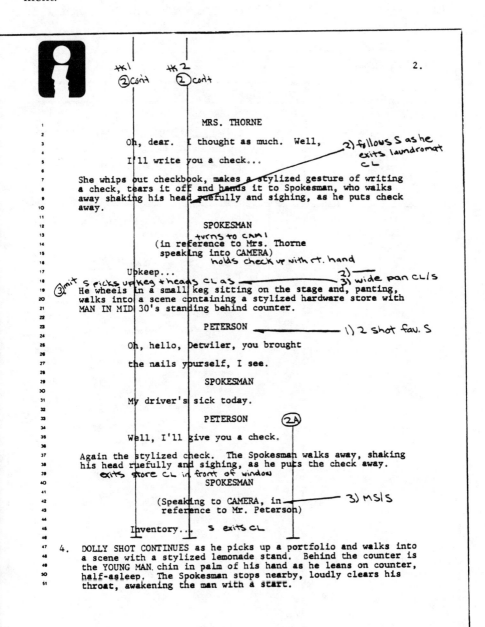

The third portion of the sequence numbered scene 4 also was covered from three contrasting views. The continuity notes indicate where each iso camera switched to a new angle. These notes help the editor determine alternatives if something goes wrong with the program. Because scene 4 overlaps scene 2, its camera switching notes had to be distinguished.

TITLE FM1 segment 8 _____ page 2 _____

SCENE	CAM/REEL	IN	OUT	TAKE	TIME	ACTION
2A	101 201 301 P1			①	:15	2124 PROGRAM ACTION: Pickup for scene 2. Cross after check to "inventory." Director prefers 2 to 2A
4	101 201 301 P1			①	:45	edge of hardware store in frame at end of shot
				②	:45	burn iso on 2nd take 2124 PROGRAM ACTION: S takes check from P, exits CL from hardware store, holds check up to CAM for "inventory." S walks CL, takes portfolio out of air, continues CL to lemonade stand, hands portfolio to BYM. BYM wakes, then looks at contents. DIAL. Through check business. S walks to CAM, holds check up: "Advertising" + exits CL white frame.

On line 42, the switching note, "3) MS/S," refers to scene 2 and pickup 2A. The note, "1) pans CL to stand—2 shot," applies to scene 4. The action in the end of scene 2 also differed from the action in the beginning of scene 4. Scene 2 ended with the spokesman exiting the frame camera left while scene 4 began with the spokesman crossing camera left and continuing with the rest of the scene. This distinction must appear in the continuity notes.

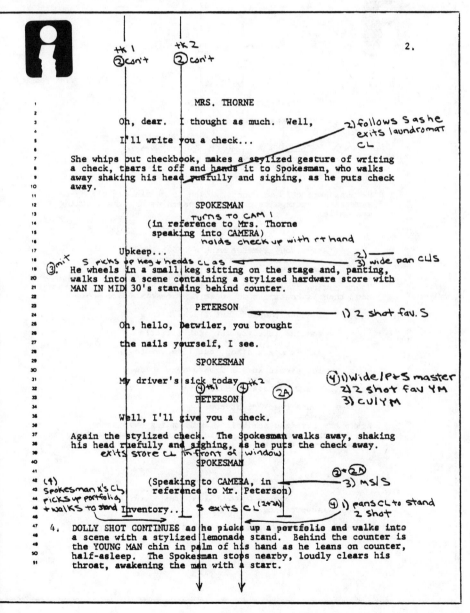

Dialogue deviations from one take to another also should be noted. On line 9 of scene 4, the actor said "Sure did" in take 1 and "You bet I did" in take 2. On line 23, he said "Oh thanks" in take 1 and "Sure thanks" in take 2. Neither deviation merited a retake or pick-up, but the script supervisor supplied the editor with the information anyway.

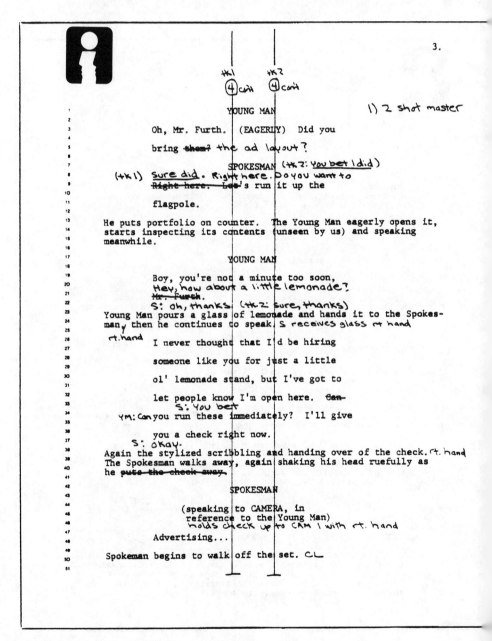

In post production, the editor may find that it's necessary to look beyond the master program to find better coverage options. This is why the continuity notes in our sample devote more attention to the slaves than the program tapes.

The following graphics illustrate how rapidly the program switches.

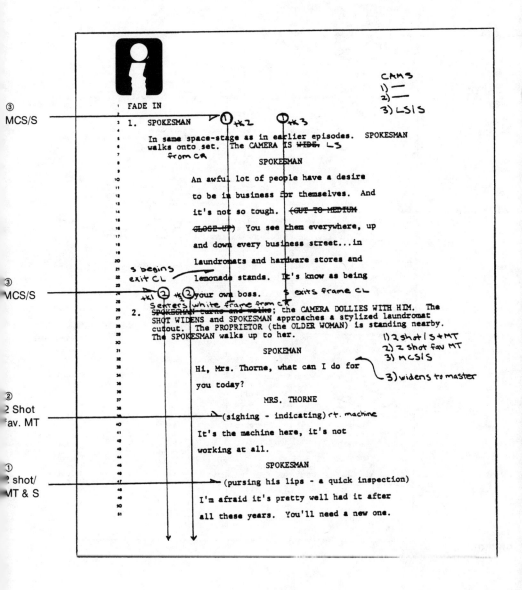

The notes on the left indicate where the program cuts from one view to another. The notes on the script pages mark the camera changes. Trying to observe and note both sets of records would be impossible. No script supervisor would ever have time.

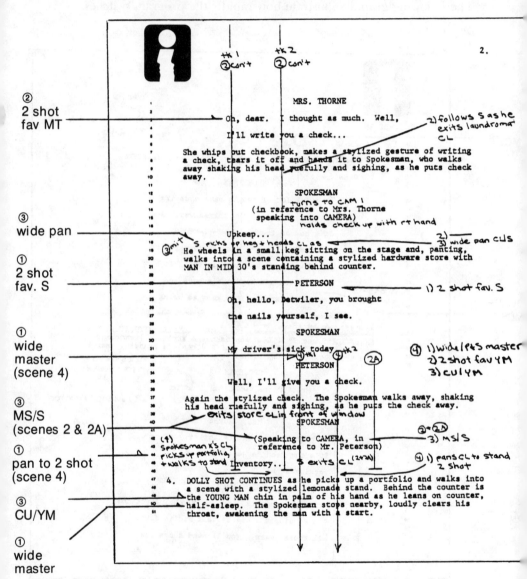

Most video script supervisors concentrate on the iso because the director's script is available as a record of program switching. The continuity script, on the other hand, is the only record of the slaves. It is common practice in video for both the director's script and the continuity script to be used during post production editing.

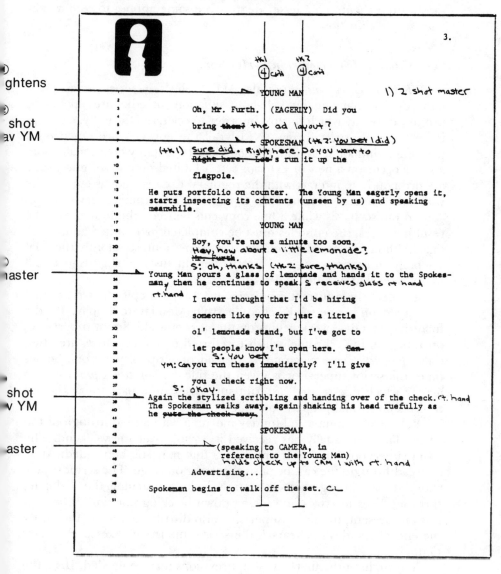

The preceding sample notes merely show one method of keeping continuity records when time codes are added later. There are many others as well. The problem with generalizing about videotape production is that, unlike film, there is no precedent. This seems especially true of industrials where anything goes as long as the finished product satisfies the client. To a lesser degree, the same applies to commercial television production.

Four-Camera Iso Television Series Sample

WKRP in Cincinnati, a popular MTM television series, is representative of how many quality half-hour situation comedies are taped. It is produced weekly which means, in order to operate efficiently, each episode follows a strict format. Nearly all the episodes are taped on a permanent indoor stage with regular characters. Only occasionally does a scene occur on a new or exterior set. A limited number of guest stars are brought in to interact with the regulars. Each episode is taped twice with four cameras. During both tapings, all four camera views are recorded on iso slaves while a line copy cuts between the four. From the resulting tapes, the episodes must be completed in a limited amount of time. Although network mandates vary from month to month, the final assembly must time out to a precise length, usually slightly over 23 minutes, excluding titles and commercials.

To meet these format requirements, a typical episode is rehearsed and taped on a one-week schedule from Monday to Friday. By the following Monday, work begins on the next episode. Script supervisors operating on this schedule, which is referred to as *back-to-back,* are often called *production assistants* or *PAs* instead of script supervisors. Sometimes the script supervisor is given the title *assistant to the producer.* No matter which title is used, a script supervisor on a back-to-back series receives no formal preparation time.

Rehearsals commence Monday morning with a readthrough of the script. The cast usually has received its scripts over the weekend. The script supervisor hands out any scripts that may still be needed. After the readthrough, the cast begins rehearsing on stage. The script supervisor's duties during these rehearsals include watching the dialogue, throwing lines to actors and taking down blocking notation. When extras are present, the script supervisor also distributes release forms. By the end of the day's rehearsal, the script supervisor takes preliminary timings.

Throughout the first day, script revisions may be needed. If so, the script supervisor takes down notes on all desired changes in dialogue as they occur during the rehearsal. These notes are then given to a second production assistant or a secretary who presents the proposed changes to the producers. If the changes are acceptable, the second production assistant types them, and returns copies to the script supervisor.

In order to keep track of the rewrites, a color system is used, not just on *WKRP* but on many films or television projects. New rewrites are printed on different colored papers. Only original pages are white. By the time typical television and film writers have completed all the necessary revisions, a script may include pages in nearly every color. If there were a cheap way of printing white letters on a dark paper, some pages would even be printed on black. The result is called a *rainbow script.*

The script supervisor distributes the rewrites. Sometimes a check list helps ensure that everyone gets their revisions. Other script supervisors write the names of the cast and crew members on the front pages. With a relatively small cast, such as the one on *WKRP in Cincinnati,* neither method is usually necessary. The script supervisor has a fairly easy job distributing the rewrites on the first day of rehearsal and on the days to follow.

The cast continues rehearsing all day Tuesday. The script supervisor performs similar duties to Monday's rehearsal by throwing lines, matching dialogue and recording blocking. At the end of the day, the cast performs a run-through for the producers. During the run-through, the script supervisor records rough timings which will help the producers, director and writers determine what further rewrites are necessary. In addition to noting total scene timings, the script supervisor marks 15-second intervals which will become invaluable at the next meeting later that evening.

Tuesday night, the writers, producers and director meet to finalize rewrites. The script supervisor rarely attends this meeting, but the second production assistant or secretary is present to take notes. Using the script supervisor's continuity notes as a guideline, the script is revised through the course of the evening.

By the next morning, the new scripts are ready for rehearsal. The second production assistant gives typed copies to the script supervisor for distribution. If the changes are extensive, rehearsal begins with another read-through; otherwise, the rest of the day is devoted to rehearsing with the new scripts. Again, the script supervisor watches dialogue, throws lines, records blocking and times scenes. Unlike the earlier timings, Wednesday's timings are usually fairly indicative of the final program. At the end of the rehearsal, the director may want to see the continuity notes or have them copied into the director's script in preparation for Wednesday evening.

Wednesday evening is reserved for planning camera blocking. The director and assistant director together pencil camera angles onto their scripts. *WKRP* scripts are typed in a split-page format which leaves the right hand side free for camera instructions.

The following example is one scene from "The Patter of Little Feet" episode of MTM Productions' television series, *WKRP in Cincinnati.* The episode was written by Blake Hunter. The handwritten notes on the

---

```
#9010 - FINAL                                                    30.
(9/19/79)                                                        (G)


INT. DJ BOOTH - IMMEDIATELY FOLLOWING     200    MED   V         ①
(Venus, Carlson)

(VENUS IS ON THE AIR)

                VENUS

    So, my children, say good-bye

    to the left side of your

    brain -- which keeps telling

    you the rules -- and say hello

    to the right side of your brain

    which keeps telling you to just

    lie back and float with it...
(VENUS HITS HIS CHIMES AND PLAYS A MELLOW CUT)  201  MASTER    ②

SFX: A MELLOW CUT

(CARLSON APPEARS AT THE WINDOW)

(VENUS WAVES HIM IN)

(CARLSON ENTERS, TURNS ON THE LIGHT)

                CARLSON

    Hi, Venus. How's it going?

                VENUS

    I don't know. I just got here.

                CARLSON

    I've been sort of wandering around.  202  C.U. V    ③

                VENUS

    Uh-huh.                             203  C.U. C     ①

                CARLSON

    In a daze, I guess.                 204  C.U. V     ③
```

right side of the page are the camera angles. The first number indicates the shot number. The center note describes the shot composition. The circled number tells which camera is involved. The line points to where the camera switches in.

```
#9010 - FINAL                                              31.
(9/19/79)                                                  (G)

          VENUS
Yeah, how come?└────────   205    MASTER              ②

          CARLSON
Venus?

          VENUS
Yes, sir...

          CARLSON
Do you have any idea how
old my wife is? └────────   206   Tite X₂ V          ④
          VENUS
I beg your pardon? └──────  207   Tite X₂ C          ①
          CARLSON
I'd like a girl, Venus.
          VENUS
We all would, Mr. Carlson.
          CARLSON
Or a boy would be nice. └── 208   C.U. V             ③
          VENUS
Pardon me, sir. └────────   209   C.U. C             ①
          CARLSON
I'd prefer a girl.  But I'd
take a boy.  I don't care.
How 'bout you? └────────    210   C.U. V             ③
          VENUS
Uh..a girl.
```

#9010 - FINAL   32.
(9/19/79)   (G)

                    CARLSON
          Yeah. I'm not really choosy
          though. └─────────────   2ll   X₂ V   ④
                    VENUS
          Apparently not.
                    CARLSON
          See, Venus, she knows how
          excited I am about this...
          so even if she were really
          frightened...she wouldn't   2l2   X₂ C   ①
          say. ⌐We're like that, her
          and me. We spend most of
          the time trying to make the
          other one happy. My mother
          says it's not an honest
          relationship, but we like
          it. And we certainly don't
          need a baby. It would just
          be a bonus. └─────────────   2l3   50|50 2shot   ③
          (HE RISES)
          Well, nice speaking with
          you, Venus. └───────────   2l4   MASTER   ②
                    VENUS   tighten on exit
          Nice speaking with you, sir.
          (CARLSON EXITS)
                    (MORE)

```
#9010 - FINAL                                              33.
(9/19/79)                                                  (G)


                    VENUS (CONT'D)

            Well, no mental problems

            there...

      CUT TO:
```

The rest of the script is broken down in the same way. By the end of the evening, a complete shooting script is ready for Thursday.

Thursday's rehearsal is devoted to camera blocking. Throughout the day, the cast walks through the action while stopping and starting frequently to set the cameras. Generally speaking, the cameras remain in more or less the same physical spot of the studio but their focus and angles are constantly changing. During this rehearsal, the script supervisor usually can't make extensive camera blocking notes because the iso cameras are not set yet. At the end of the day, the cast performs on camera for the producer. Although the cameras do not record the performance, the producers can watch a live transmission on the studio monitors. The script supervisor records accurate timings of this run-through. These timings are of key concern before the cast and crew move into Friday.

Friday begins with a late call. Starting in the afternoon, the entire episode is blocked and taped in sequence without an audience. The taping serves as a dress rehearsal for the evening performance, and gives both the actors and the crew a sense of continuity. The iso camera action is set between the assistant director and camera operators during the taping. Pick-ups are shot as the need arises while the actors are still dressed and in the mood. Time-consuming set changes are avoided by taping pick-ups in sequence. With no audience present, the director can repeat a scene as many times as desired. The dress provides at least one complete taping of the program without the pressure of an audience. This is where *WKRP in Cincinnati* differs from many other popular situation comedies.

Most situation comedies tape the dress in front of an audience as well as the evening air performance. The aim is to shoot straight through with all cameras. When a mistake occurs and the director doesn't stop, the script supervisor marks the spot carefully for a pick-up. Sometimes the pick-up is taped in front of the audience to save time. If it's getting late, the pick-up is taped after the audience leaves. This is an individual choice on the part of the director and producers depending on the atmosphere of the audience. Generally speaking, younger audiences or a group of tourists tend to be more responsive to watching multiple retakes and pick-ups. There are also instances where no fluffs happen but the director feels dissatisfied. These problems are most often corrected after the audience has left, and they are referred to as retakes rather than pick-ups.

WKRP in Cincinnati avoids many problems by taping the dress without an audience. By the air performance, the pressure is diminished because the cast and crew know they have one complete show in the can. The producers feel that by reducing this pressure, the actor and crew performances tend to be better in front of the live audience.

Using the *WKRP in Cincinnati* system, the afternoon runs pretty much the same from episode to episode. The script supervisor sits in the control booth at the director's side. All crew members in the booth, including the script supervisor, watch the action on monitors. The script supervisor's monitors have character generators so the time codes can be read directly off the screens. This eliminates the need for excessive communication with the video engineers. The only information that the script supervisor needs from the video engineers is notification when a reel has been changed. On a half hour show such as *WKRP Cincinnati,* the engineers usually use a 90- or 60-minute load which enables them to record an entire session on one reel. For the afternoon taping, camera one signals go to reel 11, camera two signals go to reel 12, camera three signals go to reel 13, camera four signals go to reel 14 and the program signals go to reel 10. If the reels are switched, then the signals would go to reels 21, 22, 23, 24 and 20 respectively. The script supervisor only records the time codes and reel identification numbers. Unlike film, the script supervisor never assigns shot numbers.

The following pages are the continuity notes from the afternoon taping.

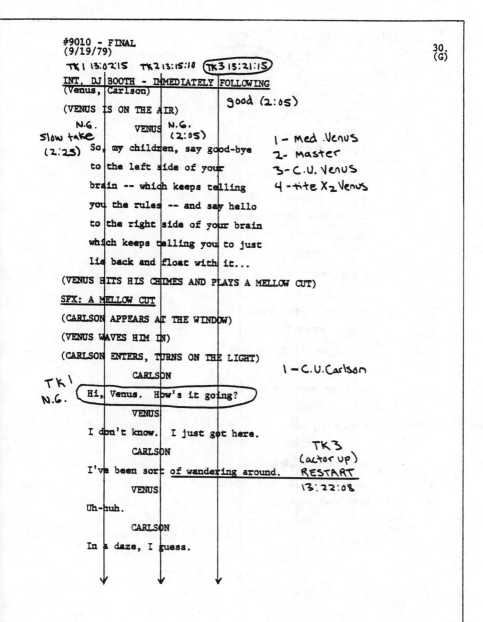

#9010 - FINAL
(9/19/79)

30;
(G)

TK1 13:02:15   TK2 13:15:10   (TK3 13:21:15)

INT. DJ BOOTH - IMMEDIATELY FOLLOWING
(Venus, Carlson)

good (2:05)

(VENUS IS ON THE AIR)

N.G.   VENUS   N.G.
slow take   (2:05)
(2:25)   So, my children, say good-bye
         to the left side of your
         brain -- which keeps telling
         you the rules -- and say hello
         to the right side of your brain
         which keeps telling you to just
         lie back and float with it...

1 - Med .Venus
2 - Master
3 - C.U. Venus
4 - tite X2 Venus

(VENUS HITS HIS CHIMES AND PLAYS A MELLOW CUT)

SFX: A MELLOW CUT

(CARLSON APPEARS AT THE WINDOW)

(VENUS WAVES HIM IN)

(CARLSON ENTERS, TURNS ON THE LIGHT)

                    CARLSON

1 - C.U. Carlson

TK1
N.G.   Hi, Venus. How's it going?

                    VENUS

         I don't know. I just got here.

                    CARLSON

         I've been sort of wandering around.   RESTART

TK3
(actor up)

13:22:08

                    VENUS

         Uh-huh.

                    CARLSON

         In a daze, I guess.

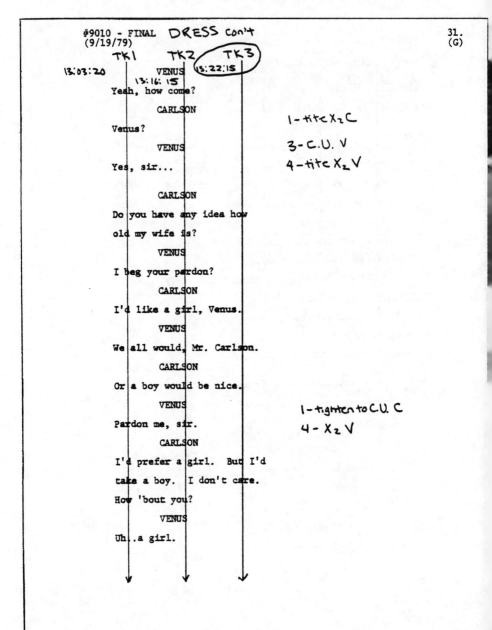

#9010 - FINAL **DRESS** con't
(9/19/79)

TK1   TK2   TK3

13:03:20   VENUS   13:22:15
                13:16:15
          Yeah, how come?

                CARLSON

          Venus?   1-tite X₂ C

                VENUS   3-C.U. V

          Yes, sir...   4-tite X₂ V

                CARLSON

          Do you have any idea how
          old my wife is?

                VENUS

          I beg your pardon?

                CARLSON

          I'd like a girl, Venus.

                VENUS

          We all would, Mr. Carlson.

                CARLSON

          Or a boy would be nice.

                VENUS   1-tighten to C.U. C

          Pardon me, sir.   4-X₂ V

                CARLSON

          I'd prefer a girl. But I'd
          take a boy. I don't care.
          How 'bout you?

                VENUS

          Uh..a girl.

                                          31.
                                          (G)

#9010 - FINAL DRESS con't
(9/19/79)

32.
(G)

TK1 13:03:50   TK2   TK3 13:22:45
                13:16:45

         CARLSON

Yeah. I'm not really choosy   1-X₂C

though.

         VENUS

Apparently not.

         CARLSON

See, Venus, she <u>knows</u> how

excited I am about this...

so even if she were really

frightened...she wouldn't

say. We're like that, her

and me. We spend most of

the time trying to make the   TK2-AUDIO W.G

other one happy. My mother

says it's not an honest

relationship, but we like

it. And we certainly don't

need a baby. It would just

be a bonus.

(HE RISES)

Well, nice speaking with

you, Venus.

         VENUS   2- Master tightens
                                on exit

Nice speaking with you, sir.

(CARLSON EXITS)

         (MORE)

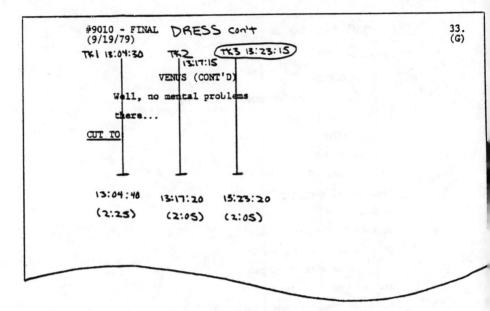

These notes differ from our earlier video example in two basic ways. First, the script supervisor doesn't rely on an editorial form for take-result information. Notes such as "n.g. Carlson's first line" are added right onto the lined page. Secondly, all tape units are identified by the time code numbers. As mentioned before, time codes correspond to actual time of day so all iso and program tapes that run simultaneously are identified by the same codes. Even frame numbers correspond to actual time; but unfortunately, frames change at such a fast rate that they can't be read while taping. For the purposes of the continuity records, frames are left off.

Time codes serve other functions in addition to supplying identifications. Instead of running the stopwatch, a script supervisor can time a scene by substracting the starting time code from the final code. Take one ended on 13:04:40 and began at 13:02:15. This means that it ran two minutes and 25 seconds. A third advantage is that management can determine how efficient the taping went by studying the time codes. Take one began at 13:02:15 or about one o'clock. Take three finished at 13:23:20 or before one-thirty. Such information is comparable to the data supplied by a script supervisor on the film daily production report.

Some script supervisors use the opposite side of the lined page to duplicate the iso information in the right margin. This method provides an at-a-glance reference to where each camera is focused at all times. Although the system provides some advantages, it is not used by

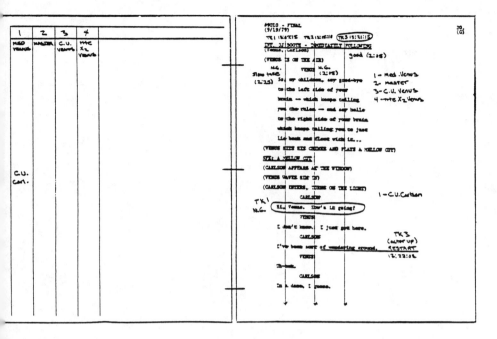

the majority of video script supervisors.

Friday evening, the entire episode is taped for a final time in front of a live audience. The script supervisor's procedure remains the same as in the afternoon. The script supervisor sits in the booth next to the director and records the action from the monitors. The taping starts at 7:00PM and is usually finished by 8:30. The entire show is taped in sequence with identical camera coverage. Only rarely does the camera blocking change between shows. The main difference between the afternoon and evening tapings is that the evening's show includes audience reaction.

The audience affects the taping in two ways. To a certain extent, the performances are altered because actors naturally tend to play off audience response. The audience has an even more obvious effect on the sound tracks. Audience reactions are recorded separately from the performance so that the two can be mixed to an appropriate balance in post production. Despite the separation, there is always an unavoidable amount of bleed-through. Both the differences in sound track and subtle performance result in a distinct tonal difference between the afternoon and evening tapings.

The script supervisor records the continuity notes for the evening's taping on the same script page as the afternoon's records. The right hand side of the page is reserved for the evening or "Air" lines. Air records are sometimes further distinguished from the dress records by using a color system which we will go into later [See pg 268 "Other Scripting Styles"]. For now, the records are kept in one color and they appear as follows:

Notice how the opposite side of the script page is blank for pick-up notes. Unlike the dress where the director can start and stop at will, pick-ups and restarts are used sparingly during the air performance. If

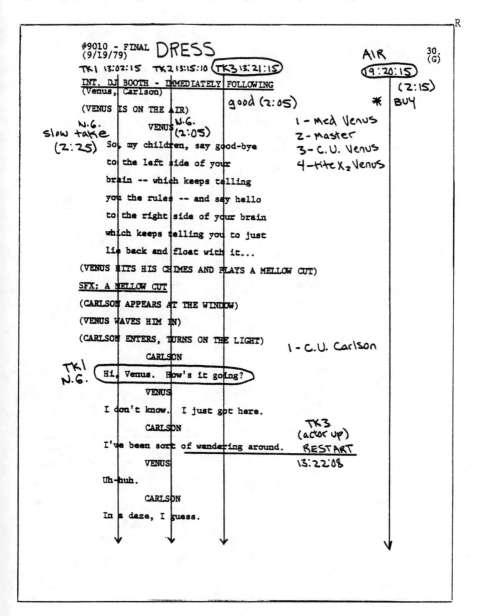

an acceptable shot can be found in one of the afternoon takes, then the air pick-up usually isn't taped. At the bottom of page 31, the director decided that a pick-up of Carlson's line was unavoidable.

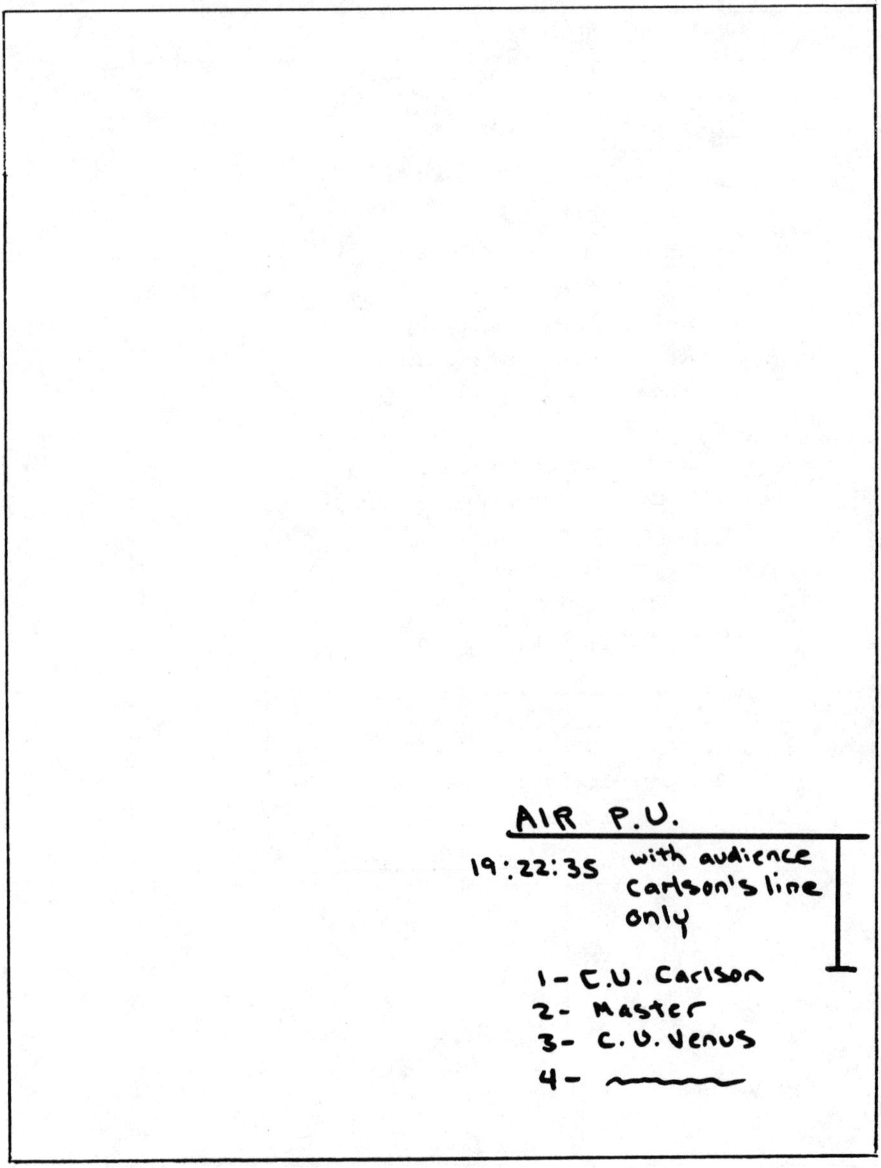

AIR P.U.

19:22:35   with audience
           Carlson's line
           only

1- C.U. Carlson
2- Master
3- C.U. Venus
4-

Only three of the four cameras were used to cover the pick-up. Running the fourth camera would be pointless because it focuses on Venus.

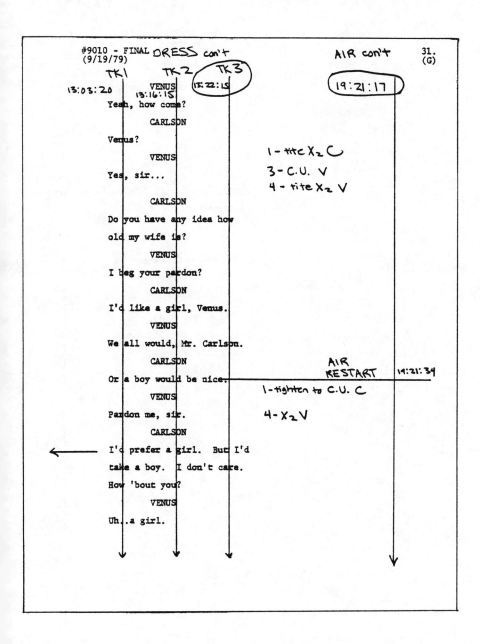

In comparison, the pick-up on the next page was taped with all four cameras because both characters were integrally involved. The latter method is more common. Both pick-ups were taped directly following

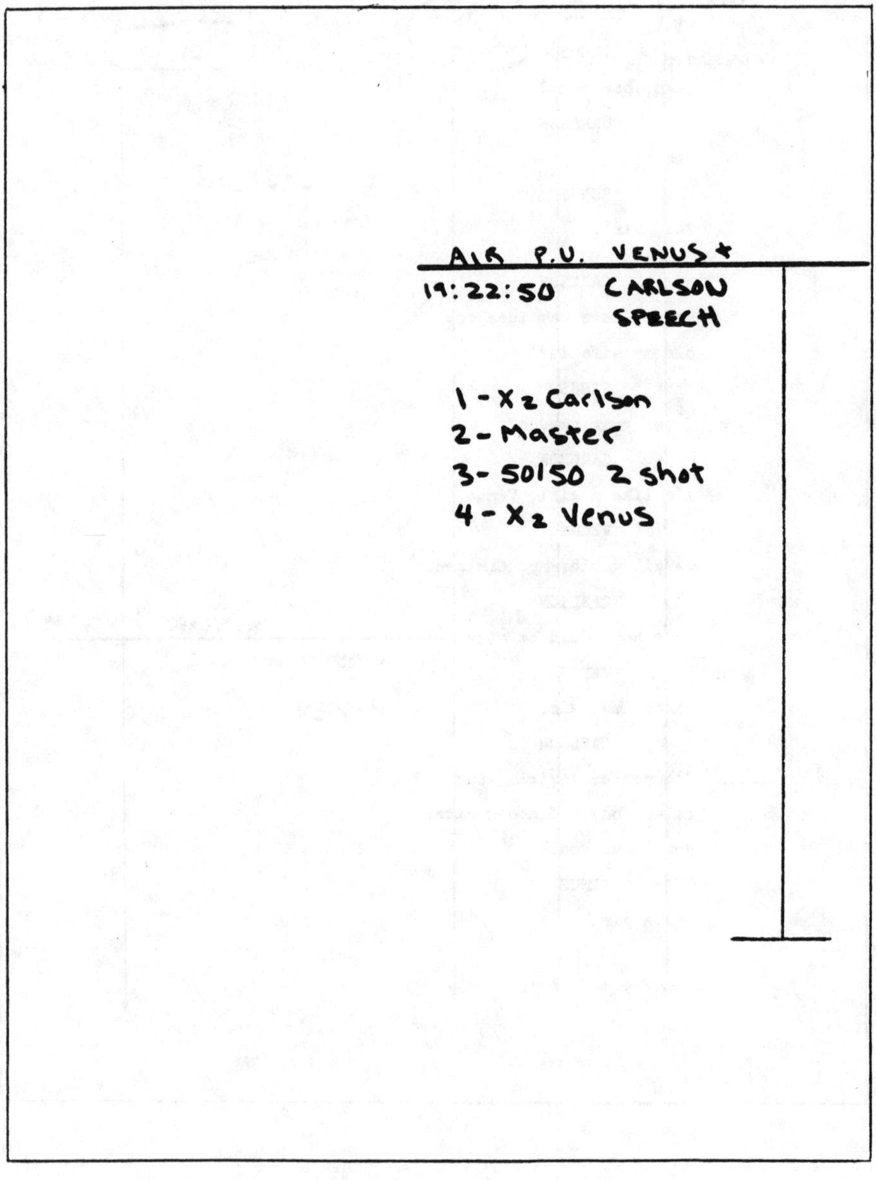

AIR P.U. VENUS +
19:22:50   CARLSON
                SPEECH

1 - X₂ Carlson
2 - Master
3 - 50/50 2 shot
4 - X₂ Venus

the scene which accounts for the short, five minute gap, between the ending air time code and the beginning pick-up codes.

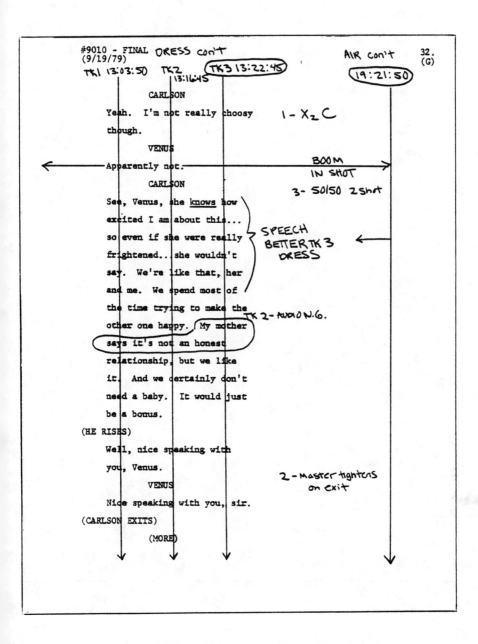

Whenever the evening's blocking fails to match the afternoon's blocking, the performance is seldom interrupted. Instead, the script supervisor merely notes the discrepancy.

In our example, the script supervisor comments that Venus' prop was missing at the air take. The director decided not to shoot a pick-up because the missing prop made no significant difference.

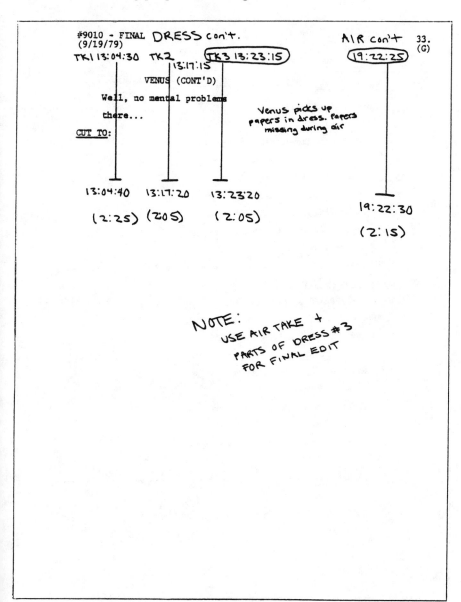

By the end of Friday evening, all taping is completed, but the script supervisor has one more script to line. Saturday morning, the director and editor view the tapes using the continuity records and the direc-

```
#9010 - FINAL                                                    30
(9/19/79)                                                        (G)
          AIR 19:20:15
INT. DJ BOOTH - IMMEDIATELY FOLLOWING └── 200    MED  V      ①
(Venus, Carlson)

(VENUS IS ON THE AIR)

          VENUS

So, my children, say good-bye

to the left side of your

brain -- which keeps telling

you the rules -- and say hello

to the right side of your brain

which keeps telling you to just

lie back and float with it...
                DRESS +K3 13:22:05
(VENUS HITS HIS CHIMES AND PLAYS A MELLOW CUT) └── 201  MASTER   ②

SFX: A MELLOW CUT

(CARLSON APPEARS AT THE WINDOW)

(VENUS WAVES HIM IN)

(CARLSON ENTERS, TURNS ON THE LIGHT)

          CARLSON

Hi, Venus.  How's it going?

          VENUS

I don't know.  I just got here.

          CARLSON
          AIR 19:21:20
I've been sort of wandering around. └── 202    C.U. V      ③

          VENUS

Uh-huh. └──────────────────────── 203    C.U. C      ①

          CARLSON

In a daze, I guess. └──────────────── 204    C.U. V      ③
```

tor's shooting scripts as guides. The script supervisor is present as they select the preferred takes. The script supervisor lines the assistant director's script which includes camera instructions. The time codes are

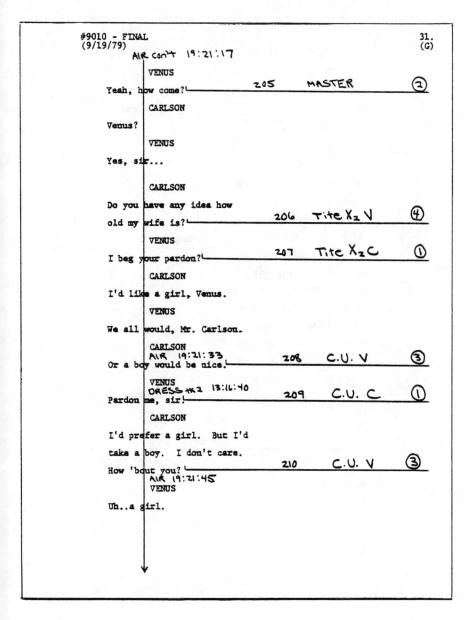

#9010 - FINAL   31.
(9/19/79)   (G)
                    AIR cont 19:21:17

                    VENUS
Yeah, how come?└─────────────── 205   MASTER   ②

                    CARLSON
Venus?

                    VENUS
Yes, sir...

                    CARLSON
Do you have any idea how
old my wife is?└────────────── 206   Tite X₂ V   ④

                    VENUS
I beg your pardon?└───────────── 207   Tite X₂ C   ①

                    CARLSON
I'd like a girl, Venus.

                    VENUS
We all would, Mr. Carlson.

                    CARLSON
                    AIR 19:21:33
Or a boy would be nice!└────────── 208   C.U. V   ③

                    VENUS
                    DRESS #K2 13:16:40
Pardon me, sir!└──────────────── 209   C.U. C   ①

                    CARLSON
I'd prefer a girl. But I'd
take a boy. I don't care.
How 'bout you? └──────────────── 210   C.U. V   ③
                    AIR 19:21:45
                    VENUS
Uh..a girl.

used to identify each selected take. The reels are distinguished by the labels, "dress take 2" or "dress take 3." In our example, most of the final program was selected from the air take. A few shots were pulled

---

#9010 - FINAL   32.
(9/19/79)   (G)
        AIR con't 19:21:50

                │ CARLSON
Yeah.   I'm not really choosy
though.   │   211   X₂ V   ④
                │ DRESS tk.3 13:16:48
                │ VENUS
Apparently not.
                │ CARLSON
See, Venus, she knows how
excited I am about this...
so even if she were really
frightened...she wouldn't   212   X₂C   ①
say. We're like that, her
and me. We spend most of
the time trying to make the
other one happy. My mother
says it's not an honest
relationship, but we like
it. And we certainly don't
need a baby. It would just
be a bonus.   213   50/50 2shot ③
(HE RISES)
Well, nice speaking with
you, Venus.   214   MASTER   ②
                │ AIR 19:22:19   tighten on exit
                │ VENUS
Nice speaking with you, sir.
(CARLSON EXITS)
                │ (MORE)

out of dress take 3 as anticipated, but one short scene numbered 209 unexpectedly had to be retrieved from dress take #2. After the takes are chosen, the script supervisor's job is done.

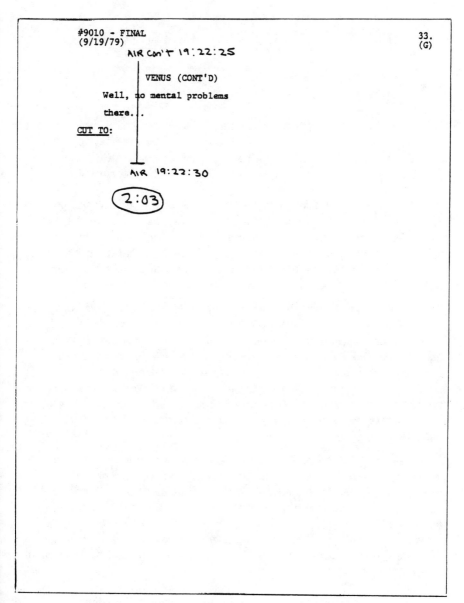

THELMA PREECE INTERVIEW

While the other interviewed filmmakers have expressed their opinions about qualities desirable in script supervisors, our final interview speaks from a different point of view. Thelma Preece spent more than 30 years representing script supervisors. We'll allow her to explain her background herself.

PREECE: When I first began working for the script supervisors' guild in 1937, there had been no paid employees. The elected secretary took notes while the elected president concentrated mostly on negotiating. This arrangement soon had to cease. Both were working script supervisors and they didn't have the time to handle the work as well as their other jobs. As a result, it became necessary to hire a business representative.

Previously, I had taught shorthand and typing in the Hollywood Secretarial School until I married. I was busy raising children when my neighbor, Trudy Wellman, approached me. Trudy Wellman was the first president of the Script Supervisors' Guild. She knew of my teaching and shorthand experience and she asked if I would be interested in working for the Guild. She also understood that, having two children, I didn't want to go out of the home to work. They didn't have an office so it worked out well. I was able to do most of the work at my house. It was a part-time job in the beginning, but only for a while.

It had never occurred to those first elected officers how much would be involved. They didn't understand, for example, that a clearing house to locate script supervisors would be needed. Producers who wanted to hire script supervisors needed a list of available people with a description of their backgrounds. Naturally, this involved longer hours for me. Eventually, we were able to rent an office, and they were able to pay me a small salary. The salary and responsibilities increased, and I became the business manager for the next 32 years.

STUDENT: As the script supervisors' business manager for such a long period, you must have witnessed first-hand the evolution from a small guild to a member of one of the largest entertainment unions. Can you give us a little background on how it all began?

PREECE: *Trudy Wellman was working as a secretary at Paramount and RKO for $25 or so a week when someone asked her if she would like to go down to the set and take notes. They would pay her $27 a week, which was a good increase in salary in those days. She accepted the job. There was no formula for the work at the time. The emergence of a script supervisor was born of necessity.*

Just as the emergence of script supervisors was born of necessity, so was the need for a guild. Trudy Wellman, Meta Stern, Babs Hoagland, Rose Loewinger and a few of the other women who were active at the time began to feel the need of a contract with the producers. They simply realized that they had no protection or unity. In the beginning, they met in each other's homes to discuss the possibility of formulating a guild. They decided that, for their own protection, they would officially unite in an attempt to keep their salaries at a certain standard. They all agreed not to work for less than $55 a week. If a studio said to a script supervisor, "I can get plenty of others for $50 so I won't pay you $55," that script supervisor would refuse the job. When the studio called the next script supervisor, he or she would also insist on $55. As the studio went down the list of candidates, they realized that the script supervisors had established $55 as their minimum rate. Observing the $55 minimum would give the script supervisors a basis from which to negotiate in the future.

I remember when we finally got the contract up to $75 a week, and some of the women claimed that $75 was a sufficient salary for the job. They felt that, if they tried for more money, the men were going to want their jobs— $75 in those days was enough to support a wife, so they'd better stop before their job looked too inviting to the men.

STUDENT: *Can you tell us about the first male script supervisor?*

PREECE: *No, because there has been a misunderstanding through the years. I have heard so many of the older women say, "We didn't used to have men;" but from the beginning, MGM, for one, hired nothing but male script supervisors.*

It wasn't until the Second World War when someone from MGM first called me to say, "We're losing all of our script supervisors to the war. I guess we're going to have to try female script supervisors. We have no choice." So MGM hired two or three in rapid succession. Much to their surprise, they found the women could do the work just as well. That seemed to break down the barrier. As I started to say a moment ago, the claim that we used to have almost all women was never true. The percentage stayed at about 30 percent men. There might have been a few months when we took in more men than women, but the men often would go on to something else which brought the percentage back. In the early days, very few women went on to anything else. You could count them on the fingers of one hand. Script supervising was usually a dead end for women.

STUDENT: *Since the beginning, how many script supervisors that come to the top of your head went on to become directors?*

PREECE: *Don McDougal who directs* The Dukes of Hazzard, *Les Martinson of* Eight is Enough, *Ken Gilbert who does* Barnaby Jones *and* The Incredible Hulk, *Don Weis directed* Body and Soul, Red Pony *and a number of* M.A.S.H. *episodes. In the early days, Mervyn LeRoy, who directed* Little Women, No Time for Sergeants, Random Harvest, Anthony Adverse *and too many others to mention, boasts he was a script supervisor. And then there is Bernie Kowalski, Bruce Kessler, Richard Michaels, Wally Bennet and Arnold Laven who have all directed a number of features and television. I'm sure there are many more. There were production managers such as Morris Abrams, Herb Coleman and Sam Freedle. Jules Levy went on to produce. And I mustn't forget Michael Preece. My son is directing* Fantasy Island *this week. Just the other day, he went in to watch the shooting because this was his first time with the Fantasy Island company, and the director was Don Weis, one of our former members. It was old home week. Today, there are even more script supervisors becoming directors. Let's see. Some of the more recent ones are Linda Day, Joan Tewkesbury, Richard Kinon, Joanna Lee, Cliff Bole and many others. These, of course, were much later, after the guild was formed. While the early script supervisors were still meeting in living rooms, they decided to form an independent guild; so they hired an attorney, legally formed the Guild and negotiated the first collective bargaining agreement with the producers.*

Unfortunately, those script supervisors were inexperienced in negotiations. They hired an attorney for the specific purpose of drawing up a contract. The salary rate the producers offered was significantly lower than the other film crafts, for the most part. The producers claimed that the script supervisors should be satisfied with the amount offered because it would be increased through the years. Still, you'll never catch up if you start with too low a base. Under normal circumstances, the unions are given a percentage increase. The higher-paid crafts prefer a percentage increase to a dollar increase; for example, a 10 percent increase of $2.00 is worth $.20, but if you're making $1.00 an hour, you're getting only a $.10 increase. The next time you negotiate, the first group gets 10 percent of $2.20, while the second group gets ten percent of $1.10. The gap widens as the years pass. The script supervisors were simply a naive group who accepted the bad counsel of that first lawyer.

STUDENT: *Is that the reason why the script supervisors were, for a long time, one of the lowest paid of all crew members?*

PREECE: *Probably, except for one or two others. It is a sad commentary when the responsibility entailed in this job was no better paid for than that of the janitors (not that there's anything wrong with janitors). Mr. Boren, who was the producers' representative, used to say to me, "Every craft comes in with legitmate arguments from their point of view. It reaches a point where you simply cannot give one union any more than you give the others without creating more problems." I asked if the producers would reconsider, provided the other locals agreed not to invoke the so-called "favored nations clause," and he said I would never get the other locals to agree. In an effort to combat this argument, during the next negotiations, I approached all of the other business agents with a typed statement to the effect that they would not make any kind of protest to the producers if the script supervisors were granted a one-time greater increase than was given to their locals. I knew they understood our position and hoped for cooperation.*

I started with the Teamsters because the Teamsters were strong. Ralph Clare, the Teamsters' representative, said, "Thelma, I wouldn't dream of standing in your way. My people wouldn't care." I said, "Would you be the first to sign?" He responded with, "I'd be glad to," and he did. I went to Herb Aller of the cameramen and John Lehners of the film editors, and right down the list from the highest paid people to the lowest. Finally, I met with the teachers' representative, who said, "My members would have my neck. We're as underpaid as you are, and I wouldn't dream of signing." One other of the underpaid groups refused to sign; nevertheless, I asked for an appointment with Mr. Boren and he read the signatures on my statement with his eyebrows raised. He then looked at the two blanks and said, "You couldn't get these?" I answered, "No, they feel underpaid, too, but I don't think that matters. You can certainly handle them. If necessary, give the teachers a little more too." The teachers represented only a few people but the other represented a good many more. He answered, "Giving three locals more than the other 19 or 20 would be setting a precedent. I can't do it. I'd like to, Thelma, but by the time the news went from mouth to mouth, all hell would break loose." And so we were behind the eight ball. As I look back now, if the first little group had stood firm so that their basic hourly rate was not so low, the percentage increase would not have been so inequitable.

STUDENT: *In the beginning, how many members were there?*

PREECE: *We had a low of about 87 members at one time. It went up to an average of 100 to 125. We didn't have a closed shop; we simply had high standards for entrance. The industry couldn't employ everyone who wanted to be a script supervisor, so we felt the only fair way to handle the problem was to set standards. Apparently, this is no longer possible because of new laws, but that doesn't provide work. I heard, for instance, that this week there are 86 people on the available list. In the old days, that would have been practically the entire membership. When we were a Guild, we tried to keep the membership down to a reasonable number so that the members would have a chance at being employed at least part of the year.*

STUDENT: *How did the Guild end up joining the IATSE union?*

PREECE: *The time came that while there was a good-sized minority who would have liked to remain an independent guild, it wasn't in the cards. We gradually learned that what we were doing was negotiating with the producers after they had finished with the IATSE. No matter what we asked for, we wound up getting exactly what the IA had negotiated. And the IA felt we weren't carrying our share of the weight.*

STUDENT: *Did they force you to join?*

PREECE: *No, we weren't forced. There were some who were bitterly opposed to being swallowed up by the IA. They felt that they had everything that the IA could offer without paying the IA dues. We were a small organization without much money. Obviously, dues would have to be increased in order to pay the per capita dues into the union. But they didn't pressure us in any way. As a matter of fact, when the IA representative spoke to the membership, he said, "We are not seeking you. If you want to join, we'll be glad to have you. We will answer your questions." They explained what membership in the IA meant. Before negotiations started with the producers, there were meetings of the business agents, Teamsters and other unions in which a list of demands were drawn up. The only advantage the IA offered the script supervisors was that the script supervisors would have a voice in those discussions. The outcome of the meeting was that the majority voted to join the IA. Looking back, I think there were a few people who always regretted not remaining as that little independent guild. It was more pleasant, but union business is not a club. I imagine some would say that we didn't gain enough to make all the expense worthwhile. But I think if the same election were held today, the majority would vote to stay in the IA.*

In both of our multiple-camera videotape examples, the script supervisor has had to re-orient his or her thinking from a film projection system to an electrical system. The continuity notes in the preceding pages reflected this difference. While some techniques used for scripting single camera film remained appropriate to scripting videotape, others found no place in the new medium. Yet, the uses of videotape and film are not always mutually exclusive. The advantages of videotape are being applied more and more to film production.

VIDEOTAPE INFLUENCES ON FILM PRODUCTION

As video technology advances, there is an increased desire to make use of video techniques to simplify film production. At the present, few of these systems have succeeded in a commercial way. The majority can only be viewed as experimental, and they usually have proved less economical than the existing film systems. The efforts to integrate film and video, on the other hand, should not be dismissed. There is no question that sooner or later, with further development, video technology will find an integral place in film production. The integration has already taken place with highly effective results in a few limited areas. The first of these systems is called the video tap.

Video Tap

The *video tap* or *video assist* is a small black-and-white video camera which can be mounted on nearly any model film camera. Attached to the prism of a film camera's eyepiece, the video tap captures exactly the same images as the film camera during filming. A cable runs from the tap to a small video cassette recorder. The VCR records the signal on conveniently-sized ¾-inch, ½-inch or even ¼-inch cassettes. Usually, a 9-inch monitor is positioned on the set near the director, but sometimes larger monitors are provided when more people must view the action. These recordings can be viewed during the take or at any time afterwards to check composition and details.

On rare occasions, video taps are used on features as a directing tool, but they are more frequently reserved for commercial production. On a commercial set, the director, clients and agency producers often must view the action simultaneously, [see commercials page 245]. The video monitor allows all of the decision-makers to check the composition of each shot without delaying production by looking through the camera lens. If questions arise regarding how a product was held during a particular take or whether the actor smiled while drinking the product, the cassette can be relayed to settle disagreements. Video taps definitely help simplify production on commercials.

From the script supervisor's standpoint, the video tap is a mixed blessing. While it's helpful to have the monitor available for checking framing, timing and larger physical elements, most details are too unclear for matching. As the film camera's shutter opens and closes, the video monitor flickers. The flickering makes observing most details and nuances on long, full, wide or even medium shots difficult. Although the cassettes are available as a back-up to check continuity problems, a script supervisor should never rely on them. In fact, the video tap technician who helped us research this subject said that in the three years he has worked with video taps, no script supervisor has ever asked to replay a cassette for continuity reasons. Only an inadequate script supervisor would waste time replaying the tapes to confirm information that should already be in the continuity notes.

Using a video tap is one way in which video technology has helped simplify film production. The advantages of tape's immediacy help to avoid costly problems with the film. A second videotape advantage, electronic editing, has also been applied successfully to filmmaking, only this time during post production.

Editing Film on Videotape

Occasionally, film companies transfer film to videotape before editing in order to maintain the quality of film while exploiting the convenience of electronic editing. This method is practiced mostly on film projects in which the end product remains on videotape, such as commercials or television documentaries. Films intended for theatrical release prior to a television sale, or television films released theatrically abroad are rarely edited on tape. Eventually, nearly all films are transferred to videotape before airing on U.S. television. (Some foreign television stations are still geared toward a film chain so their films are never transferred to tape, but this is unheard of domestically.) Because the edited videotape cannot be transferred directly back to a theatrical print without sacrificing considerable quality, most films even partially intended for theatrical release ultimately must be cut on film. What prevents these films from using videotape is that there is no widely accepted way to conform film negative to the corresponding videotape in the U.S.

New editing systems are being developed to provide the missing solution for matching film negative to videotape footage. Currently, when editing a final film, a negative cutter duplicates each cut of the assembled work print by matching the numbers printed on the edge of the film. A picture that has been edited on videotape, instead of on a workprint, has no edge numbers for identifying cuts. By laying an identification track similar to a SMPTE time code on the film optically, identification numbers can be translated into electrical codes and transferred to a video control track. These identifications also could serve to sync dailies automatically. Most editing systems which have been proposed to conform negative to video rely on this sort of solution, but none is commercially perfected yet.

Editing film on videotape has rarely affected the script supervisor's job in the past because it has occurred exclusively in post production. The only difference in continuity involves the timing of commercials, which will be discussed later during Chapter Five, [see commercials page 243]. A recent breakthrough by Francis Ford Coppola threatens to change not only the script supervisor's role on the set, but also the role of all crew members. The Coppola system, although already discontinued, has a much greater potential significance on the future of film production.

The Coppola System

Numerous filmmaking innovations of late have been attributed to Coppola's Zeotrope Studio. The first attempt at combining electronic editing techniques with film production in a grand scale was achieved on Coppola's feature, *One From the Heart*. Before filming *One From the Heart*, the entire picture was shot on videotape with the hope of limiting expensive production costs by virtually cutting the picture before filming.

The screenplay was first fed into a word processor which simplified making deletions, additions and revisions in the script. From this detailed script, sketches were drawn and photographed, and the actors were recorded reading their parts. The videotapes were then compiled into a rough sequential storyboard in order to gain a feeling of the film as a whole. By analyzing the electronic storyboard. Coppola was able to determine which scenes were unnecessary, whether he could avoid building a set and in what ways a scene could play better. All this was accomplished in pre-production in order to improve the movie and to save money.

Next, they rehearsed the entire action on improvised sets while videotaping. The videotapes were assembled, and then shown to the cast and crew. Although only crudely assembled, the videotapes gave them a sense of how the individual pieces of the picture should flow together. Rehearsals were also taped on location in Las Vegas which gave the cast a clear feeling of the environment. (The scenes were later filmed on a soundstage.)

Technical rehearsals for the cast and principal crew came next. Again, the rehearsals were taped to correct story problems, experiment with camera placement, polish acting nuances and accomplish any number of beneficial changes before principal photography. Finally, after all the questions had been worked out, *One From the Heart* was filmed following closely the revised storyboard and script. By using a video tap, monitors were made available on the set for cast and crew as well as for the director. Composition, lighting, in-camera special effects and general performance could all be evaluated immediately.

After filming, the dailies were transferred to color videocassettes. Since video runs at 30 frames per second, a coding system was invented to account for the discrepancy. (This is not true in Europe where 60-cycle power changes the video rate to 25 frames per second.) SMPTE time codes were burnt into the tape along with video frame codes, the corresponding film frames, and also scene, take and reel numbers. The original idea was to edit on tape and cut the film to match. A team of editors worked with a combination of electronic video and traditional film editing equipment. The problem of conforming the negative to the tape became so cumbersome and costly that they were finally forced to abandon the video and cut the picture on a Kem table and a standard moviola.

The pioneering efforts of Coppola should not be viewed in any way as a failure. Even though his experiment proved impractical and prohibitively expensive for most companies due to the excessive lead time required, Coppola's system is a truly revolutionary innovation in its infant stage. It was the first successful step toward a grand-scale integration between video technology and film production. A system such as Coppola's which relies so heavily on preparation time may have been more practical in the early days of the big studios when economic pressures didn't play as active a role as today, but at the time, the necessary video equipment was unavailable. Dismissing Coppola's system on the basis of its shortcomings on *One From the Heart* is like dismissing the early attempts at flying when all the inventors lacked was rip-stop nylon and lightweight aluminum. The early flying machines were not so different from today's hang-gliders.

At present, film production hasn't advanced that far from the early days of the "talkies," outside of special effects. While the equipment goes through constant upgrading, production is slow to follow suit. From computerized film cameras capable of achieving special effects such as the Magicam, to the Movicam which offers digital diagnoses of electrical circuitry malfunctions, to the eventual conversion of optical houses to computer technology, equipment will continue to evolve. Eventually, the script supervisor, together with every member of a film crew, will have to adjust their working methods to accommodate the new technology. What all these innovations have in common is that they are not intended to replace film, but to use the advantage of videotape and computer technology to improve film production.

Our next chapter continues on this line. While the formats discussed more closely resemble a traditional single camera film style, their inherent problems call for specialized scripting techniques.

Chapter Five

Other Scripting Styles

Multiple camera film projects and commercials are usually scripted in standard styles unique to their formats. Specialized production techniques, on the other hand, such as musical numbers, stereo filming, process shooting and cross mediums call for simple variations on the single camera film scripting style. In both cases, the nature of the format or technique ultimately causes problems for the editor if the script supervisor doesn't take appropriate continuity records. How the script supervisor prevents these problems from occurring will be explained in depth as we illustrate several examples of alternative scripting styles.

MULTIPLE CAMERA FILM

The filming of a television show or motion picture often involves more than one camera. In Chapter Three's *Return to Macon County* example, a difficult stunt sequence was shot with two cameras. Dangerous or expensive stunts, action filmed under time limitations such as a sports event, performances in front of live audiences, unpredictable animal action, highly emotional impromptu acting, and the like often utilize multiple-camera filming because pick-ups are difficult or impossible. Our first example presents a popular script notation system designed for three-camera "live" film.

Three-Camera "Live" Film

From the early days of Desilu Productions to the current Paramount Pictures television, the three-camera format has been used on a regular basis to film weekly episodic comedy shows. Paramount Pictures' long-running hit series, *Happy Days*, provides a perfect example. Similar to *WKRP in Cincinnati*, *Happy Days* operates on a one-week schedule. The script supervisor works back-to-back episodes from Monday to Friday. In the early Desilu days, the script supervisor used to work only four days, but now five days is the rule for multiple-camera film. The following is a composite sample of the day-to-day continuity duties on a filmed situation comedy using *Happy Days* episode "No Tell, Motel."

Monday morning, the cast and crew receive their scripts when they meet for the first time. The cast reads through the entire script in the presence of the director, writers, producers and script supervisor. During the read-through, the script supervisor times the script. This timing is turned over immediately to the producer who heads the rewrites. After the read-through, a discussion takes place before dismissing the cast and script supervisor. The writers stay behind to rework the script.

Tuesday morning, the cast and director begin blocking the action. Because the cast is so experienced, their pacing doesn't vary much from this first rehearsal to the final performance. The script supervisor records the timing as well as action, dialogue changes, and rewrite suggestions. By the afternoon, the cast is dismissed, and the script supervisor turns in the proposed changes to the director's secretary. The director's secretary in turn submits the notes to the episode's producer. All approved changes appear on the script revisions delivered to the cast first thing Wednesday.

Wednesday morning, each scene is rehearsed twice. If a guest star has a small part in the episode, the guest star rehearses for the first time Wednesday morning; otherwise, the guest star starts Tuesday. After lunch, the cast runs through the full script for the producers and writers. Up to now, rehearsal of all scenes taking place on one set are finished before moving on to the next set. Starting Wednesday afternoon, all rehearsals are run in sequence. During the runthrough, the producers and writers take notes. A discussion follows, in which requests are made for final changes. The script supervisor's timings are also mentioned. These timings are for the most part definite by now, and they will be of prime importance for rewrite night, Wednesday night. The production secretaries attend the rewrite meetings, leaving the script supervisor free to go home.

Sometime during the evening, Wednesday, the script supervisor prepares a *light plot*. A light plot is a one-page breakdown which lists each scene as day or night and its location. The script supervisor leaves room at the side for lighting and sound details. The locations are identified by letters. Not all letters of the alphabet are used. The reason certain letters are left out is because in the confusion of hurrying to their marks, dolly grips may mistake M for N, E for F, or I for 1. Consequently, dating back to the '50s, someone at Desilu decided to exclude the letters F, I, and N. The following example light plot breaks down our "No Tell Motel" episode.

			Light Plot
PROD. NO.: *170*	TITLE: *No Tell Motel*		
SCENE	SET	DAY/NITE	REMARKS
A	INT. Living Rm.	Nite	
B	INT. Kitchen	Nite	
C	INT. Living Rm.	Nite	
D	INT. Living Rm.	Nite	
E	INT. Arnold's	Day	
H	INT. Motel Rm.	Nite	Light change
J	INT. Motel Rm.	Nite	
K	INT. Motel Rm.	Day	
L	INT. Living Rm.	Day	
M	INT. Living Rm.	Day	Tag

The light plot is turned in early the next morning.

Using the revised scripts, the cast and crew walk through the action in order to set camera blocking Thursday morning. This can take anywhere from a half day to a full day. After the blocking is set, the cast and crew run the show for the producers and writers with the cameras but no film. A list is compiled of angles that can't be covered during the initial performance. Say, for instance, that a section of one scene requires four views when only three cameras are available. The fourth view will have to be picked up later. After the rehearsal, the camera crew goes home while the cast and producers meet to discuss last minute changes.

By Friday morning, a final script is set. The show rehearses from beginning to end in sequence unless there is an obvious reason to do otherwise. At four o'clock that afternoon, the first audience comes in—usually made up of young children and teenagers. The episode is filmed in entirety, and pick-ups are shot whenever possible as the need arises. After the show, the producers and writers who have attended the performance meet with the cast for final revisions. The cast then breaks for dinner before the evening performance.

Friday evening, last minute preparations are usually limited because everything should be ready. The show commences at eight o'clock in front of a live audience. An episode without many wardrobe and set changes runs about one and a half hours while a more complicated episode lasts two hours. Pick-ups are shot in sequence if the show is going smoothly. When a show runs long, pick-ups are shot after dismissing the audience. What is interesting about both tapings is the simplicity of the continuity notes.

At the time the three-camera film scripting technique was devised, an editing machine called the "three-headed monster" was used. The three-headed monster was a moviola that ran three reels of film simultaneously on side-by-side screens. There was no need for any continuity notes to show where a close-up cuts into a master. As a result, the continuity script was usually marked with a single line. If a pick-up was shot, the pickpup added another single line. Today, a script supervisor who is unfamiliar with three-camera film procedure may look at lined script and think the continuity notes are inadequate. What the inexperienced script supervisor fails to realize is that the simple system was devised back in the early days and has survived as the precedent.

Everyone involved on a three-camera film show realizes that the episodes are shot in a specific manner from week to week. The three cameras are labeled A, B, and C. The B camera, or center camera, nearly always shoots wide to master the scene. The outside cameras, A and C, shoot over-the-shoulders, close-ups, or any other view outside of the master. Although the A and C cameras change in composition frequently within one continuous take, the B camera usually remains a master throughout the scene. Keeping this in mind, a continuity script with single lines should be adequate.

Multiple-camera scenes are also numbered differently than for single-camera film or even multiple-camera video. Each shot is identified by the location letter. The first scene that takes place in location L is called L. In the majority of scenes, all three cameras shoot the entire scene through one time, and their combined blocking covers the action sufficiently. For the sake of illustrating typical scripting techniques, we've chosen a scene where a fourth camera view was required.

47.
(L)

L

master

L

INT. CUNNINGHAM LIVING ROOM - DAY

HOWARD AND MARION ARE LISTENING TO JOANIE EXPLAIN HER STORY.

                    JOANIE

        And we kept one foot on the floor at

        all times until Fonzie got there. So

        nothing happened.

                    MARION

        Well, that's good enough for me. Isn't

        that good enough for you, Howard? (TO

        JOANIE) I'm sure that's good enough for

        him, Joanie. So, now that everything

        is all settled down and back to normal,

        I'm going to go start lunch.

SHE EXITS TO KITCHEN.

                    JOANIE

        (HESITANTLY) You're not still angry, Dad?

-L   con't   48.
                                                        (L)

                    HOWARD

          Oh, no... I'm not angry.

               L | JOANIE

          (RELIEVED) Good.

DOORBELL RINGS. JOANIE ANSWERS IT TO REVEAL A MAN FROM
THE PHONE COMPANY.

                    PHONE MAN

          Phone company. Where's the phone you

          want taken out?

                    HOWARD

          It's upstairs.

                    PHONE MAN

          Sure. Upstairs. They're always

          upstairs.

HE EXITS UPSTAIRS.   L2

                    JOANIE   PICK UP

          Dad! I thought you said you believed

          me.

                    HOWARD

          I do. And I'm proud of you for

          behaving the way you did at the motel.

                    JOANIE

          Then why are you having my phone taken

          out?

                    HOWARD

          Because you broke your contract. I

          called the phone company as soon as I

          found out you went out with Chachi.

L con't

L2 con't

49.
(L)

JOANIE

Aw, come on, Dad. I'll make a new

deal. Let me keep my phone and I won't

go out with Chachi for three weeks...

(HOWARD IS SILENT) ... four weeks. Two

months. Come on, Dad.

HOWARD

I've got a better deal. You ever go

to a motel with a guy again and I'll

board up your room with you in it.

JOANIE

(GLAD TO BE ALIVE) That's fair.

HOWARD

I thought you'd go for it.

HE EXITS TO KITCHEN.

FADE OUT.

1^{so}

END OF ACT TWO

In the sample scene, Ll was a tight two-shot of Joanie and the phone man which was not included in the first filming of scene L. During L, camera B shot wide to master most of the action while cameras A and C captured singles of the stars. An additional pick-up was needed to cover problems in the latter half of scene L, and all three cameras were used.

The following editorial form is turned in with the lined script to supply print instructions.

DAILY LOG

SHOOTING DATE_____ DAY_____

TO:_____   FROM: Dottie Aldworth
(EDITORIAL DEPARTMENT)   (SCRIPT SUPERVISOR)
SERIES: Happy Days   PICTURE TITLE: No Tell Motel
                      PRODUCTION NO: 170

SCENE NO.	CAMERA	TAKE	SCENE NO.	CAMERA	TAKE
A	3	1			
A1	A,C	2			
A2	B	1			
B	3	1			
B1	3	1			
C	3	1			
D	3	1			
E	3	1			
E1	B	2			
E2	A	3			
E3	A,C	1			
H	3	1			
J	3	1			
K	3	1			
L	3	1			
L1	B	1			
L2	3	2			
m	3	1			

The marked script, the shot list with print instructions, and the final timings noted at the bottom of each scene on the lined script are turned in to the film editor at the end of the evening. Methods for turning in records differ from show to show, but the *Happy Days* script supervisor leaves hers at the studio gate where the editor comes in the next morning.

In many ways, the scripting of *Happy Days* resembles the scripting of multiple-camera video shows. Scripting multiple-camera film action scenes, on the other hand, more closely resembles the style of single camera film. The following example was taken from the records of a unique picture entitled *Roar*.

Multiple-Camera Action Sample

Many of the scenes in Noel Marshall Production's feature film, *Roar,* were shot with multiple cameras due to unusually complex production conditions. Lions and tigers play integral roles throughout the entire film. A sequence may include as many as 20 large cats at any given time. Sometimes the animals appear alone on the screen, while other times they interact with humans. The difficulty of working with the cats created special requirements which directly affected the script supervisor's job.

Noel Marshall's philosophy departs from that of other animal film directors in that Noel preferred to shoot his film more in the style of a documentary than an average feature. Instead of scripting specific animal action and then training the cats to perform the tasks, Noel Marshall chose a more natural approach. He observed what the animals were capable of untrained, and then integrated their natural tendencies into the story. As a result, the script was constantly revised after filming the sequences. The continuity notes were used as the basis for those revisions.

The following examples are the partial records from a particularly complex scene where a dozen lions interact with one of the film's main characters, John. Four cameras were used for scene 291N to capture contrasting views which could be intercut without a matching problem. If only one camera were used, it would be nearly impossible to get the cats to repeat the action close enough to match the cuts. Scene 291P was shot with only one camera, but it didn't pose as critical a matching problem since the camera was mounted on the handlebars of the motorcycle to focus on John. The final scene in our example, scene 296A, was even more complex. In addition to the problems of controlling the animals, scene 296A also involved a difficult stunt. This time, the action was covered with five cameras rolling simultaneously. Without the use of multiple cameras, filming compatible views would not be possible.

DAILY EDITORIAL REPORT

CAMERA ROLLS:
A 379
B 313-314
C 231-232
D 108-111
E 62
F 11

SOUND ROLLS:
339

PRODUCTION   ROAR

PRODUCER   MARSHALL

DIRECTOR   MARSHALL

SCRIPT SUPERVISOR _____

DATE   11/1/77

1st CALL   7 AM

1st AM SHOT   9:20

LUNCH   NOON

1st PM SHOT   2:15

WRAP   3:30

FINISH   6:00

CAM ROLL	SCENE	TK	SND ROLL	PRINT	TIME	LENS	ACTION
A 379 B 313 C 231 D 108	A,B,C,D 291N						John drives around the yard near the logs chased by the cats.
						60 to 250	A cam N. side of rd. next to lion compound (Allan shooting south. Low (200mm)
						500mm	B cam behind log in front of house (Tar shooting east. Low (500mm)
						30 mm	C cam among the trees by picnic table (Jan shooting south)
						35mm	D cam mounted on handlebars facing forward (remote lockdown (35mm)
		①	WILD 339	all cams	:30 :55		Action repeated because of confusion of cats. John couldn't always make the perfect circle.
D109	D 291 P					35mm	John rides from the garage down into yard, circles, and drives out toward river tree bridge. C.U.
							D cam only mounted on handlebars facing John (remote lockdown / 35mm at 18 FPS because bike running slower)
		1	WILD 339	—	:18		bike stalled as it reached road
		②	WILD 339	D cam	:30		went down road, should have gone south of log in front of the house. Didn't make the circle.
D110		③	MOS	D cam	1:32		MISSLATED AS 296 tk3 but tailslated correctly as D 291 P tk 3. several starts: 1) bike stalled on hill 2) good run 3) good run, did circle twice

DATE 11/1/77

PAGE 2

CAM ROLL	SCENE	TK	SND ROLL	PRINT	TIME	LENS	ACTION
A379 B314 C232 D111 E62 F11	A,B,C,D,E,F 296A						The jump from the roof of the house west side. Porch of roof cheated to hide ramp and include barrel. ALL DIRECTIONS = CR to CL
						110mm	A cam at foot of tree to 2nd floor (Allan. pantilt - 110mm / 35 FPS)
						30mm	B cam in water box facing the house (Eric. lockdown - 30 mm / 35 FPS)
						20mm	C cam on water platform facing house (Tar. low ang. tilt - 20mm / 35 FPS)
						40mm	D cam on roof in SW corner angling toward John breaking through railing (Mark. remote lockdown - 40mm / 46 FPS)
						30mm	E cam on shore east of cement treed. (Steve. Low angle pantilt - 30mm / 34 FPS)
						35mm	F cam in pilings underneath jump (Jan. pan w/ hispeed cam - 35mm / 80 FPS)
		1	WILD 339	–	:15		false start
		②	WILD 339	all cams	:35		Excellent. As John swims back to the house, he is very near the floating rungs of railing. His shirt has torn and shows the wet suit concealed underneath.

REVISED 11/17/77   94A

290   EXT. FRONT OF THE HOUSE--DAY

      Just as John takes off, out the double doors, a full grown male lion jumps
      off the roof onto the moat bridge. The lion hits the bridge only yards in
      front of John as he "roars" out of the house.

291   EXT. THE FRONT YARD--DAY

      He makes it across the high grass in front of the house and up the hill,
      when no less than ten lions come piling out of the windows of the garage
      barely fifty yards ahead of him. John spins the bike around and heads back
      downhill. On his way down, John accidentally jumps the bike over,
      but John is up before the lions can overtake him. They do, however, get
      close enough to engage John and his motorcycle in a mad chase around the
      clearing in front of the house.

      He rides his bike by the front of the house with the pack of lions right
      on his tail. He rides down by the tree bridge and sails across the
      river. He wanders around aimlessly, unable to find help, manages to get lost
      and again is on the house side of the river and he comes barreling along the
      path to the front yard. He spills the bike just before he gets to the moat
      bridge. But again he quickly mounts his bike and is off again, back to the
      house.

292   EXT. THE FRONT OF THE HOUSE--DAY

      As John crosses the yard, Madeline opens the front door.

                              MADELINE
                          John! Hurry!

      John makes the bridge but misses the door forcing him to turn right at the
      porch. Pursued by several lions, he races up the ramp around the second floor
      porch and up the ramp to the roof. Races a couple of times.

      On the roof, John slides and crashes backward into the railing. He remains on
      his bike, but it hangs on the eaves out over the water. One of the lions
      approaches and takes hold of the front wheel in his mouth, nearly shaking John
      off the bike. John holds the clutch and cranks the throttle wide open. The
      noise makes the lions jump back. John pulls his bide off the eaves, and the
      lions head toward him. He rides toward the porch on the roof:

293   OMITTED (most of the original 293 put into 292)
294   OMITTED
295   OMITTED

296   ANOTHER ANGLE--THE ROOF--DAY

      An elephant crosses the river, also interested in the noisy activity, trumpets
      his excitement. John makes   wide turn, too wide, and sails off the roof, some
      thirty feet into the river below. The lions watch him go, look down curiously
      for a moment, then, the chase is over, so they go back down the ramp as Jerry
      looks on.

After the filming was completed, the script was revised to reflect
the filming. The revised script was used by the editor in lieu of a lined
script. Without lined pages, many of the community duties normally

handled by a script supervisor unavoidably fell into the hands of the editing assistants. Long hours were spent in the editing room just to sort through the ample footage of this single sequence. The value of complete and accurate continuity records couldn't be better illustrated than by the comparison to the *Roar* records. At the same time, this statement should under no circumstances be taken as a criticism of Noel Marshall's film. The decision to devote the time and expense in bringing the continuity records up to date after the filming was a choice made by the producer-director in order to maintain the integrity of his film where it counted—during the filming.

The *Return to Macon County* truck stunt, the *Happy Days* scene, and the unusually demanding *Roar* sample are three different uses of multiple-camera film. All pose their own requirements for scripting. Although our next sample uses only one camera, the format dictates yet another contrasting style.

COMMERCIALS

Commercial production calls for a specialized continuity style. The form that we are going to present in our sample is considered the most universally accepted. Before tracing the steps of the sample, however, we must offer an explanation of the differences between commercials and other motion picture/television production. In order to hold script on a commercial effectively a script supervisor must first have this basic understanding.

Differences in Commercial Production and Other MP/TV Production

The problem with commercial production is that the chain of authority is muddled. The process of producing a commercial starts with a client who has a product or service to advertise. If the client is a large corporation, the advertising department handles the responsibility of delivering the commercial. This department may or may not have to obtain all go-aheads from the "brass" of the corporation. On the other hand, the large corporation may be a subsidiary of a larger corporation. In either case, the client usually sub-contracts the commercial to an advertising agency. Depending on the corporate attitude, the creative input such as script development, marketing strategy and artwork may remain with the client or it may be turned over to the agency. If the department delineates the responsibility to the agency, it's still fairly safe to assume that all final decisions are cleared with the department. The ad agency in turn is in contact with the producers of a production company. How much input the production company executives have in the development of the commercial again depends on too many factors to begin listing. Finally, the ultimate job of filming the commercial ends up in the hands of the production crew which has its own hierarchy of command. As a non-decision-making crew member, the script supervisor's involvement doesn't usually begin until the first day of the shoot when theoretically all the details have been worked out.

As with most theory, the reality never seems to work out quite as smoothly as anticipated. On a typical commercial set, the agency representatives, producer, client executives, writer, star, director and countless others are all present or only a telephone call away, ready to voice their ideas. Sometimes, a lucky crew encounters a group which has already worked out their differences before the day of the shoot; but more often, the decision process is both time-consuming and nerve-wracking. A cameraman once threatened to invent a camera with six eyepieces so that all the decision-makers could see a shot at the same time. As long as the script supervisor appreciates this problem, he or she will be equipped to deal with the massive ambiguities.

Just as the chain of command affects the crew, so does the format. A commercial can be shot in 16mm, 35mm or on videotape. This difference will have a substantial effect on other crew members but not on the script supervisor. What concerns the script supervisor more is the length of the commercial.

Commercials usually run approximately 10-, 20-, 30- or 60-seconds. A 10-second commercial or *spot* actually plays only 8 seconds on film. Similarly, a 20-second spot times out to 18 seconds, a 30-second spot times to 28, and a 60-second spot times out to 58. A taped commercial or a commercial which is finished off on tape can run one second longer than filmed commercials. These should time out during production to 59-, 29-, 19- and 9-seconds respectively. Often, more than one version of a commercial is filmed at the same time; for instance, a 60-second version could be shot during the same shooting session as a 30-second version. The format will determine how a shoot is scheduled.

Commercials are scheduled anywhere from one day to two weeks. A simple commercial's schedule usually runs a day or two. A larger budget commercial or a more complicated commercial may run up to five days or more. When several different spots are shot at the same time or when the script involves many locations, the schedule tends to run longer. Regardless of the schedule, the script supervisor works on a daily rate.

With no advance preparation time, the script supervisor starts working from the moment of arrival on the set. The script supervisor should begin establishing rapport by introducing him or herself to the various crew members. Working methods have to be even more flexible than on a feature. With such a short shooting schedule, there will be no time to iron out idiosyncracies.

While the crew lines up the first shot, the script supervisor carefully times the script. Commercial timing is critical. Each shot must be planned in advance down to the half- or quarter-second. Once the timing is set, the filming must conform precisely. A shot that runs even one second over could create terrible problems in the cutting room. The timings should be presented to the director or agency representative for approval.

In some cases, the company has already set the timings. The script supervisor should use these timings if possible, but they should always be double-checked. The director may expect a horse to pull the cart of beer up to the camera in two seconds when the old nag can hardly pull the load in five. Any potential problems in timing should be pointed out as soon as possible.

In general, a commercial company is much more meticulous in lining up shots than a feature company. With such a short script, the slightest detail becomes significant. Lighting the first shot of the day, for instance, often requires literally hours. Even though breaking down the script and establishing working relationships sounds like a lot to accomplish in the morning, the set-up time for the first scene is usually adequate. Understanding the different attitudes of commercial filmmakers and how these attitudes dictate priorities will help the script supervisor put the morning to its best use.

Attitude Differences

The attitude of commercial filmmakers differs from the attitude of other filmmakers in that commercial filmmakers are not story tellers as much as they are advertisers. Different objectives and qualities are important. Although the specifics vary from company to company, these differences can be broken down into four broad areas—the importance of time accuracy, product visibility, localized marketing, and advertising copy. All four will directly affect the script supervisor's job.

The *importance of time accuracy* cannot be over-estimated. As we began to explain earlier, the script supervisor must ensure that each scene of a commercial times out precisely as planned. When a scene involves dialogue, the script supervisor may have to rehearse lines with the speakers until their pace matches the timing. While shooting the scene, the script supervisor's timings have to be so precise that a fractional second stopwatch is recommended. In addition to split-second timings, the script supervisor must accurately sense when a scene starts and stops. Remember that on features, a script supervisor also observes the difference between picture time and actual time, but in commercials the observations have to be all the more precise. The script supervisor is in complete charge of maintaining time accuracy.

Attitudes about *product visibility* affect the script supervisor's job as much as time accuracy. *The script supervisor must keep in mind at all times that the product is the star.* Anything that either draws attention away from the product or makes the product less attractive is considered detrimental. Say, for example, that an actress holds up a bottle of dishwashing liquid in a full shot, and then the camera cuts to a close-up of the product in her hand. The objective of the commercial is defeated if the ring on her finger upstages the product in the close-up. To avoid this problem, script supervisors should be conscious of extraneous jewelry or any distracting physical detail. The same applies to matching mistakes such as finger placement when holding a product. Ensuring product visibility is an important part of the script supervisor's job on commercials.

Similar to time accuracy and product visibility, *localized marketing* poses additional concerns for the script supervisor. When a commercial airs on television, it usually runs in a specific region of the country or *market*. A car commercial may air in the New York area, for example, and not in Southern California. If the license plates on the cars are California plates, the script supervisor should draw attention to the potential discrepancy. Other examples of localized marketing concerns are regional laws. Some states, for instance, require drivers to wear seatbelts. The actors in commercials intended for these locals must use their belts. Many states don't allow beer and wine to be sold in supermarkets. A housewife rolling her cart down the beer aisle on the way to the toilet paper section would be inappropriate in one of these states. Although no one can be expected to know all the laws affecting marketing, the script supervisor can ask questions such as "Do you want the license plate taped?", or "Do the palm trees in the background bother you?". A little common sense on the part of the script supervisor can save the day.

The script supervisor has little control over *changes in advertising copy.* As explained earlier, at least five or six people nearly always play a part in the decision-making of commercials. While shooting or rehearsing, even the slightest change in dialogue should be mentioned immediately. Say, for example, an actor or director wants to change a single word in copy. The writer, producer, advertising agency representatives, and everyone present finally agree on a revision after a laborious debate. Even then, a call still has to be placed to the home office before shooting can resume. Our only advice is to be patient and flexible. Adding another opinion only makes the process take longer. Changes in advertising copy should be left to the others.

Changes in advertising copy, localized marketing, product visibility, and time accuracy are all examples of the attitude differences between commercial production and feature film production. The differences affect how the script supervisor observes continuity. Just as the methods for observing continuity change on a commercial, so do the methods for script notation. The following example is designed to show how a typical commercial is lined.

Commercial Sample

"Hero II" is a 30-second commercial spot representative of how many commercials are scripted. The product advertised is Recipe Beef Chunks dog food and the commercial features Lassie. The advertising agency involved is Needam, Harper, and Steers and the client is the Campbell Soup Company. All rights to Lassie are owned by Lassie Television, Inc., a subsidiary of the Wrather Corporation. The commercial was produced through a well-known commercial production company called Bill Hudson Films Inc. with John Hazard in charge of production and Bill Hudson directing. Get the picture?

During the filming of most commercials, the script supervisor lines both a storyboard and a split-page script. The split-page and storyboard formats divide the action into audio and visual parts. On the split-page script, the visual is on the left side of the page while the audio is on the right. On the storyboard, pictures represent the visual of each scene while the audio is typed below. In the lining of the "Hero II" script, the distinction between the audio and visual was observed.

A widely accepted coding system was used to number the shots. 60-second spots are usually coded in the 100s, such as 101, 102, 103, 104, and so on. A 30-second spot's scenes are numbered in the 200s. 20-second and 10-second spots use numbers in the 300s and 400s respectively. As a 30-second spot, the "Hero II" scenes were assigned a 200 series.

The first three scenes of the sample script were covered from four different angles: The first shot was a master number 201. 201A captured a close-up of the boy followed by a close-up of the dog numbered 201B, and finally a two-shot numbered 201C.

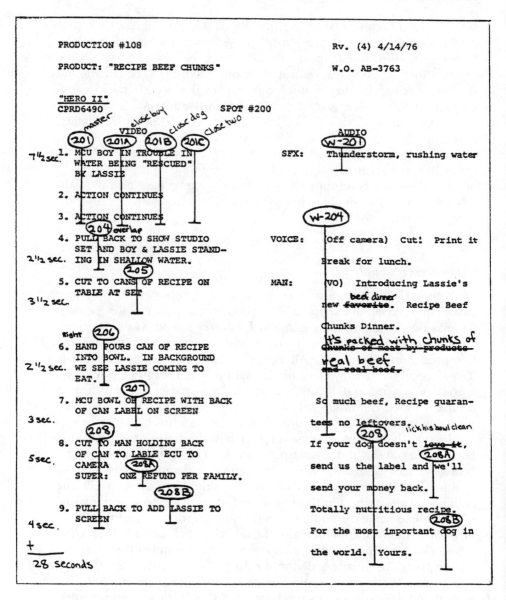

PRODUCTION #108   Rv. (4) 4/14/76

PRODUCT: "RECIPE BEEF CHUNKS"   W.O. AB-3763

"HERO II"
CPRD6490   SPOT #200

VIDEO	AUDIO

master close boy close dog close two

(201) (201A) (201B) (201C)   (W-201)

7½ sec. 1. MCU BOY IN TROUBLE IN   SFX: Thunderstorm, rushing water
        WATER BEING "RESCUED"
        BY LASSIE

2. ACTION CONTINUES

3. ACTION CONTINUES

                                            (W-204)
(204) overlap

4. PULL BACK TO SHOW STUDIO   VOICE: (Off camera) Cut! Print it
   SET AND BOY & LASSIE STAND-
2½ sec. ING IN SHALLOW WATER.   Break for lunch.

(205)

5. CUT TO CANS OF RECIPE ON   MAN: (VO) Introducing Lassie's
   TABLE AT SET   beef dinner
3½ sec.   new ~~favorite~~. Recipe Beef

                                             Chunks Dinner.

Right (206)   It's packed with chunks of
                                             ~~chunks of meat by-products~~
6. HAND POURS CAN OF RECIPE   real beef
   INTO BOWL. IN BACKGROUND   ~~and real beef.~~
2½ sec. WE SEE LASSIE COMING TO
   EAT.

(207)

7. MCU BOWL OF RECIPE WITH BACK   So much beef, Recipe guaran-
   OF CAN LABEL ON SCREEN
3 sec.   tees no leftovers. lick his bowl clean

(208)   (208)

8. CUT TO MAN HOLDING BACK   If your dog doesn't ~~love it~~,
   OF CAN TO LABLE ECU TO   (208A)
5 sec.   CAMERA (208A)
   SUPER: ONE REFUND PER FAMILY.   send us the label and we'll

                                             send your money back.
                  (208B)
9. PULL BACK TO ADD LASSIE TO   Totally nutritious recipe.
   SCREEN   (208B)
4 sec.   For the most important dog in

                                             the world. Yours.
+
28 seconds

All three were shot M.O.S. The thunder and rushing water effects were recorded previously from a sound library and numbered W201. The last two script scenes required a little more coverage due to the sound synch.

The following is the corresponding story board:

The story board script is lined in the same manner except the distinction between the audio and visual was not made. Script supervisors usually draw the lines through the dialogue boxes instead of the picture frames so they're easier to see.

DAILY EDITORIAL REPORT   PG 1

JOB # 108   TITLE RECIPE BEEF CHUNKS DIRECTOR HUDSON

SHOOTING DAY final   DATE 4/14/76   SCRIPT SUPERVISOR ULMER

SETS/LOCATIONS STUDIO

W.O. AB-3763   30 SECOND SPOT

SC	TAKE	TIME	COMMENTS	ACTION
201 MOS	1	7½"	N.G. action of dog	Master full shot Boy + Dog rescuing him in rushing water
	#2	7½"	Fair	
	3	2"	N.G. Bad Cam. start	
	④	7½"	Excellent	
201A MOS	1	7½"	N.G. bad for director	close up Boy through all three scenes
	2	2"	false start	
	③	(7½")	okay	
201 B MOS	1	7½"	N.G. Bad action of Dog	close on Dog through all three scenes
	2	5"	N.G. Camera	
	③	(7½")	okay	
201C MOS	#1	7½"	fair	close two-shot Boy + Dog through all three scenes
	2	7½"	N.G. rescue part only fair	
	③	(7½")	okay	
204 MOS	1	2½"	N.G. Camera	Overlaps 201 - camera pulls way back showing studio set with Boy + Dog in water
	2	2½	N.G. Director	
	3	1"	false start	
	④	2½"	Fair	
	⑤*	2½"	Excellent	
205 MOS	①	3½"	possible high-light	M.C.U. Cans of Recipe on set
	②	3½"	okay	
206 MOS	1	2½"	N.G. hand shook too much	Hand - close pours Recipe food into bowl
	②	2½	okay	

At the end of each day, the script supervisor turns in the lined script, storyboard, and accompanying editorial notes in a manilla envelope. Because many commercial shoots last only a few days, a daily continuity report is unnecessary. When the filming is completed and the script supervisor turns in the final records, the job is over.

DAILY EDITORIAL REPORT PG 2

JOB # 108   TITLE RECIPE BEEF CHUNK DIRECTOR HUDSON

SHOOTING DAY final   DATE 4/14/76   SCRIPT SUPERVISOR ULMER

SETS/LOCATIONS STUDIO

W.O. AB - 3763   30 SECOND SPOT

SC	TAKE	TIME	COMMENTS	ACTION
207 mos	1	3"	N.G. Camera	MCU of full bowl. Back of can label seen
	2	3"	N.G. Camera	
	③	3"	Excellent	
WILD TRACK				WILD TRACKS for 201 through 207 numbered W-201 + W-204
208 sync	1	5"	N.G. false start	Man holding back of can with label in ECU to camera
	#2	5"	fair hold	
	3	4"	N.G. Dial "Money back"	
	④	5"	okay	
208 A sync	1	no timing. To inter- cut 208 + 208B	Bad label	C.U. label saying " One refund per family to intercut 208
	②		Fair	
	③		good	
208 B sync	1	4"	N.G. Camera	Camera- pull back from 208 to include Lassie in studio set
	②	4"	Fair	
	③	4"	Excellent	
				Note to Editor all times noted here are what are to be used to total 28 seconds
				201 (A,B,+C) 7½ In 208,
				204 2½ Break up the
				205 3½ 9 seconds with
				206 3½ 5" for 208 +
				207 2½ 208A + 4"
				208 3 for 208B
				+ 9
				28 seconds

By comparing all of the various continuity styles from commercials to feature films, it's obvious that scripting techniques are tailored to the requirements of their formats. Commercials are scripted on both storyboard and split-page scripts with careful attention paid to split-second timing and product visibility. Single camera film is usually scripted on a full-page script with the concentration shifting to detail and matching. Videotape has the advantage of immediate replay which makes matching less problematic. The multiple-camera formats used in episodic television have very defined scripting requirements in order to operate efficiently from week to week as opposed to industrial training programs where anything goes. Just as scripting techniques are dictated by individual formats, various production techniques demand specific clarification.

SPECIALIZED NOTATION

A list of all the production techniques requiring specialized notation would undoubtedly be lengthy and useless. Script supervising is not the kind of job where a person can merely memorize a few facts and expect to get by. As we've emphasized throughout this book, the script supervisor has to be able to handle any situation that arises by first recognizing a potential problem and then solving it with a successful record-keeping system. The following scripting techniques offer solutions to a representative sample of tricky production areas, starting with musical scenes.

Musical Scenes

Although the days of filming large-budget musicals are virtually over, many films still feature musical scenes. Instead of stringing together a series of production numbers with just enough plot to get by, the new breed of films integrates music into the story in a more realistic manner. The techniques for filming both are the same for the script supervisor. The sample we've chosen to illustrate some of the scripting problems involved in musical scenes is from Columbia Pictures/Rastar Productions' feature, *The Competition*, written by Joel Oliansky and William Sackheim. The scene provides a perfect example because of the complex coverage selected by the director, Joel Oliansky.

The Competition is a love story set against a world-class piano competition in which as many as 85 different playbacks were used. A *playback* is a reproduction of the studio-quality musical recording which is used as a guide during filming. Musical scenes are usually filmed M.O.S. with playbacks so that dancer movements or singer lips match the music. The original track is added to the picture in post production. Using playbacks avoids the need of an orchestra and optimum recording conditions on location.

In the case of *The Competition*, various competitors play complex piano concerti throughout the entire film. Many are accompanied by a full-scale symphony orchestra. Each concerto was first recorded in a top-quality recording studio to ensure sound excellence. Playback copies

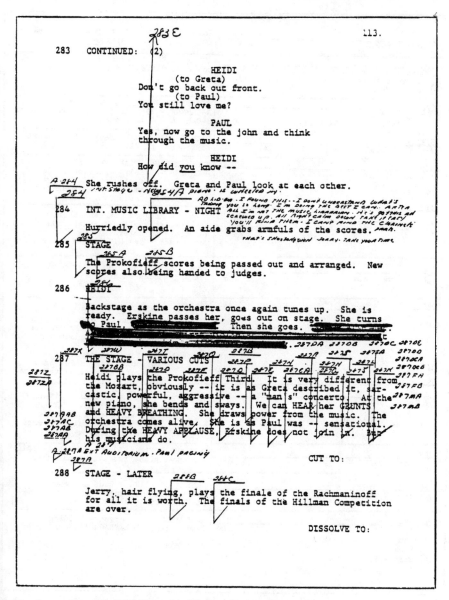

283   CONTINUED: (2)   113.

                        HEIDI
                     (to Greta)
          Don't go back out front.
                     (to Paul)
          You still love me?

                        PAUL
          Yes, now go to the john and think
          through the music.

                        HEIDI
          How did you know --

          She rushes off. Greta and Paul look at each other.

284   INT. MUSIC LIBRARY - NIGHT

          Hurriedly opened. An aide grabs armfuls of the scores.

285   STAGE

          The Prokofieff scores being passed out and arranged. New
          scores also being handed to judges.

286   HEIDI

          Backstage as the orchestra once again tunes up. She is
          ready. Erskine passes her, goes out on stage. She turns
          to Paul,   Then she goes.

287   THE STAGE - VARIOUS CUTS

          Heidi plays the Prokofieff Third. It is very different from
          the Mozart, obviously -- it is as Greta described it, sar-
          castic, powerful, aggressive -- a "man's" concerto. At the
          new piano, she bends and sways. We can HEAR her GRUNTS
          and HEAVY BREATHING. She draws power from the music. The
          orchestra comes alive. She is as Paul was -- sensational.
          During the HEAVY APPLAUSE, Erskine does not join in. But
          his musicians do.

                                                    CUT TO:

288   STAGE - LATER

          Jerry, hair flying, plays the finale of the Rachmaninoff
          for all it is worth. The finals of the Hillman Competition
          are over.

                                                    DISSOLVE TO:

were used during the filming to match the pianist's keyboard action. During example scene #287, the film's leading lady, Heidi, plays the Prokofieff piano concerto onstage during the finals of the Hillman Competition. The entire movie builds up to the moment when Heidi finally performs the winning concerto. The concerto's three move-

Scene		Date / Time	Description
287F	Comp - PRINT	4/2 2:45	50mm - TATIANA AND KARNOW - plus two KGB'S - PLAYBACK #16X
287D	1. Comp audience too dead / 2. ng gobo shake / 3. Comp - PRINT	4/2 :40 :20	AUDIENCE REACT o.s. C.L. to Heidi PLAYBACK #16X
287E	Comp - PRINT - NOTE: SEE PICKUP 287EA	4/2 1:50	TWO CAMERAS - PLAYBACK #16XB A-CAMERA - 29mm DiSalvo's plus audience B-CAMERA - 40mm - audience
287EA	Comp - PRINT	4/2	PICKUP 287E - PLAYBACK #16XB - last 15 seconds of Playback
288B	Comp - PRINT	4/2	TWO CAMERAS - PLAYBACK #18X A-CAMERA - DiSalvo reaction of Jerry 29mm B-CAMERA - 35mm Over f.g. daughter to Mrs. DiSalvo
284	Comp - PRINT	3/25 :20	24mm CAMERA IN CORNER - Shooting down aisle - 1st violinist enter from b.g R-L cross to camera and Pan L-R to music rack - see NICHOLS IN doorway (L)
284A	Comp ng focus	3/25 :28	50mm - CAMERA HOLDING - 1st violinist hands grabbing music
285	1. Comp / 2. Comp - PRINT	3/31	TWO CAMERAS A-CAMERA - Shooting toward audience men come in with music and piano - Dolly R-L see Nichols passing out score B-CAMERA - at far side of stage - on opposite door - See Bass players and cellos take their seats
287G	Comp - PRINT	4/2 3:05	TWO CAMERAS- PLAYBACK #16XB A-CAMERA - SINGLE TATIANA - FINALE B- CAMERA - 40mm - KARNOW- TATIANA TWO KGB'S plus audience React C.L. Heidi -audience rise for Bravos
287H	1. Comp - PRINT	4/2 :55	A-CAMERA ONLY - 50mm - Two shot-PB#16 Karnow-Tatiana react to each other
287A	Comp - PRINT	3/6	CAMERA ON PORCH - Paul to camera- Dolly back and Pan R-L into building PLAYBACK 16X -NO SYNC
A-287A	1. Comp - A shoot only / 2. Comp / 3. F.S. / 4. Comp - PRINT	3/6 2:00 2:00	A - CAMERA - on crane - Holding Paul pacing - PLAYBACK 16X - NO SYNC B- CAMERA - on

ments were recorded separately and numbered 16X, 16XA, and 16XB. Most of the camera angles used to cover the scene were filmed to one of these three playbacks. It's the script supervisor's job to note in the continuity records which playback was used for which action. This information is vital to the editors especially in a complex scene such as

288B ① Comp - PRINT	4/2 1:16	29mm - TATIANA - KARNOW - plus Two KGB'S - PLAYBACK #18X
287J ① Comp - PRINT NOTE: SEE 287K	4/2	TWO CAMERAS - PLAYBACK #16 A-CAMERA 24mm - on deck to Judges B- CAMERA - 35mm from stage to Judges see Greta b.g. last 15sec playback
287K ① Comp - PRINT	4/2	A-CAMERA ONLY Same as 287J - No Playback
287L ① Comp - End marks B	4/2 3:05	TWO CAMERAS - AS ABOVE - PLAYBACK #16 FINALE - NOTE: B CAMER TURN ON LATE
288C ① Comp - PRINT	4/2	TWO CAMERAS AS ABOVE - Judges PLAYBACK 18X - SAINT SAENS
285A ① Comp - PRINT	4/2	CAMERA SHOOTING FROM STAGE - Mrs. Doneallen passes out new scores R-L B- 35mm wide
287AA 1. Inc ng shadows 2. Inc ng camera ③ Comp - PRINT	4/2 1:40	24mm - PAUL ENTERS AND CROSSES C.R. He prodeeds down outside aisle - Dolly shot - PLAYBACK #16XA
287AB 1. Inc ng camera ② Inc - PRINT	4/2 1:08	24mm - PICKUP AT TOP OF AISLE C.R.
287AC ① Inc ng PRINT	4/2 :27	PICKUP AS HE APPROACHES EXIT
287N 1. F.S. 2. Comp ng collasped key - PRINT 3. F.S. 4. Inc ng sync ⑤ Comp - PRINT	4/7 :10 2:30	PLAYBACK 16X - Over piano Hi angle to orchestra - Erskine conducting - back reveal Heidi f.g. L frame - arm down and Hold Heidi and keyboard 1ST MOVEMENT
287P 1. Comp ng sync on arm down 2. Comp cue late 3. Comp sync ng at end 4. Comp " " " 5. Comp ng camera at end ⑥ Comp - PRINT	4/7 1:00 :50 :50 :50	STAGE CRANE - PLAYBACK 16X - profile Heidi hands on keyboard - arm up shooting down on Heidi - as she near finish a dramatic arm drop 1ST MOVEMENT
287Q 1. Comp 2. F.S. 3. F.S. ④ Comp - PRINT	4/7 2:40	STAGE CRANE - PLAYBACK 16XA - Low profile Heidi - arm up to orchestra Pan to Erskine he looks at her L -R arm back down to Heidi profile 2ND MOVEMENT

#287. Although scene 287's five pages of records may appear as excessive coverage, every bit was used in the final cut of this highly dramatic scene.

Musical scenes such as the example for *The Competition* are scripted

	Date	Time	Description
287R 1. Comp ngC at end 2. Comp 3. Comp didn't get in soon enuf 4. Comp ng zoom control fails 5. Comp need to be in sooner ⑥ Comp - PRINT	4/7	1:35	HIGH ANGLE OVER ORCHESTRA - PLAYBACK #16XA - arm down and slide across piano R-L.to Heidi in profile arm up tilt down for finish - 2ND MOVEMENT
287S ① Comp - PRINT	4/7		STAGE CRANE - Erskine (L) frame and Orchestra turn look under lens Pan over so Erskine is in (R) frame
287SA ① Comp - PRINT	4/7		50mm - PICKUP 287S PLAYBACK 16X
287T ① Comp - PRINT	4/7	1:40	ERSKINE & Orchestra PLAYBACK #16XA
287U 1 Comp HOLD ② Comp PRINT	4/7		ERSKINE AND ORCHESTRA PLAYBACK #16XB
287V Comp End marks ng sync ③ Comp - PRINT	4/8	1:40 :30 1:35	TWO CAMERAS- PLAYBACK 16X A-CAMERA-From behind strings to Heidi and audience B-CAMERA - 40mm same action
287W 1. Inc ng look Same 2. ng sync ③ Comp - PRINT	4/8	:15 1:20 2:20	TWO CAMERAS - PLAYBACK 16XB A- CAMERA - ZOOM - On Erskine Pan L-R Dolly in to Heidi and Erskine B-CAMERA - 50mm - Heidi and audience
287X ① Comp - PRINT	4/8		CLOSE HEIDI AND AUDIENCE ABOVE KEYS - PLAYBACK 16XB
287BB 1. ng sync ② Comp - PRINT	4/9		TWO CAMERAS - PLAYBACK #16X A- CAMERA - OVER ERSKINE TO AUDIENCE B- CAMERA - HOLDING STRINTS - ZOOM IN
287Z ①. Comp - PRINT B ONLY ②. Comp - A and B PRINT	4/10		TWO CAMERAS - PLAYBACK #16X A- CAMERA - Low on violins arm up for over view Pan over to Violas for piccato - Dramat arm down BCAMERA - 150mm - Camera on dolly various shots orchestra
285E 1Inc ngCamera ② Comp- PRINT	4/11		A ONLY - SPLIT DIOPTER SHOOTING TO PERCUSSION AREA - General melee getting ready for beginning of Prokofieff
287ZA ① Comp - PRINT	4/10		A ONLY - SPLIT DIOPTER - CASSTANETS AN TYNPANY PLAYBACK 16X

similarly to any other single-camera film with the addition of playback numbers. These numbers help identify the footage for matching the picture to the corresponding sound track. Just as the continuity records for musical numbers require additional identifications, so does cross-medium coverage.

287DA ʟ Comp ② Comp - PRINT	4/11	A CAMERA ONLY - Start on a 40mm over audience to Heidi - widen and reveal MORE Audience - 24mm - PLAYBACK 16X
287DB ① Comp - PRINT	4/11	A CAMERA - Low over audience to Heidi - PLAYBAC K #16XB - arm up and widen lwns.
287DC ʟ. ng sync 2. ng sync 3. F.S. 4. ng arm down ⑤ Comp - PRINT	4/11 3:10	Hi angle over audienct to Heidi - arm down - scene goes thru bow with Erskine PLAYBACK #16XB
287AAB ʟ. ng 2. ng ③ Comp - PRINT	4/11	PAUL'S P.O.V. HEIDI - Over audience PLAYBACK 16XA
287DE ① Comp - PRINT		PLAYBACK 16X Start on violins 20mm - Pan R-L to Heidi - Zoom to 37mm Hold audience in b.g.
287DD ʟ. NgCamera down sooner hair late 2. ngCamera ③ Comp - PRINT	4/11 :55 1:00	STAGE CRANE - In front of stage Start close on fingers then arm up and widen - hold all of Heidi and keyboard - start down and zoom in to hands - Continue very low up to hands - PLAYBACK 16XB
287DCA ʟ Comp ② Comp- PRINT		PLAYBACK 16XA - CLOSER FOR BOW
287DCB ① Comp - PRINT	4/11	PICKUP 287DCA - NO PLAYBACK
287FA ʟ ngA ② Comp - PRINT	4/16	ERSKINE AND BALCONY - PLAYBACK 16X
287FB ʟ. ng sync ② Comp - PRINT	4/16	ERSKINE AND BALCONY - PLAYBACK 16XB
287MA 1. ng people in shot 2. Comp - 3. ng b.g. 4. ng Camera lose speed ⑤ Comp - PRINT ⑥ Comp- PRINT - End ID. for take 6	4/19 :05 :40 :20	PLAYBACK #16X - Wide angle Greta and Paul listen to o.s. Heidi playing
287MB ʟ. Comp ② Comp - PRINT	4/19	AT DOORWAY - Close Greta leaning against wall (R) - Paul lookout door and exit R-L

Cross-Medium Coverage

Many film crews take into account while still in production the need for *cross-medium coverage*. Any time a film or tape is intended for one medium before being released in another, additional coverage may be necessary for the transition. In one example, a major studio picture filmed two versions of certain key scenes so that the picture could be

---

page 78

2/7 SL # 188
#1 1:45 compl. fair
#2 1:45 compl. fair
    camera questionable
3 1:35 compl. N.G.
    tk 1 better
4 :20 N.G. false start
⑤ 1:45 good
	SC 188 - INT LIBBY'S CABIN - NIGHT
	Master love scene between
	Libby + Harley on bed all through
	with all dialogue

2/7 SL # TV 188 ① 1:50 good	SC 188 - INT LIBBY'S CABIN - NIGHT Master TV version of love scene between Libby + Harley action same as 188 except Libby wears bra
2/7 SL # 188A #1 1:30 compl. 2 :35 N.G. start ③ 1:35 ④ 1:35	SC 188 - INT LIBBY'S CABIN - NIGHT close Libby. Harley in + out all through
2/7 SL # TV 188A 1 :20 N.G. start ② 1:38	SC 188 - INT LIBBY'S CABIN - NIGHT close Libby with Harley in + out Same as 188A only Libby wears bra

2/7 SL # 188 B
① 1:34 compl. sound off
    and on
② 1:35 compl. good
    but tk. 1 better
	SC 188 - INT LIBBY'S CABIN NIGHT
	close Harley with Libby in +
	out all through.
	At ends a two-shot taking them
	out the door

released with both a R rating and a PG rating. In our next sample scene, additional coverage was shot for *Return to Macon County* in order to pass television obscenity restrictions.

The following script notes show two versions of Scene #188. Shot #188 was intended for the feature release while shot #TV188 was filmed for television broadcast. In #TV188, the female character wears a bra. Shot #188, on the other hand, is performed partially in the nude. Notice that both shots were lined individually in the same manner as any other additional camera view. The editorial notes explain.

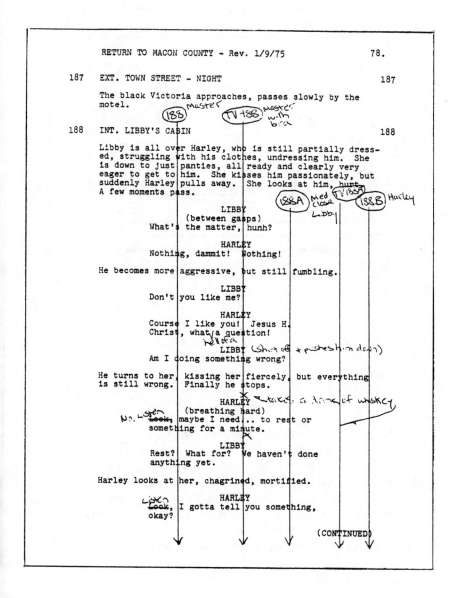

RETURN TO MACON COUNTY - Rev. 1/9/75   78.

187   EXT. TOWN STREET - NIGHT   187

       The black Victoria approaches, passes slowly by the
       motel.   188) Master   TV 188) Master with bra

188   INT. LIBBY'S CABIN   188

       Libby is all over Harley, who is still partially dress-
       ed, struggling with his clothes, undressing him. She
       is down to just panties, all ready and clearly very
       eager to get to him. She kisses him passionately, but
       suddenly Harley pulls away. She looks at him, hurt.
       A few moments pass.   188A) Med Close TV 188A 188B) Harley
                                    Libby

                        LIBBY
                   (between gasps)
              What's the matter, hunh?

                        HARLEY
              Nothing, dammit! Nothing!

       He becomes more aggressive, but still fumbling.

                        LIBBY
              Don't you like me?

                        HARLEY
              Course I like you! Jesus H.
              Christ, what a question!
                        LIBBY (Shirt off + pushes him away)   he likes
              Am I doing something wrong?

       He turns to her, kissing her fiercely, but everything
       is still wrong. Finally he stops.

                        HARLEY takes a drink of whiskey
                   (breathing hard)
       No, Look, maybe I need... to rest or
              something for a minute.

                        LIBBY
              Rest? What for? We haven't done
              anything yet.

       Harley looks at her, chagrined, mortified.

                        HARLEY
       Look, open I gotta tell you something,
              okay?

                                        (CONTINUED)

In addition to identifying alternate footage, the script supervisor should also watch for framing problems due to cross-mediums. Different model cameras have various aperture markings on their viewfinders indicating alternate medium formats.

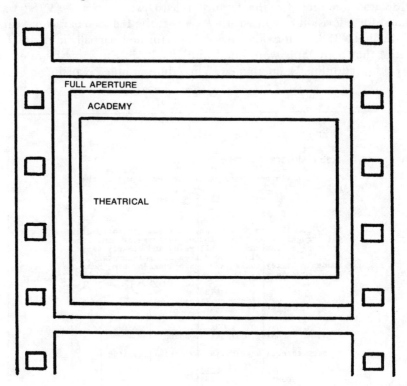

The full screen aperture shows the entire exposed frame (or in other words, what would be visible if no sound track reduced the size of the frame). The Academy is equivalent to the average television format which is smaller in height and width than the full screen aperture. The current wide screen theatrical format includes the smallest area of the exposed frame.

On the first day of the shoot, the script supervisor should find out which format is being observed. A film intended for a theatrical release before a television sale, for example, should usually be protected for Academy. Whenever checking the frame through the camera's viewfinder, the script supervisor should observe the appropriate lines. A larger format such as the Academy poses significantly different requirements for the art department as well as the sound and camera teams. Sets must be built, lit, and dressed higher and wider. Microphones have to be held further away from the speakers in order to stay out of the frame. The differences in coverage requirements are especially evident when converting a theatrical feature to a telefeature.

Each shot of the theatrical picture must be composed so that all important details will be visible on typical television screens. Different models of television sets (and even different adjustments on the same model), vary in how much of the total picture appears. In addition, the curved surfaces of most screens cause distortion problems at the extreme edges and corners. If a crucial clue appears too far out in the frame, the clue may be lost or distorted in transmission. A standard-accepted *safe area* was devised, based on the average color home receiver, to accommodate these discrepancies. Observing the Academy usually solves most television conversion problems with the exception of the opening and closing titles.

Anyone who has ever tried to watch one of their favorite movies on television has probably noticed that their heroes appeared tall and skinny through the titles as if they had pituitary disorders. As soon as the titles were over, the heroes were miraculously cured. Sometimes, instead of optically narrowing the images during the titles, a black bar appears along the top and bottom of the screen. The *title safe* area is due to distortion at the curved edges of the television screen. For economic reasons, titles are often optically corrected after completing the film for the television version.

It is by no means the script supervisor's job to line up shots or make demands about dialogue changes, but a conscientious script supervisor should be aware of the problems involved in cross-medium coverage. On rare occasions, the cinematographer may ask where in the frame an important action occurred in order to determine whether it was in the safe area. A director may ask the script supervisor to prepare a list of vulgar dialogue lines for pick-ups. Awkward composition or coverage disrupts the flow of a program as much as any other continuity mistake. A similar principle applies to filming stereo. While it's not a continuity duty to decide when to use stereo, information provided by the script supervisor may prove useful.

Stereo Filming

On rare occasions, a film track is recorded in *stereo*. Recording stereo is usually very difficult, time-consuming and expensive; however, sometimes story requirements such as overlapping dialogue make stereo recording unavoidable. Most filmmakers who want to achieve a stereophonic effect mix their films in stereo rather than actually recording in stereo while filming. Because of the complexity of stereo production, good continuity records are invaluable to the sound editor.

Continuity records for stereo reflect sound perspective. The term, *perspective* refers to the location in which a sound comes from. Say, for example, a rock group performs onstage in front of a screaming audience. One perspective is from the stage. In the background, the audience screams and cheers, but the main sound is the music. The screaming is in the foreground from an audience perspective while the music plays faintly in the background. Editorial notes should list the two perspectives.

The following sample of stereo notation illustrates the previous example. Four cameras were used in scene 95 to shoot the concert. Each

DATE __1/3__

PAGE __42__

CAM ROLL	SCENE	TK	SND ROLL	PRINT	TIME	LENS	ACTION
204ᴺ 205ᴱ 221ᴰ 214ᴰ	95	1	54ᵃ 48ᵇ	① cam C N.G. first few seconds cam	1:55	100 28 30 Various zoom	1/3 Concert - Michigan - Night Johnny plays guitar solo in the spotlight center stage while the audience goes wild. CAM A - CAM ROLL 204 SND ROLL 54 Johnny close all through CAM B - CAM ROLL 205 SN. ROLL 54 full stage band CAM C - CAM ROLL 221 SN. ROLL 48 audience watching concert CAM D - CAM ROLL 214 SN. ROLL 48 various audience members at operator's discretion. Hand slates in between SN ROLL 54 - stage perspective SN ROLL 48 - audience perspective
204	96	1 H2 3 4	MOS	③ ④★	:20 :20 :21 :21	100	1/3 CONCERT BACKSTAGE - NIGHT C.S. Sara watching Johnny with tears in her eyes note: mix sound from scene 95 to cover with WT 96 tk 1 N.G. light knocked tk 2 Hold comd. tk 3 fair tk. 4 best take
204	98	1	MOS	①	:15		1/3 CONCERT BACKSTAGE-NIGHT establishing shot of Sara backstage while stagehands mingle. (use SN. from 95 & WT96)
206	99	1 2	MOS	②	:17		1/3 CONCERT BACKSTAGE-NIGHT Hal observes Sara medium shot. (use sound from 95 & WT96)
48	WT 96						WILD TRACK BACKSTAGE NOISES

of the four views corresponds to one of the two perspectives. Scenes, #96, #98, and #99 were shot M.O.S. with the intention of mixing the concert tracks to a desired balance with backstage wildtrack #WT96. Notice that the records also indicate both sound roll numbers. The perspectives are designated to the proper sound roll.

These simple additions to the continuity notes should answer any questions the editor may have.

Process Shots

In order to save time and money, or to achieve a special effect, many companies film *process shots*. Process photography involves shooting a live scene in front of a projected background or *plate* to form a combined picture. The background plate is usually projected from the rear onto a translucent screen. The projected images can either be stationary or moving. Typical backgrounds include anything from the view out a car window to a beautiful lake to an oversized witch's castle. Interlocking the camera and projector ensures that their shutters open and close at the identical rate; otherwise the filmed image would appear to flicker. Special attention is paid in order to preserve the illusion of the combined picture such as that paid to the physical relationship between camera, screen and projector; the balance of light between screen and live action; the angle and intensity of the light; perspective; relative values; and many others. The only details script supervisors concern themselves with are the plate numbers.

In the following example from "The Hot Rod" episode of Lorimar Productions' television series, *The Waltons,* process photography was used to film scene #44.

SCENE NO.	TIME	SND	LENS	DESCRIPTION 1/8/81
44-1 N/G C	:45	SYNC	40mm 10'6"	MASTER - PROCESS - 4 SHOT (VERDIE, JODY, JOHN-B, MARY)
(44-2) PRINT	:51			PLATE 55
44A-1 N/G A	:13	SYNC	35mm	2 SHOT (JOHN-B & MARY)
44A-2 N/G A	:16			
(44A-3) PRINT	:54			
44B-1 N/G CAM	:48	SYNC	47mm	2 SHOT (VERDIE & JODY)
(44B-2) PRINT	:53			

The corresponding script pages appear on the following pages.

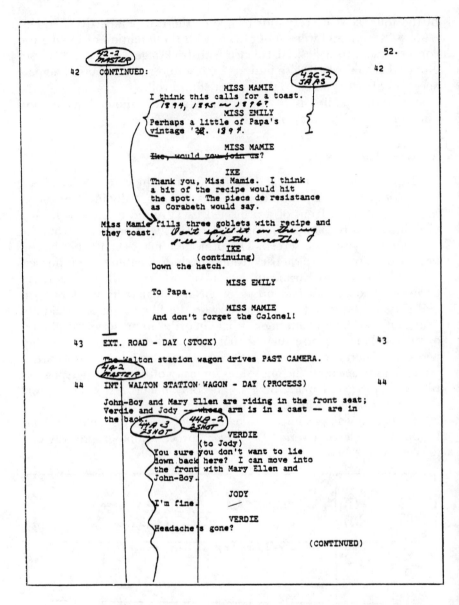

The actors performed the scene inside a station wagon while the background outside the car was rear-projected onto a screen. The script supervisor noted the plate numbers in the continuity records.

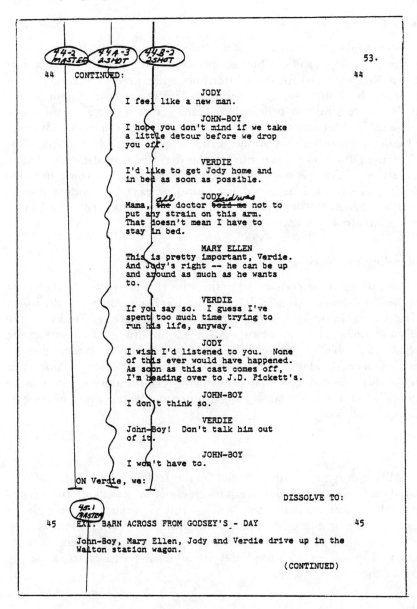

It's also interesting to see how the script supervisor numbered the shots. The take number was incorporated into the shot number in both the lining and the editorial records. Although unusual, it was a system that worked well for *The Waltons*.

Color Coding

Sometimes *a color coding system* is used to simplify continuity notes. In the past, single camera film scripts were often lined in three colors of ink. Red was used for the master lines while green was reserved for medium shots and blue for close-ups. The three-color system is currently obsolete in film production. Many script supervisors still use a comparable three-color system for multiple-camera video production. All editorial records that apply to the air taping are in red ink. Blue ink is used for notes taken during the dress rehearsal taping. Information regarding pick-ups is written in green ink. In some notation systems, green ink is reserved for sound notes. Color coding doesn't have any benefits other than providing an at-a-glance reference to information already provided in the notes.

Attending the Rushes

Similar to color coding, attending the rushes is usually the script supervisor's choice. After each day's film has been processed, the uncut footage is available for viewing. These screenings are referred to as the *dailies* or *rushes*. The script supervisor should attend. By viewing the footage, valuable insight into the director's intentions can be gained. Lists of needed retakes or pick-ups are made. The script supervisor may notice some details that previously went unnoticed. On a more general level, the script supervisor can become better aware of the picture's overall flow.

Typing

Although typing is discouraged by the IATSE union, it is still very common. Certainly an editor has a much easier time working from typed notes than handwritten notes, but a script supervisor doesn't always have the time or energy to type up continuity notes after a long day on the set. If a script supervisor has sloppy handwriting, typing is mandatory. Typing, color coding, and attending the rushes are all at the script supervisor's discretion.

Clips

Whenever a perfect match is essential, the script supervisor can ask either the assistant director or editor for a *clip*. A clip is a short piece of printed film used to match lighting, set dressing, props, costumes, makeup, hair or the like when enough time has elapsed for the film to return from the lab. Similar to the videotape cassettes mentioned in Chapter Four, [see page 225], clips should only be used as a last resort.

Most of the time, the script supervisor's notes and photographs provide necessary matching informaton, but sometimes a discrepancy appears in the notes or clear instant photographs aren't available. A clip is the only perfectly accurate matching guide. Whenever using clips, the script supervisor must remember to return the clip to the editing room as soon as possible.

If there is one theme that could be applied to everything discussed in this book, it's *flexibility*. In Chapter One, we emphasized how providing compatible footage allows the editor flexibility to cut sequences in any number of desirable manners. In Chapter Two, we stressed how a script supervisor, by taking a problem-solving approach, can be prepared for most problems that arise on the set. A helpful script supervising technique can be developed to solve nearly any problem by first recognizing the potential problems involved in a film project. Chapters Three and Four illustrated several alternative scripting methods, each appropriate to varying styles of production. The interviews interspersed throughout the preceding pages show how a script supervisor must tailor continuity duties to co-workers' likes and dislikes, and how continuity is valued differently by each crew member who works closest with the script supervisor. In this chapter, our stress has been similar. By recognizing the requirements of a production technique format, the script supervisor can devise the best possible scripting system.

Conclusion

This book has been intended as an introduction to script supervision. We've tried to provide the novices with all the basic knowledge of filmmaking necessary in understanding the script supervisor's job on a film or television set. The script supervisor's responsibilities have been outlined in detail for such varied formats as features, episodic television, industrial training films or tapes, and commercials. Scripting tips have been provided for such varied techniques as single-camera film, videotape, multiple-camera film and videotape, process photography, musical productions, and many more. The theories explained throughout these chapters and the representative samples of the most common scripting styles have been offered to give a novice the common sense to meet nearly any situation that arises.

In concluding, we'd like to leave you with a final thought. Besides knowing all your tools and responsibilities and being blessed with good health, patience and a sense of humor, the key word is *Dedication*. Way back in the '40s, Shirley was staying at a small hotel on location in New Jersey. She brought her infant daughter, Arianne, and a nurse along with her. In the middle of the night, a fire broke out. Half asleep, she jumped out of bed, grabbed her script and was more than half way down the fire-escape before remembering to wake the baby and nurse. With the aid of a bewildered fireman, she returned and rescued them, after leaving the script with an amazed assistant director trying to get himself out.

There are innumerable human experiences that could be related, but all we're trying to relate is how stimulating a job script supervision can be. So please "forward march" onto a set as soon as you can with your knowledge and ability bringing good fortune, and especially if you feel you have a talent for this vocation. Remember, "talent obliges." It obligates the mightiest efforts to achieve the goal of being a responsible, respected and vital part of your crew—a great script supervisor.

Glossary

ACTION 1. The command given by a director for the actors to begin the scene. 2. Any activity performed by a subject whether actors or scenery that is being filmed. 3. In the case of script supervisor notes, camera movements in addition to activity in front of the camera.

ACTION SAFE The portion of a video picture that can be transmitted to the average home color receiver without distortion. Action safe is a larger area of the full aperture than title safe.

ACTUAL TIME An estimation of the amount of time out of the total time filmed that will be included in the picture after editing. Same as ESTIMATED TIME, CREDITED TIME, or PICTURE TIME.

ADDED SCENE 1. Any scene filmed that is not in the script. 2. When tallying total added scenes, a sequence which was shot in 10 setups but the script only allotted 8 has 2 added scenes.

AERIAL SHOT 1. Any camera viewpoint from the air. 2. An art or model shot from above or on an animation stand.

ALTERNATING SCRIPT SUPERVISORS Two script supervisors on a back-to-back series that alternate episodes. One prepares while the other shoots, then they switch and the first works the shoot while the second prepares.

ANGLE The direction from which the camera is aimed at the subject being filmed. Same as CAMERA ANGLE.

APERTURE An adjustable lens opening which varies in size to allow more or less light to pass through to the film.

APPROACH The continuous camera movement from a relatively long shot to a closer shot of the same subject. Same as DOLLY, TRUCK, and ZOOM.

A.S.A. RATING A number system which rates a film's speed or sensitivity to light. The higher the number, the less light is needed to expose the film correctly. Same as FILM SPEED.

ASSEMBLY Editing together the film units into a desired sequence.

ASSEMBLY VIDEOTAPE EDITING The process of building a desired sequence of scenes by editing the tape segments together one by one in consecutive order.

ASSISTANT DIRECTOR or A.D. The crew member to whom the script supervisor gives the daily continuity records. The a.d. is responsible for supervising activity on the set. Main duties include recording employment times, calling actors and crew, turning in nightly production reports to the production offices, and maintaining silence and discipline on the set. An a.d. may also be responsible for calling out instructions during filming.

AUDIO The sound portion only or concerning sound, whether effects, dialogue or music.

AUDIO-DUBBING A form of electronic videotape audio editing in which an old signal is replaced with a new signal. The original sound is erased when the new sound is recorded in its place.

AUDIO SWEETENING A form of electronic videotape audio editing in which the original recordings are retained. The originals are copied onto a second tape or composite master audio recording. Their levels can be mixed to a desired balance.

BACK-TO-BACK SERIES A television series that films or tapes its episodes one after another without more than a few days in between.

BACKGROUND or B.G. The portion of a scene that is not the center of attention and often farthest from the camera.

BEAT A momentary pause in an actor's movement or dialogue usually associated with strong emotional motivations.

BIG CLOSE-UP or B.C.U. A camera view very close to the subject, filling the frame. Where a shot of a man's face is a close-up, a shot of the scar on his nose is a big closeup. Same as EXTREME CLOSE-UP.

BLOCKING 1. The movement patterns that performers follow during a scene. 2. The movement pattern of the camera.

BLOW-UP 1. The technique of enlarging a smaller gauge film to a larger such as 8mm to 16mm or 16mm to 35mm. 2. The blowing up of one portion of the frame to the same format. This is an optical process that is often cheaper to use than reshooting to achieve a desired image size or to hide a mistake.

BOOM A support from which a microphone is suspended that can follow an actor's motion. A boom can be a large machine or a simple telescoping pole. Script supervisors often note that a shot is ruined because the boom was seen by the camera.

BROADCAST MASTER A composite master tape assembled through on-line electronic videotape editing. The broadcast master drops only one generation from the original recording which enables it to retain its broadcast quality.

BURN IN A laboratory term for an optical effect where a title or other subject is photographed over previously exposed film.

CAMERA ANGLE The direction from which the camera is aimed at the subject being filmed. Same as ANGLE.

CAMERA CREW Sometimes refers to all crew members involved in the photography as opposed to sound technicians, etc. Other times, the term refers only to the director of photography, the cameraman and camera assistants, and not the script supervisor or other crew members.

CAMERA LEFT or C.L. Static or movement direction as viewed through the camera rather than by the subject being filmed. A ballerina on the left side of the frame is camera left no matter which way she faces.

CAMERA OPERATOR The crew member who actually operates the camera. If the director of photography doesn't operate the camera, then there is usually a director of photography, a camera operator, and assistant cameramen.

CAMERA REPORT A daily record which describes what is included on the exposed film. This form is filled out by an assistant cameraman and sent into the lab with the exposed film.

CAMERA RIGHT or C.R. The opposite of camera left. The static or movement direction as viewed through the camera rather than by the subject being filmed.

CAMERA ROLL NUMBER The number assigned to a roll of film stock as it is loaded into the camera.

CAMERAMAN The crew member responsible for the photography of the picture. The cameraman has the option of operating the camera or supervising the operation. Same as DIRECTOR OF PHOTOGRAPHY, and sometimes confused with CAMERA OPERATOR.

CHROMA KEY a system for matting one subject over another by shooting the foreground subject against a specially colored background. The background becomes transparent through an optical process, and a second camera's subject takes its place.

CLAPPERBOARD A board or chalkboard that is attached to a clapstick. The scene and take number in addition to other identifying information is either chalked on the board or temporarily labeled with tape markings so that it will be recorded on the film before each shot. Same as SLATE.

CLAPSTICK A hinged pair of sticks used to synchronize the film with the sound. When the sticks are clapped together, the sound of the clap is aligned with the image of the clap so that all consequent images match their corresponding sounds. Most frequently referred to as SLATE; also known as CLAPPERBOARD and NUMBER BOARD.

CLIP A short piece of printed film used for matching lighting, props, set dressing, costumes, make-up, hair, or any other production detail.

CLOSE SHOT or C.S. A shot which highlights only one portion of the action by excluding the surrounding detail. A shoulder up view of a person is one example. The term close shot is often used erroneously as interchangeable with close-up.

CLOSE-UP or C.U. A shot which highlights only one portion of the action by excluding the surrounding detail, only closer than a close shot. If shoulders up is a close shot, then head only is a close-up. A close-up reveals more detail than a close shot.

COMMENT CUTAWAY A thematic comment made by a film cutting away to a seemingly unrelated shot. Cutting from a sloppy eater to a shot of a pig would constitute a comment cutaway.

COMMENTARY Dialogue spoken by an off-screen speaker. See also NARRATION, VOICE OVER, and OFF-SCREEN DIALOGUE.

COMPILATION SEQUENCE A sequence of stock footage or excerpts from other films and tapes.

COMPLEMENTARY TWO-SHOT A camera view of two subjects that complements a second view of the same two subjects. One of the two shots favors one subject, while the other favors the opposite subject.

COMPLETE TAKE A take that is filmed from beginning to end of the planned action without stopping. A complete take can be printed or n.g.

COMPOSITE MASTER A master videotape achieved by copying portions of original recordings onto another videotape in a desired sequence.

CONSECUTIVE NUMBERING SYSTEM A continuity numbering system where the first shot filmed is numbered one; the second shot, two; and so forth until all the filming is completed.

CONTINUITY The smooth and logical progression from one shot to the next without mis-matches of costumes, props, directional movements, and the like.

CONTINUITY GIRL or BOY. a crew member responsible for the care and maintenance of continuity. Same as SCRIPT CLERK, SCRIPT GIRL, and SCRIPT SUPERVISOR.

CONTINUITY NOTES Records kept by the script supervisor including continuity information on each shot filmed, editorial reports, daily production reports and costume, set, and prop requirements.

COVERAGE The collection of shots filmed to represent the action of a scene. A master shot with various close-ups might be considered adequate coverage of a particular scene.

CRAB DOLLY A dolly which has front and back wheels that can move smoothly in any direction.

CRANE A large camera mount that enables vertical, horizontal, and diagonal camera movements from high up.

CREDITED TIME An estimation of the amount of time out of the total time filmed that will be included in the picture after editing. Same as ACTUAL TIME, ESTIMATED TIME, or PICTURE TIME.

CROSS-CUT To edit two or more scenes together by alternating them portions at a time. Same as INTERCUT.

CROSS DISSOLVE or X-DISSOLVE An optical effect where one scene fades out as a second scene fades in. Same as LAP DISSOLVE.

CROSSING THE LINE or CROSSING OVER THE ACTION AXIS Terms refer to using inconsistant camera angles while covering a single event or from sequence to sequence.

CUE A command given by a director or an actor which means the script supervisor should tell the actor the next line or movement.

CUE TRACK A sound track that is recorded during filming when the conditions are somehow inadequate, making a clean recording impossible. The cue track is used as a reference for later dubbing of dialogue or for adding effects.

CUT 1. A command given by the director indicating that the camera operator should stop filming. 2. The point in the scene where it abruptly ends before the next scene starts, determined by the editor.

CUTAWAY A shot inserted between two others of the main action. Cutaways are often used to add visual variation, to show a reaction, to make a comment, to help express a time lapse, and to highlight aspects of the action.

CUTTER A technician who is responsible for assembling the film units into a finished movie. Same as EDITOR.

DAILIES An uncorrected and unconnected series of prints of the film shot from which the best portions will be selected for the finished film. Same as RUSHES.

DAILY EDITORIAL REPORT A script supervisor's daily record of what scenes are shot, how long each take is, which take is good, a description of the action in each shot, the camera and sound information.

DAILY PRODUCTION REPORT A script supervisor's daily record of editorial information as well as running lists of total estimated picture time, set-ups, retakes, added scenes, footage, sound tracks, scenes covered, meal breaks, and miscellaneous notes.

DEPTH OF FIELD The distance from nearest the camera to the farthest that subjects appear in focus.

DIALOGUE COACH The crew member responsible for cueing actors, helping actors prepare their dialogue, and sometimes serving as an acting coach.

DIRECTOR The person who is responsible for the entire concept of the film, choosing locations, selecting camera angles, directing actors, blocking the camera, and supervising the entire crew.

DISSOLVE An optical effect where one scene gradually blends into the next scene until the second scene replaces the first. Same as LAP DISSOLVE and CROSS DISSOLVE.

DISTANT LOCATION Technically, any location over 300 miles from the home studio.

DOLLY A mobile platform with four wheels that the camera is mounted on.

DOLLY SHOT A shot where the camera, on a dolly, moves along with, toward, or away from the subject. Same as TRUCKING SHOT or TRAVELING SHOT.

DOLLY TRACKS Metal or wooden tracks on which the dolly wheels roll, assuring a smooth and consistent movement from take to take.

DOUBLE Stunt actors who perform in the place of the main actors. Doubles are common when the action is physically demanding or dangerous.

DOUBLE EXPOSURE or DOUBLE RUN When the film is exposed twice on the same frames of film.

DROPOUT A loss of video information caused by imperfections in the raw videotape stock.

DUB-DOWN A transferring of master videotapes to lesser quality video cassettes before off-line electronic video editing.

DUBBING 1. The addition of one sound track to the film's soundtrack. 2. The replacement of a film's dialogue track with another track in a different language.

EDIT To assemble the film units into a desired order.

EDITING SCRIPT A description of shots in the order they will appear in the completed film.

EDITOR The person who is responsible for assembling the various film units into a desired order. Same as CUTTER.

EFFECTS 1. Any recorded sound other than dialogue or music. 2. Transitions between scenes that don't cut directly like wipes, fades, dissolves, and other optical processes.

ELECTRON GUN The device in a television camera which breaks down the electrical image on the target area in the vidicon tube into the television signal.

ELECTRONIC VIDEOTAPE EDITING The process of assembling the pieces of a videotape program into a desired sequence without physically cutting the tape.

ENDSLATE An up-side-down slate that appears at the end of a shot rather than at the beginning. Same as TAILSLATE.

ESTABLISHING SHOT A shot that is used to establish a new subject or location which appears near the beginning of the total time filmed that will be included in the picture after editing.

ESTIMATED TIME An estimation of the amount of time out of the total time filmed that will be included in the picture after editing. Same as ACTUAL TIME, CREDITED TIME, and PICTURE TIME.

EXPOSURE. The adjustable amount of light permitted to pass to the film resulting in the process of photographing.

EXTERIOR Any location filmed outside.

EXTREME CLOSE-UP or E.C.U. A camera view very close to the subject, filling the frame. Where a shot of a man's face is a close-up, a shot of the scar on his nose is an extreme close-up. Same as BIG CLOSE-UP.

EXTREME LONG SHOT or E.L.S. A camera view very far from the subject encompassing a large expanse of land. A panoramic view of the mountains or a New York skyline are examples of an extreme long shot.

FADE IN An optical effect where each frame of film receives progressively less exposure until it fades to black.

FADE OUT An optical effect where each frame of film receives progressively less exposure until it fades to black.

FAST MOTION A scene which appears to be faster than normal because it is shot in less than the standard amount of frames per second is described as being in fast motion.

FIELD One half of the lines which comprise the television picture. A field is recorded by a single sweep of a video head in a helical scan videotape recording system.

FILM SPEED A number rating system that measures a film's sensitivity to light. Same as A.S.A. RATING.

FIRST GENERATION The original videotape recordings only are referred to as first generation. SAME AS MASTER.

FLASH PAN A camera movement that occurs when the camera jerks between two actions in one shot causing a blur in between. Same as WHIP PAN or SWISH PAN.

FOCAL LENGTH The distance from the optical center of the lens to the film surface when the lens is focused on a distant object. This distance determines the field of view with a short length resulting in a wide angle view and a long length resulting in a narrow view.

FOCUS PULL A camera shot where the focus shifts from the background to the foreground or vice-versa without altering the framing. See also RACKING or RACK SHOT.

FOOTAGE The unit of measurement used for film.

FOREGROUND or F.G. the portion of a shot nearest to the camera.

FRAME 1. A complete television picture which is comprised of two fields. 2. A single image on a length of film. See also X.

FRAMES PER SECOND or F.P.S. The rate at which each frame is either exposed or projected.

FREEZE FRAME Stopping the action abruptly by freezing on a single frame for a designated period of time. Same as STOP MOTION.

F-STOP The theoretical measurement of the lens opening which allows light to pass through to the film, (not to be confused with the actual measurement or T-stop).

FULL SHOT A shot which includes all the action in the scene as opposed to a long shot which views the full subject in focus but not always the background.

GLITCH A low frequency noise signal which appears usually as an interruption of the television picture. A glitch is caused by physical imperfections in the oxide coating of the raw videotape stock.

HAND-HELD SHOOTING Filming is considered hand-held when the camera is not on a tripod or dolly camera mount, but instead is mounted on the camera operator's shoulder.

HELICAL SCAN VIDEOTAPE RECORDER A videotape recording system in which the tape is wrapped around the head drum in a slanted or helical pattern.

HIGH ANGLE The camera view with the camera mounted higher than the subject, angling down.

IN THE CAN The phrase used to mean the scene or project is finished.

IN-CAMERA EDITING An imprecise term which refers to editing while switching between multiple video cameras in production.

INCOMPLETE TAKE A take that is interrupted before the end of the planned action. An incomplete take can be printed or n.g.

IN-HOUSE Tapes or films intended for use exclusively within a company rather than a commercial release are referred to as in-house.

INSERT VIDEOTAPE EDITING The process of recording new material into a videotape of existing material.

INSERTS Close up of written or printed legend which must be seen in large detail, or a full screen shot of an important prop. Inserts usually can be shot separately from the scene in which they appear, and edited into the scene later.

INTERCUT To edit two or more scenes together by alternating them, portions at a time. Same as CROSS CUT.

INTERIORS Any scenes shot indoors.

I.A.T.S.E. or I.A. A major theatrical engineering union called The International Alliance of Theatrical Stage Employees and Motion Picture Machine Operators of the United States and Canada.

ISOLATED A videotape term used during multiple videotape production to indicate the signals which are being recorded separately from the program or composite master. SAME AS ISO.

JOB NUMBER A number assigned to the film project by the management. Same as PRODUCTION NUMBER.

JUMP CUT A cut between two shots where a portion of the action is left out, resulting in actors appearing as if they "jump" into a different position in the frame.

KEYING The combining of the dark portions of one video signal with the light portions of another signal to form a composite picture.

LAP DISSOLVE An optical effect where one scene fades out as a second scene fades in. Same as CROSS DISSOLVE or DISSOLVE.

LAPSE OF TIME CUTAWAY Cutting away to a secondary action and then returning to the primary action to help express a short lapse of time.

LEFT Same as CAMERA LEFT.

LIBRARY FOOTAGE A segment of film that is purchased from a film library rather than shot specifically for the film, or footage from a previous episode in the case of television. Same as STOCK FOOTAGE.

LINE COPY or LINE FEED The program master of a multiple camera videotaping. See also ON THE LINE.

LINES OF RESOLUTION Horizontal lines or scans of the electron gun over the target surface within television cameras and monitors. The quantity of lines determines the capability of displaying greater picture detail.

LIP SYNCHRONIZATION or LIP SYNCH The matching of the sound track to the picture; for example, lip movements precisely match the sounds of speaking.

LOCATION Any filming site other than a studio.

LONG SHOT A camera view which includes the full subject in focus but not all of the background.

LOOP An endless loop formed by attaching the ends of a segment of film permitting it to be projected over and over. Loops are used to match words to lip movements and effects to their visuals.

LOW ANGLE The camera view with the camera mounted lower than the subject, angling up.

MAGNETIC TAPE DEVELOPER A chemical solution that is painted on videotape in order to make the tracks visible.

MARK IT The command given by the assistant director, director, or camera operator cueing the second assistant cameraperson to clap the slate, identifying the take.

MASTER SHOT A shot which contains most of the action included in a scene in one continuous take.

MATCH DISSOLVE A lap dissolve from one scene to another where the central subject remains the same in both locations. A scene may focus on a broken foot in the playing field, then match dissolve to the broken foot in the hospital waiting room.

MEDIUM-CLOSE SHOT A camera view which includes a larger portion of the screen than a close shot like heads and shoulders of two people. See also TIGHT TWO SHOT.

MEDIUM SHOT The most common camera view where the subject and the background are focused but the surrounding locale is out of focus.

MEDIUM-TO-CLOSE PAN A camera move that pans with a general subject first, and then moves in on a specific detail of the same subject or a nearby detail. An example might be a medium shot panning with a detective as he walks toward a table, tightening on a bloody knife atop the table after he passes.

MIX The process of blending together the dialogue, effects and music of a film onto mono or stereo tracks that synchronize with the picture.

MONTAGE A sequence of related or unrelated shots, often expressing the passing of time or a speeded-up version of an event. A collection of various rodeo shots might be a montage presentation designed to express that the rodeo occurred.

M.O.S. ("MIT OUT SOUND") To film a scene without the accompanying sound.

MULTIPLE EXPOSURE More than one image exposed on the same segment of film.

N.A.B.E.T. A major engineering union called the National Association of Broadcast Employees and Technicians.

NARRATION Same as COMMENTARY.

N.G. The notation used to indicate that a take is unacceptable or no good.

NUMBER BOARD A board or chalkboard that is attached to a clapstick. The scene and take number, in addition to other identifying information, is either chalked on the board or temporarily labeled with tape markings so that it will be recorded on the film before each shot. Same as SLATE.

OFF-LINE EDITING The process of assembling a video program by using copies of the original tapes. The off-line master is used as a guide for on-line editing.

ON-LINE EDITING The process of assembling a video program using the original recordings by duplicating the cuts on the off-line master. The on-line master only drops one generation.

ON THE LINE A phrase used to indicate the program master of a multiple camera videotaping.

OPTICALS Visual effects such as wipes, dissolves and fades that are added during or prior to the process of printing the film. In the case of multiple camera videotape, opticals can be recorded during the taping process through the control board.

OUT-TAKES Any footage that is not used in the completed picture.

OVER-CRANK To film at a speed over the standard rate, causing the action to appear as if it is moving slower than normal.

OVER-EXPOSURE Permitting more light to strike the film than necessary, resulting in a washed-out image.

OVER-SHOULDER SHOT The camera view over the shoulder of one player toward another. By shooting over the shoulder, the physical relationship between the player and the second is preserved. See also RAKING.

OXIDE The iron oxide coating used on video- and audiotape onto which the electrical signals are recorded.

PAGE For script supervisors' purposes, each script page is divided into eighths. A page worth of script is made up of 8/8's of script regardless of how much appears on one sheet of paper.

PAN Camera movement from one side to the other on the vertical axis during filming.

PARALLEL ACTION Two scenes appearing to happen at the same time by alternating portions of one with portions of the other. See also CROSS CUT and INTERCUT.

PAY-OFF PAN A camera movement where the camera pans with one subject without holding to that subject so that the camera can hold on a different subject, permitting the first to move out of frame.

PHYSICAL VIDEOTAPE EDITING The process of physically cutting the videotape and re-assembling it into a desired sequence. Physical editing is nearly obsolete except in the case of repairing torn tape.

PICK-UP 1. When a scene breaks or goes wrong before completion, it can be "picked up" before the break and continued to the end. 2. Any added angles to cover these mistakes in a master shot or to add cinematic variety and emphasis to the action in the master shot.

PICTURE TIME An estimation of the amount of time out of the total time filmed that will be included in the picture after editing. Same as ACTUAL TIME, ESTIMATED TIME, and CREDITED TIME.

PLATE NUMBERS The numbers assigned to the background projection during a process shot.

PLAY-BACK or P.B. A reproduction of the actual recording to be used in the film. If a musical number is being shot M.O.S., then a play-back is used so that the dancing and singing will match the orchestration. A singer mouths the words of the song and the dancers move to the taped music so that an orchestra and optimum recording conditions won't be needed on location.

POINT-OF-VIEW SHOT or P.O.V. The camera angle from a designated viewpoint; i.e. a character's p.o.v. or the p.o.v. out the car window.

POLAROID Originally a trade name and now a term used to refer to all cameras that are capable of processing the photograph instantaneously.

POST-PRODUCTION Any work done after principal photography like editing, adding opticals, mixing, finding stock footage, filming some inserts, dubbing, musical scoring, etc.

PRE-PRODUCTION Any work done before principal photography in preparation of filming.

PRESENCE Ambient sound of a given locale recorded during production so as to match the room tone of the dialogue synch track. The presence recording is used in post-production sound editing.

PRINCIPAL PHOTOGRAPHY The majority of filming involving the body of the script excluding second unit photography, inserts, and some re-takes.

PRINTS 1. Those takes which the director chooses to develop. 2. Any copy of the film or portion of a film.

PROCESS PHOTOGRAPHY A type of cinematography that consists of filming live action in front of a projected background or plate to form a combined picture.

PRODUCTION ASSISTANT 1. A loose term referring to any assistant during pre-production, production, or post-production. 2. In the case of videotaping in a studio, the term is used for a script supervisor.

PRODUCTION BOARD The breakdown of each shot onto a narrow strip within a specially designed holder. Each strip includes the date the shot is scheduled to be filmed, the characters in the shot, the location, and all physical requirements necessary to film it.

PRODUCTION NUMBER A number assigned to the film project by the management. Same as JOB NUMBER.

PRODUCTION UNIT The collective term which refers to the entire crew involved in filming.

PROTECTION SHOT Any additional take or camera set-up that is filmed or taped with the intention of avoiding unforeseen problems.

QUADRAPLEX VIDEOTAPE RECORDER A videotape recording system in which the tape travels in a uniform horizontal path past one or two rotating heads. Same as TRANSVERSE SCAN VIDEOTAPE RECORDER.

RACK SHOT or RACKING SHOT A camera shot where the focus shifts from the background to the foreground or vice versa without altering the framing. See also FOCUS PULL.

RAINBOW SCRIPT A script that has been rewritten numerous times so that each rewrite appears on a different color paper. The resulting script pages appear in the colors of the rainbow.

RAKING Angling the camera past one subject to another such as an over-the-shoulder shot.

REACTION CUTAWAY A single camera shot that captures a secondary subject's reaction to the main action, taking the attention away from the main action only momentarily.

REACTION PAN While the main action is happening, the camera pans to capture the reaction from a second subject.

REACTION SHOT A camera shot that captures a subject's reaction to another action. Unlike a reaction cutaway, the reaction shot is not limited to a secondary subject.

RECORDIST The crew member who is responsible for recording a film's sound effects, dialogue, and music. Also known as PRODUCTION MIXER, LOCATION MIXER, or SOUND MIXER.

REHEARSAL Any practice run of either camera movements or performer actions without filming or recording. Same as RUN-THROUGH.

RELATED CUTAWAY A single camera shot that captures a minor action related to the scene. Cutting from a classroom of students taking a test to a short shot of the clock, and back to the classroom would be a related cutaway.

RE-TAKE Re-filming a shot after the camera set-up has been struck because of previously undetected problems.

REVELATION PAN A camera move where the camera pans across an area and holds on a significant detail.

REVERSE ANGLE 1. The 180° opposite camera angle than a previous angle. 2. The corresponding angle to an established camera direction like, if the subject looks toward the left, the reverse angle has the subject facing toward the right.

REVERSE PAN A camera movement where the camera pans in one direction then pans in the other direction within the same shot.

RIGHT Same as CAMERA RIGHT.

ROOM TONE The tonal quality of a desired room necessary for assembling background presence.

RUN-THROUGH Any practice run of either the camera movements or the performers' actions without filming or recording. Same as REHEARSAL.

RUSHES An uncorrected series of print takes of the film shot from which the best will be selected for the finished film. Same as DAILIES.

SCANNING The process of breaking down a picture image into a electronic signal.

SCENE A portion of the film that takes place within a single location and one time period. It can be a series of shots or a single shot.

SCENE NUMBER For a script supervisor, scene numbers are those numbers that appear in the script rather than the numbers assigned to the various shots. When the forms ask which scenes are covered, the list of scenes that are included within the shots filmed should be listed. On the slate, the term scene refers to the shot rather than the scene in the script. These may or may not coincide.

SCRATCH TRACK A duplicate voice or effects recording which is used when filming M.O.S. to help ensure that the timing will work in the scene after the audio is added.

SCRIPT A detailed shooting plan of a film which includes a description of the shots as well as the text to the dialogue and action.

SCRIPT SUPERVISOR A crew member responsible for the care and maintenance of continuity. Same as CONTINUITY GIRL in England, SCRIPT CLERK, and SCRIPT BOY or SCRIPT GIRL.

SECOND UNIT A secondary film crew which films scenes simultaneously with the primary crew but at a different location. Stunts and incidental scenes are often second unit shooting.

SEQUENCE A series of shots that are concerned with one particular event in the story after the film is edited.

SET A specially constructed or existing scenery where the action takes place during filming.

SET DRESSING Any portable object on a film set that is not part of the scene other than to dress up the set.

SET-UP Each new camera position or significant change in the camera operation, focal length, lens, or lighting.

SFX Sound effects.

SHOOTING Another term for photographing.

SHOOTING SCHEDULE A list or description of the shots in a film script categorized by the date they are supposed to be filmed.

SHOOTING SCRIPT 1. A detailed shooting plan which includes a description of the shots as well as the text to the dialogue and action. 2. The same, only the shots are arranged in the order in which they will be shot instead of the order they will appear in the completed film.

SHOT The term used to refer to a segment of film within one take or without stopping the camera.

SHOT LENGTH For a script supervisor, the amount of time the shot will appear in the movie rather than the time from "action" to "cut."

SHOT NUMBER The number assigned to the shot by the script supervisor which may or may not coincide with the number assigned in the script to the corresponding scene. Same as SLATE NUMBER.

SIDE ANGLE The camera view with the camera mounted to the side of the subject angling toward the subject.

SLATE A board or chalkboard that is attached to a clapstick. The scene and take number in addition to other identifying information is either chalked on the board or temporarily labeled with tape markings so that it will be recorded on the film before each shot. Less frequently referred to as CLAPPERBOARD or NUMBER BOARD.

SLATE NUMBER The number given to each shot during filming. Same as SHOT NUMBER.

SLAVES Isolated videotape recordings. Same as MASTERS.

SLOW MOTION Action which appears as if it's slowed down because it was shot at a rate faster than the standard frames per second.

SMPTE TIME CODES Eight digit numbers which are automatically laid down onto a videotape in the form of electrical signals on the control track.

SOUND EFFECT Any audio track other than dialogue or music.

SOUND REPORT A daily record of the sound tracks recorded during the day's filming.

SOUND ROLL NUMBER A number assigned to each roll of audio tape as they are used during filming.

SOUND TRACK 1. The audio portion of a final print. 2. Any portion of the film's sound that will eventually be compiled into the completed sound track.

SPECIAL EFFECTS Any visual or audio effect achieved through optical or physical manipulation of color, size, timing, and composition.

SPECIAL EFFECTS GENERATOR or SEG A videotape vision-switcher that has a capacity for adding special effects such as wipes, fades, crossfades, and superimpositions.

SPEED The term used by the sound recordist that indicates that the tape is turning at the desired speed.

SPLIT SCREEN An optical effect where a portion of the screen has one scene while another portion has a different scene.

SPOTS The term used to refer to commercials.

STAND-INS Actors who walk through the action while being lit or while blocking camera movements in the place of the main actors.

STICKS 1. Clappers with no slate or numberboard attached. 2. A slang term for tripod in the phrase "camera on sticks."

STOCK FOOTAGE A segment of film that is purchased from a film library rather than shot specifically for the film, or footage from a previous episode in the case of television. Same as LIBRARY FOOTAGE.

STOP MOTION Stopping the action abruptly by freezing on a single frame for a designated length of time. Same as FREEZE FRAME.

STORYBOARD A series of sketches and their corresponding descriptions for each shot of the film, arranged in the order of the story sequence.

STUDIO LOCATION Any filming shot within the confines of the studio building.

SUBJECTIVE PAN A camera move that approximates the look of a subject scanning an area like eyes scanning a room or a closed-circuit television camera scanning for intruders.

SUPER Superimposing one scene over another on the same length of film.

SWISH PAN A camera movement that occurs when the camera jerks between two actions in one shot causing a blur in between. Same as FLASH PAN and WHIP PAN.

SYNC Regulating the scanning beam in multiple camera videotaping with each other to achieve an uninterrupted picture on the program as required by the FCC.

SYNCH or SYNCHRONOUS SOUND Synchronizing the film images with the corresponding sounds.

TAILSLATE A slate held upside down that appears at the end of the take rather than at the beginning. Same as ENDSLATE.

TAKE A single attempt at photographing an action. Every attempt is a separate take.

TARGET AREA A light sensitive surface within the vidicon tube which becomes electrically charged by the light rays from the taped image.

TILT A vertical pan camera movement.

TIME OF THE FIRST SHOT For a script supervisor, the time that the first shot is completed.

TIME OF THE WRAP For a script supervisor, the time that the wrap begins rather than when the crew is finished wrapping.

TITLE SAFE The portion of a video picture that can transmit titles to the average color home receiver without distortion. Title safe is a smaller area of the full aperture than action safe.

TITLES Any printed material added after production or during principal photography like opening credits, closing credits, foreign translations, or relevant information like dates and commentary.

TRACK To move the camera toward, away from, or with the subject during filming.

TRANSITION The change from one shot to another.

TRANSITION FLASH PAN The transition between one shot and another when both use the flash pan technique. The camera jerks away from the action at the end of the first scene, causing the images to blur. At the beginning of the second scene, the camera jerks toward the action again blurring the images. When the two scenes are cut together, they form a transition flash pan.

TRANSVERSE SCAN VIDEOTAPE RECORDER A videotape recording system in which the tape travels in a uniform horizontal path past one or two rotating heads. Same as QUADRAPLEX VIDEOTAPE RECORDER.

TRAVELING SHOT A camera movement beside, toward, or away from the subject while the camera is mounted on a specialized camera mount or dolly. See also DOLLY SHOT and TRUCKING SHOT.

TRIPOD A three-legged stationary camera mount. Tripods are usually made up of two parts—a fluid, friction, or geared head and metal or wooden legs or "sticks."

TRUCKING SHOT A camera movement beside, toward, or away from the subject while the camera is mounted on a specialized camera mount or dolly. See also DOLLY SHOT and TRAVELING SHOT.

T-STOP The actual measurement of the lens opening which allows light to pass through to the film, (not to be confused with F-Stop which is the theoretical measurement).

TWO-SHOT A camera view that includes two people, usually from the waist up.

UNDER-CRANK To film at a speed under the standard rate causing the action to appear as if it is moving faster than normal.

UNDEREXPOSURE To permit less light to pass through to the film than is necessary to expose the film completely.

UNRELATED CUTAWAY A thematically unrelated shot inserted between two others of the main action. An unrelated cutaway may be used to express a lapse of time or to foreshadow a coming event.

VIDEO TAP or VIDEO ASSIST A small black-and-white video cassette recording system which can be attached to a film camera in order to record the same images as the film.

VIDEOTAPE A magnetic tape that transmits electrical impulses which can reproduce a picture with an accompanying audio track.

VIDICON TUBE A device within a television camera that translates the light patterns into electrical signals.

VISION MIXER A lesser-used term for vision switcher.

VISION SWITCHER A machine that feeds multiple camera video signals to isolated and program videotape recorders. The vision switcher operator can direct any of the camera signals to the program videotape recorder at any time and switch between two or more signals at will.

VOICE OVER Dialogue spoken by an off-screen speaker. See also NARRATION, COMMENTARY, and OFF-SCREEN DIALOGUE.

WALLA Unscripted background noises which give the impression of specific locations, i.e. cafe walla, street walla, and airport walla. Walla is recorded separately from the dialogue so it can be mixed to a desired balance.

WHIP PAN A camera movement that occurs when the camera jerks between two actions in one shot causing a blur inbetween. Same as FLASH PAN and SWISH PAN.

WIDE ANGLE A camera view which includes a wide area of the set, permitting most of the action to be seen at one time.

WILD FOOTAGE 1. Picture or sound that is taken without following a pre-planned shot list in a script; for instance, improvisational shooting during a riot where there is not enough time to plan or slate the shots is called shooting wild footage. 2. Any footage shot M.O.S. is referred to as wild.

WILD SOUND Sound recorded at a different time than while the filming is going on.

WILD TRACK A sound recording that is non-synchronous.

WIPE An optical effect where a scene enters the edge of the screen while another scene is going on, and gradually moves across pushing the first scene off the screen.

X The abbreviation for film footage.

X-DISSOLVE An abbreviation for Cross Dissolve. An optical effect where one scene fades out as a second scene fades in. More frequently called LAP DIS-SOLVE or DISSOLVE.

ZOOM RATIO The ratio between the largest image size and the smallest image size possible by varying the focal length of the lens.

ZOOM SHOT A camera technique which gives the impression that the camera is moving toward or away from a subject by varying the focal length of an adjustable lens.

Index